Linux
Networking
Clearly
Explained

Linux
Networking
Clearly
Explained

Bryan Pfaffenberger
University of Virginia

**Morgan
Kaufmann**

AN IMPRINT OF ACADEMIC PRESS
A HARCOURT SCIENCE AND TECHNOLOGY COMPANY

San Diego   San Francisco   New York   Boston
London Sydney   Tokyo

Morgan Kaufmann
340 Pine Street, Sixth Floor, San Francisco, CA 94101-3205, USA
http://www.mkp.com

Academic Press
A Harcourt Science & Technology Company
525 B Street, Suite 1900, San Diego, CA 92101-4495, USA
http://www.academicpress.com

Academic Press
Harcourt Place, 32 Jamestown Road, London, NW1 7BY, UK
http://www.academicpress.com

Library of Congress Catalog Card Number 00-106073
International Standard Book Number 0-12-533171-1

Printed in the United States of America
01 02 03 04 05 06 IP 9 8 7 6 5 4 3 2 1

Contents

Part One

Part One

Connecting to the Internet

1

Creating a Dial-Up Internet Connection

Your Linux networking journey starts with the fundamentals—setting up your modem and creating an Internet
connection. This chapter fully surveys the knowledge you
will need to create such a connection successfully. You'll
start by selecting the right modem for your Linux system,
installing your modem (without zapping your system),
and configuring your modem for Internet use. Although
several types of dial-up Internet connectivity are available
from Internet service providers (ISPs), by far the most
common is the *Point-to-Point Protocol (PPP)*, which is
featured in this chapter. By the time you have finished fol-

3

lowing this chapter's steps, you should have a working PPP connection. If you are inclined to know more about the technical details, you will find a brief discussion at the close of this chapter.

As explained in the Introduction, this chapter—like all the chapters in this book—features the networking utilities available for the KDE Desktop Environment (http://www.kde.org). In particular, this chapter features KPPP, which most Linux users consider to be the best such utility available. However, you should be aware that your Linux distribution may make other modem and Internet connectivity utilities available. For example, Red Hat Linux version 6.1 and later offers a PPP connection utility that is just as easy to use as KPPP. In addition, the Red Hat utility is tailored to certain peculiarities of the Red Hat distribution. If you are having trouble getting KPPP to work, try the PPP utility provided by your Linux distribution. In addition, this chapter's closing section, "Looking Under the Hood," shows you how to use text-mode utilities to establish a PPP connection.

What You Will Need

To connect to the Internet using the instructions in this chapter, you will need the following:

- **PPP account with an Internet service provider.** Service from local and national ISPs is available in almost all areas. In the U.S., check your Yellow Pages under "Computer Networks" for ISPs that operate in your area.
- **Information about your PPP connection.** When you sign up your account, make sure you obtain the following information: the telephone number to dial,

the type of authentication (PAP or CHAP), your login name (also called username), your password, the Internet addresses of the primary and secondary DNS servers you need to use, the type of Internet address your computer will have (static or dynamic), and the IP address of your ISP's default gateway, if any. If your ISP uses static IP addressing, find out which IP address to use. It is unnecessary to worry about what all this information means just now; you just need to know this information so that you can supply it to KPPP.

- **A Linux-compatible modem.** As the next section explains, not all modems work with Linux.

Now that you know what you need, we will start with the hardware.

Getting the Right Modem

Chances are you are already familiar with modems, those all-but-essential devices that translate the 0s and 1s of your computer's internal messaging into the warbling sounds that can be carried by analog telephone systems. This process is known as modulation. A modem at the receiving computer translates the sound from the telephone back into 1s and 0s, which is a process known as demodulation.

In most cases, you can get almost any modem working with Linux in short order. As this section explains, though, it is worth learning a bit more about modems so that you can choose the ideal modem for your Linux system.

TIP If you run into trouble getting your modem to work with Linux, please bear in mind that modems are relatively cheap. Which is worth more, your time or the $50 it takes to purchase a modem that's fully compatible with Linux?

When we are talking about *modems* here, note that we are talking about *real* modems—that is, modems that are designed to work with the analog telephone system. Available today are various high-speed Internet connections, such as cable services, Digital Subscriber Line (DSL), and ISDN; the devices used to connect to such services are often called "modems," but this term is inaccurate. These services bypass analog phone connections and offer an all-digital connection. Most of these connections require you to install an Ethernet networking card. You'll learn more about Ethernet cards and these high-speed services later in this book.

Modem Speed and Modem Protocols

When you shop for a modem, the first thing you probably look at is the speed. Modems are typically rated by the number of bits per second (bps) that they can transfer, at least under ideal conditions. A bit is the basic unit of computer data, a single binary number (a 1 or a 0). Eight bits are required to represent a single character. A modem's speed is generally given in Kbps, which stands for kilobits per second (one kilobyte equals roughly 1,000 bits). Modems rated to run at 56 Kbps have now been common for several years. Although manufacturers could build faster modems, the speed is limited by the ability of telephone wires to carry sound.

Speed is not the only thing to look for. A modem's speed is partly a function of the *protocols* that the modem is designed to work with. You will learn much more about protocols in this book, but here is a short definition—a protocol is a standard that defines how computer devices communicate with each other. Some protocols are *proprietary*; that is, they are developed by a commercial vendor, who regards them as a trade secret. *Open protocols* are developed by trade industry groups that seek to enlarge the market for everyone by agreeing on openly available standards. Open protocols are generally ratified and maintained by international standards organizations. *Public protocols* are those developed with public funding and released for public use, without restriction.

You want a 56 Kbps modem, but not just *any* 56 Kbps modem. "Bargain-basement" modems may work only with certain proprietary 56 Kbps protocols, such as X2, that were offered before the current standard (V.90) was ratified. Look for a modem that conforms to the V.90 protocol.

Hardware and Software Modems

Modems do more than serve as an intermediary between the computer's digital messaging and the telephone system's analog connections. They can also perform certain additional tasks, such as compressing data for faster transfer and checking for errors and correcting them automatically. To perform these tasks, modems need guidance from software. Most modems provide the needed software by means of permanently encoded chips contained within the modem's hardware; these modems are called *hardware modems*—and, as you will see, this is the type of modem you want for your Linux system.

Because it is slightly more expensive to provide the needed software within the modem's hardware, some modem manufacturers offer "bargain" modems that won't work unless your computer is running the needed software. The problem with such modems lies in the fact that this software is designed to run on Microsoft Windows, and is not available for Linux. These modems, called *software modems*, do not work with Linux and you will not succeed in installing them successfully. Many of these modems are sold with the "WinModem" brand name— avoid them!

Examples of modems employing software for compression and error correction include SupraExpress 56K, US Robotics WinModems, US Robotics Sportster Voice/Fax (model 1785), AOpen FM56-P and FM56-H, AT&T/ Lucent WinModem, Boca Research 28.8 internal modem (model MV34AI), Boca Research 33.6 internal modem (model MV34), HP Fastmodem D4810B, Multiwave Innovation CommWave V.34 modem, Rockwell SoftK56, Zoltrix 33.6 Win HSP Voice/Speaker Phone modem, and the Zoltrix Phantom 56K, model FM-HSP56PCI, chipset PCTel (PCI).

Internal and External Modems

You can get a modem to install inside your computer (an *internal modem*) or outside of your computer (an *external modem*). Although internal modems are generally less expensive, external modems have a series of lights that can help you diagnose the behavior of a connection. For example, external modems display a light when a connection is active. Without the light, you may not be able to tell as easily whether the connection has actually been made.

External modems have their advantages, but they do take up desk space. There is another deficiency. Because external modems require their own power supply, they are more expensive—and even worse, you will need to find a place to plug in yet another of those big, bulky transformers that convert alternating current (ac) line voltage to low-voltage direct current (dc).

Weighing all these factors, most modem buyers opt for an internal modem. But *which* internal modem?

Choosing an Internal Modem

If you want to use an internal modem, the best advice sounds like something from one of the holy books of the Eastern religions: look inside. It is not navel-gazing we are proposing here; this brand of introspection involves a look inside your computer. You need to know whether you have an empty expansion slot, and if so, what type of slot it is.

Before you open your computer, please keep the following precautions in mind:

- **Make sure everything is unplugged.** You do not want any stray electricity to shock you or your computer.
- **Get a screwdriver.** Generally, you need a Phillips screwdriver (the one with the cross at the tip) to open up your computer.
- **Use a nonmagnetic screwdriver.** Magnets can destroy your data.
- **Touch a large metal object.** This is the simplest way to discharge any static electricity in your body. It does not take much to overload the wires on computer boards.

- **Do not touch computer circuits with metal objects.** If you are wearing a ring or a bracelet, take it off. The last thing that your computer needs is a piece of metal to cross its wires.

If you make a mistake, it is probably not the end of the world. It is actually more difficult to break a computer than you might think.

Now you are ready to open up your computer. Once open, you can identify the expansion slots that you can use. There are three major slots in use today:

- **ISA.** The Industry Standard Architecture slot is about 6 in long, and colored black in most computers. Even though this standard slot dates back to 1984, it is still a common option for 56 Kbps modems.
- **PCI.** The Peripheral Component Interconnect slot is the most common standard in use today. If your internal modem is not ISA, chances are good that it is a PCI modem. The PCI Slot is about 3 in long, parallel to your ISA slots, and is white in most computers.
- **AGP.** The Accelerated Graphics Port slot is generally used only for video cards. The AGP slot is just a little shorter than the PCI slot, and is colored brown in most computers.

Please note that Linux works best with ISA modems. In general, PCI Plug and Play modems are not supported by Linux; exceptions are PCI modems based on the Lucent Venus chip set (such as Actiontec PM-6500-LKI). If you have an available ISA slot, by all means get an ISA modem. If the only available slot is a PCI slot, be sure to choose a PCI modem that is compatible with the distribution of Linux you are using.

External Modems

If you decided to go the external modem route, you will need to consider how to connect your modem to your computer. Physically, there are three main types of external modems:

- **Serial.** Most current external modems plug into the serial port on your computer. Serial ports have 9 pins. Many mice also plug into serial ports.
- **Parallel.** Older external modems plug into the parallel port on your computer. Parallel ports have 25 holes; most printers also plug into a parallel port. If you need to use an external parallel modem and a printer, plug the modem into your computer first. Most parallel modems have a second parallel port where you can then plug in your printer.
- **USB.** The Universal Serial Bus is designed to allow your computer to manage up to 127 peripherals such as printers, modems, and cameras. Although version 2.3 of the Linux kernel will support USB, this kernel version is still in beta testing at this writing and is not considered stable enough for day-to-day use. Avoid USB modems for now.

If you have an external parallel or serial modem, they are almost interchangeable. Adapter cables are available that allow you to plug a parallel modem into a serial port, or vice versa.

Modems for Notebook Computers

Most notebook computers require you to use a modem designed to fit into one of the computer's PC Card slots (also called PCMCIA slot). These PC Cards are 5 mm thick and about the same length and width as a credit card. Notebook computers usually include 1 or 2 slots for PC Cards. You can insert a PC Card, case and all, directly into most laptops. An annoyance—Most PC Card modems require you to use a special telephone cable, one end of which is designed to fit into the tiny receptacle at the end of the card. If you lose the cable or break the connector, you cannot log on.

Some notebook computers come with internal modems. As these are generally WinModems, they do not work with Linux. In addition, some PC Card modems employ software for com-pression and error correction. Examples include 3Com 3CXM356/3CCM356 and 3CXM656/3CCM656 PCMCIA, Compaq 192 PCMCIA modem/serial card, Megahertz XJ/CC2560 PCMCIA, and New Media Win-surfer PCMCIA modem/serial card. If you have this type of modem, you will need either a separate PC Card or a external modem for your laptop computer.

Installing Your Modem

Now that you have selected a modem, the next step is to install it in your computer. As there are three different types of modems, the following sections include three different sets of installation instructions.

In all cases, never use excessive force to install your modem. If you would have to "cut and file," stop everything. Make sure that you have the right card for the right slot.

Installing an Internal Modem

The following steps are general and do not apply in all cases. If in doubt, consult the instructions that came with your modem. You may also find modem installation instructions on the modem driver floppy disk, or on the manufacturer's Web site.

1. Disconnect your computer from all power lines and connections to peripherals such as your monitor.

2. Remove the screws from the back of your computer, and then remove the computer cover. Remember to put your screws in a safe place.

3. Ground yourself by touching a large piece of metal. A metallic file cabinet or computer cover should be sufficient. Ground yourself frequently while you are installing your modem.

4. Look at your modem. If you have documentation available, check to see if it is an ISA or PCI modem. Look at the card. Most of the card should be green. The bottom of the green part of the card should be coated with gold or silver. You will insert this end of the card into the appropriate slot.

5. Look inside your computer. If you have an ISA card, you will install it in the black slot. If you have a PCI card, you will install it in the shorter white slot. (Hint—ISA and PCI slots are parallel.)

6. Check your computer case. If you do not see a rectangular hole next to your modem slot, unscrew or detach the cover next to the slot.

7. Now check your modem for *jumpers*. A jumper looks like a small rectangular piece of plastic that connects two adjacent wires that stick out of your card. If there are jumpers on your modem, check your modem documentation for whether this affects its COM or IRQ port.

8. Install your modem. The gold color tab goes in the slot. You may need to apply a moderate amount of force and a gentle rocking motion. If the card will not fit, check your documentation again.

9. Reinstall your computer cover, and reattach all wiring.

Now that you have physically installed your modem, you can test it out on your Linux computer. Look for the next steps after the sections on installing external and PC Card modems.

Installing an External Modem

The following steps are general and do not apply in all cases. As Linux does not yet support USB modems, these steps do not apply to such modems.

1. Look at the equipment that came with your modem. It should include a 9-pin (serial) or a 25-pin (parallel) cable, as well as an ac power adapter.

2. Look at your modem. You should be able to plug the serial or parallel cable into one of the connectors on your modem.

3. Now attach the other end of this cable. The right plug is typically on the back of your computer case.

TIP If you have a parallel modem cable, you may already have a printer attached to the parallel port. External modems commonly include a second parallel port; detach your printer cable from your computer and then connect it to the modem.

If you do not see any lights on your modem's display panel, make sure it is plugged into a power outlet as well as your computer. Then check for an on/off switch.

Installing a PC Card Modem

Installing a PC Card modem (also called a PCMCIA modem) should be easiest of all. On many laptop computers, the PC Card slot is hidden behind a small door. Sometimes you have to open the door, and sometimes you can push right through the door.

Position your PC Card next to the door, make sure it is as flat as possible, and then slide it into position. When the PC Card is most of the way inside your computer, you will need to push a bit harder to seat the PC Card into its connector. If you have to push any harder, you should probably take out your PC Card and try again.

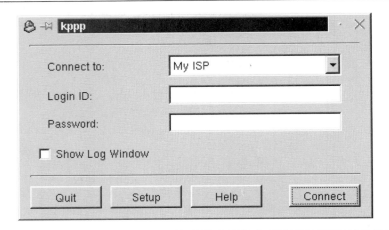

Figure 1.1 Click Setup to find out whether your modem is working.

Checking Your Installation

Now that you have installed your modem, start your system. When you have logged on, use KPPP to determine whether Linux can detect your modem's presence.

Start KPPP with the following steps:

1. Start Linux on your computer.

2. Log in and start the KDE desktop.

3. Click the Main Menu Button.

4. Point to Internet, then click KPPP. You will see the KPPP dialog box, shown in Figure 1.1.

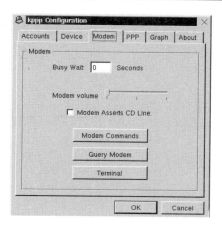

Figure 1.2 Click Query Modem to test your modem.

NOTE If you are using Corel Linux, click the Main Menu button, point to Applications, point to Network, and then click Dial-Up, which starts KPPP.

5. Click Setup. You will see the KPPP (Dial-Up) Configuration dialog box.

6. In the KPPP (Dial-Up) Configuration dialog box, click the Modem tab.

7. Click Query Modem, as shown in Figure 1.2. Linux now tests the communication setup with the modem in several different ways. If you see a series of "Modem Query Results," you are ready to set up a connection to the Internet. Otherwise, read the following sections to diagnose your problem.

If KPPP does not detect your modem on the first try, do not despair. Chances are you can solve the problem. For more information, see "Troubleshooting your Installation" on page 29.

Configuring KPPP

So far, you have used KPPP to make sure that your computer can talk to your modem. Now you can use the other parts of this powerful tool to configure the way your Linux computer connects to the Internet.

There are four basic issues to address when setting up a connection to the Internet:

1. How Linux sets up your modem. You will choose settings using the Device tab.

2. The commands Linux uses to communicate with your modem. You can configure these commands using the Modem tab.

3. What Linux does with your modem while connecting and disconnecting from the Internet. You can configure these settings using the PPP tab.

4. The account settings required by your Internet Service Provider. You configure these using the Accounts tab.

With the exception of setting up your account, you can rely on the KPPP defaults for most of these settings. Still, you should take a quick look at the existing settings; the following sections walk you through them and explain what they do.

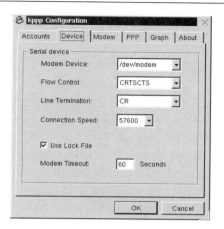

Figure 1.3 Set up the serial connection in this dialog box.

If KPPP is not already open, click on the Main Menu button, point to Internet and then click KPPP. In the KPPP dialog box, click Setup. Now you are ready to configure this powerful tool.

Choosing Device Settings

In the PPP Configuration dialog box, click the Device tab. You will see the Device settings, shown in Figure 1.3. You may have already used this tab earlier in this chapter to set the proper COM port. Now review the other options shown in Figure 1.3:

- **Flow Control.** Regulates the speed of data, so that the data are not lost between your modem and your computer. There are two basic types of flow control, hardware (CRTSCTS) and software (XON/XOFF). As most software modems do not work with Linux, this should normally be set to CRTSCTS.

- **Line Termination.** This setting is important only for text based modem communication, which you probably will not use (PPP is automatic and does not require any text-based interaction). Note, though, that you may not be able to see your commands or the answers from the remote computer if you choose the wrong setting here. The most common standard is Carriage Return/Line Feed (CR/LF). Because modems are set up differently, you may need to change this setting when you are using text based commands. Some trial and error may be necessary.
- **Connection Speed.** This is not the speed of your modem. This is the speed between your COM port and your modem, in bits per second. The typical maximum speed for most computer COM ports is 115,200 bps. If you have trouble logging on to an Internet account, you could try a slower connection speed.
- **Use Lock File.** This should be checked, to ensure that no other program tries to communicate with your modem while you are connected to the Internet.
- **Modem Timeout.** If your modem does not connect after dialing due to a busy signal or line fault, KPPP will redial the number automatically. You should specify a timeout setting so that the modem can hang up and the system can provide a dial tone again. Typical modem timeouts are 30-60 s.

Configuring Modem Setting

In the KPPP Configuration dialog box, click the Modem tab. You may already have used the "Query Modem" command to test your modem. The other commands in this dialog box include:

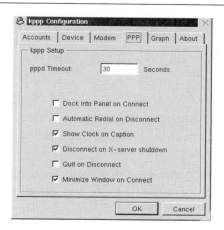

Figure 1.4 Here you control what happens during the connection.

- **Busy Wait.** If your modem gets a busy signal, Linux waits this period of time before trying to dial the phone number again.
- **Modem Volume.** The three modem volume settings correspond to: Off, Medium, and High. This applies only if your modem has a speaker.
- **Modem Commands.** Click this to see the commands that Linux uses to test your modem. Do not modify this list unless you know what you are doing.
- **Query Modem.** You used this command earlier in this chapter to test whether Linux can communicate with your installed modem.
- **Terminal.** You can click this to bring up a blank screen where you can enter text commands to your modem. You can also use this terminal to watch what's happening while KPPP is trying to connect.

TIP Enable the Terminal option so you can view the interaction between your ISP's computer and KPPP; what you see in this window may give you important clues for resolving connection problems. After you are certain you have configured your connection correctly, you can disable this option.

Choosing Connection Settings

This group of settings, shown in Figure 1.4, determines how Linux communicates with your modem from when it connects to when you end your connection. Review the settings shown in Figure 1.4:

- **pppd Timeout.** After your modem connects to a modem at your ISP, it has to set up a PPP connection. If your modem cannot set up a PPP connection, your ISP may be busy; in that case it is best to try again. A typical timeout is 30 s.
- **Dock into Panel on Connect.** Minimizes your KPPP windows once your modem has established a connection. This option overrides the Minimize Window on Connect option. This is an especially useful option if you are paying long-distance charges for your connection; the panel icon reminds you that you are connected (and paying).
- **Automatic Redial on Disconnect.** Redials your ISP if you are disconnected while you are on the Internet. Enable this option so that KPPP can restore your connection in the event of a line fault.
- **Show Clock on Caption.** Sets up a clock once you have a PPP connection to the Internet. This is useful especially when the cost of the telephone call depends on the length of your connection.
- **Disconnect on X Server Shutdown.** Ends your KPPP connection if you exit KDE.

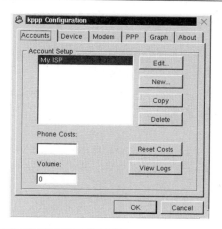

Figure 1.5 Setting Up A New Account

- **Quit on Disconnect.** Closes KPPP when you disconnect from the Internet. If you disable this option, KPPP stays on-screen after you log off.
- **Minimize Window on Connect.** Minimizes the KPPP window when your KPPP connection is established.

Configuring Your Internet Account

In this section, you will make use of the information you requested from your Internet service provider (ISP). Click the KPPP Accounts tab, as shown in Figure 1.5, and then click New. You will see a series of different tabs to configure the actual connection. To get started, click the Dial tab. You will see the Dial options. Table 1.1 discusses the various options and tells you the information you need to supply.

Table 1.1 New Account Dialog Box, Dial Tab

Item	Data Required
Connection Name	None. Enter the name of your choice, such as your ISP.
Phone Number	The local telephone number(s) for your ISP.
Authentication	Checks your password. Ask your ISP for this information. Generally, ISPs use PAP or CHAP. The other options (Script or Terminal-based) are generally used only when connecting to a UNIX computer at a public library or a university.
Store Password	KPPP stores your password for the next time you use this connection.
Execute Program	Leave this option blank.
Edit pppd Arguments	Leave this option blank.

TIP Ask your Internet Service Provider whether more than one telephone number is available. If so, you can set up KPPP to dial these numbers in sequence if one is busy. For example, if you can connect to your ISP at 555-1234 and 1-925-555-4321, enter the following in the Phone Number text box: 555-1234:1-925-555-4321. Also, if you need to dial "9" to access an outside line, enter: 9,555-1234. The comma gives your telephone time to get a dial tone for an outside line.

Now click the IP tab. You will see the IP options, shown in Figure 1.6. Here, you supply the information KPPP needs to establish an IP address (Internet address) for your computer. Most ISPs use dynamic addressing (the default setting). However, you may need to supply a permanent (fixed or static) IP address. If your ISP gave you a fixed IP address, you can supply it here. Table 1.2 dis-

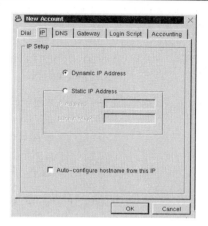

Figure 1.6 Most connections use dynamic IP addresses.

cusses the various options you will see after you click the IP tab; review them now.

Table 1.2 New Account Dialog Box, IP Tab

Item	Data Required
Dynamic IP Address	Choose this option if your ISP has not given you a permanent IP address. Also used if your ISP uses a "DHCP" Server.
Static IP address	Choose this option if your ISP has assigned you a permanent IP address.
IP Address	Type the permanent IP address as assigned by your ISP.
Subnet Mask	If you have a permanent IP address, you also need this information from your ISP. A typical subnet mask is 255.255.255.0.

Now click the DNS tab (see Figure 1.7). Here, you will supply the addresses for your ISP's domain name system

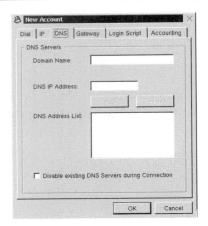

Figure 1.7 In this dialog box, supply DNS server information.

servers (also called DNS servers). In brief, the domain name system is a huge, worldwide system of linked servers that map numeric IP addresses (such as 216.32.74.53) to human-readable domain names (such as www.yahoo.com). If you do not supply valid DNS server addresses, you will need to type numeric IP addresses to access information on the Internet. Review the options for Domain Name Servers in Table 1.3.

Table 1.3 New Account Dialog Box, DNS Tab

Item	Data Required
Domain Name	Use the Domain name of your ISP. For example, if your ISP is Mindspring, enter mindspring.com.
DNS IP Address	You will need the IP address for your ISP's Domain Name Server. Many ISPs have more than one DNS Server; you can enter the IP address for each server.
DNS Address List	Contains the IP address(es) that you entered from each Domain Name Server.

| Disable existing... | If you have a larger network, you may have your own DNS Server. In this case, you may want to check this box to allow your computer to use the ISP DNS Server. |

The next tab, Gateway, is important only if your ISP told you that you needed to supply a gateway address. Review the options for the Gateway tab in Table 1.4.

Table 1.4 New Account Dialog Box, Gateway Tab

Item	Data Required
Default Gateway	This option sends all your data to the Internet through your connection to the ISP.
Static Gateway	Some ISPs require you to specify the IP address of their gateway, their connection to the Internet.
Gateway IP Address	If your ISP needs you to enter the IP address of their gateway.
Assign the Default...	Keep this on. This option sends any message to an outside network through your ISP connection.

The next two tabs, Login Script and Accounting, are for specialized situations. If your ISP does require a Login Script, consult their technical support for details.

The Accounting tab helps you work with different charges for local telephone calls. If you live in one of the countries shown under this tab, check the rules. Look in one of the following directories for the rules for your national telephone company: ~/.kde/share/apps/kppp/Rules or /usr/X11R6/share/apps/kppp/Rules.

Figure 1.8 Congratulations! You are connected!

You can use Tables 1.3 – 1.6 as a checklist with your ISP. Once they have answered all of the questions on the checklist, you can fill out the appropriate blanks in the KPPP utility.

You Are Ready To Connect!

Once you have set up KPPP, you are finally ready to connect to the Internet. If it is not already open, click on the Main Menu button, point to Internet, then click KPPP. This opens the KPPP dialog box.

In the Connect To text box, choose the name for the connection to your ISP. Select the Show Log Window option. Enter your user name in the Login ID text box, enter your password in the Password text box, and then click Connect.

If you are successful, you will see "Connect" in the Login Script dialog box, as shown in Figure 1.8. If the connection did not work for some reason, see "Troubleshooting Your Installation" for tips on resolving the problem.

Troubleshooting Your Installation

This section provides solutions for almost all of the problems you may encounter with modems. Remember, though, that some modems simply do not work with Linux, no matter what you do. Before troubleshooting your modem, make sure it is compatible with Linux; otherwise, you will be wasting your time.

An organized approach to troubleshooting pays off. Take it step by step. Remember what the great Sherlock Holmes told the baffled Dr. Watson: "When you have eliminated all of the other possibilities, whatever remains, however improbable, is the truth." Now we can start by figuring out what is wrong with the modem.

Checking Physical Connections

Make sure your modem is properly seated in the expansion slot and that all the connections are snug. Is the phone line plugged into a standard modular telephone jack?

Curing the Modem Blues

When you queried your modem with KPPP, you may have been told that your modem is "busy," and that KPPP is really sorry about this. The sympathy is nice, but you are given no clue as to how to solve the problem.

What is going on? Your modem is not busy; rather, Linux could not find it. This problem could be caused by any of the following:

- Your modem does not have Plug and Play capabilities, and KPPP does not know which serial port to use. You need to determine which serial port your modem needs.
- Two devices are vying for access to the same serial port. You will need to reconfigure one of them in order to get your modem to work.
- You or somebody else configured your computer so that one or more serial ports is disabled or has a non-standard configuration. You will need to enable the port or restore the default configuration.

The following sections detail strategies for solving these problems.

Which Serial Port Is Your Modem Using?

Start by determining which serial port your modem is trying to use. In the Windows world, serial ports are known as COM ports; a maximum of four are available (COM1, COM2, COM3, and COM4).

If your system enables you to run Windows as well as Linux, you can use Windows to find out which serial port your modem is using. In Windows 95 or 98, right-click on the "My Computer" icon, click Properties in the shortcut menu, then click the Device Manager tab. Click on the plus sign adjacent to "modem." In the properties for your modem, find the COM port under the Modem tab, the IRQ and I/O under the Resources tab.

If you are using an older modem that uses jumpers to assign the COM port, you can determine the COM port by taking a look at these jumpers. Often, the COM port is printed on the circuit board, so you can immediately see which COM port is in use.

Still unable to figure out which serial port your modem is using? Check your modem's documentation; chances are it will tell you which serial port is enabled by default.

Resolving Serial Port Conflicts

Once you have determined which serial port your modem requires, make sure no other device is trying to use the serial port at the same time. Chances are your system has only two devices that require a serial port: a *serial mouse* (a mouse that connects through a serial port) and your modem.

If you have a serial modem and a serial mouse but only one serial port, you will need to add an additional serial port before you can get your modem to work. But there might be an easier solution. On the back of your computer, look for a round PS/2 port. If you have a PS/2 port, you can get an adapter for your serial mouse that enables it to plug into the PS/2 port.

If your computer is equipped with two onboard serial ports, you may need to disable one of them in order to get your internal modem to work. Suppose your modem wants to be connected to COM2. However, your system is set up so that one of the onboard serial ports is connected to COM2. To disable the onboard serial port, start your computer and type the key (generally Delete) that enables you to view your computer's Setup menu. Locate the page that contains the port settings. Disable the onboard serial port that your modem wants to use, save your settings, and restart your computer. Try using KPPP to auto detect the modem again.

Setting the Port Manually

Did the auto detect fail again? If you are sure that no other device is trying to use the serial port your modem prefers, it is possible that you are using a modem that lacks Plug and Play capabilities, or that the Linux Plug and Play software cannot detect your modem for some reason. In such cases, you will need to specify the serial port manually.

To specify the serial port manually, follow these steps:

1. In the KPPP Configuration dialog box, click the Device tab.

2. Click the pull-down arrow adjacent to Modem Device. You can make one of five choices, as shown in Table 1.5.

Table 1.5 KPPP Modem Devices

Device	Channel
/dev/ttyS0 or /dev/cua0	COM1
/dev/ttyS1 or /dev/cua1	COM2
/dev/ttyS2 or /dev/cua2	COM3
/dev/ttyS3 or /dev/cua3	COM4

3. Select the modem device that corresponds to the COM port for your modem.

4. Click the Modem tab and try the Query Modem button again. If the modem still does not respond and you are sure you have got the serial port right, it is possible your IRQ settings are incorrect; check the next section to find out.

Is Your Modem's IRQ Configured Correctly?

Now make sure your modem is set to the correct interrupt request (IRQ) line. To determine the current IRQ assignment for the serial port to which your modem is connected, type **setserial /dev/modem** at the Linux prompt, and press Enter. You will see the current port assignment and IRQ. Now shut down your system and examine your modem. If your modem has jumpers that enable you to configure the port manually, examine the jumpers to make sure that they match the port that you are using the PPP Configuration Device Tab. If not, change the jumpers so that they match.

If this did not work, it is possible that your system's serial port settings have been altered so that they are using a non-standard IRQ configuration. To check the configuration, restart your system and press the key that enables you to enter your computer's startup menu (where you can examine the BIOS and other settings). Find the area where serial ports are listed, and make sure that these settings have not been changed from the defaults (COM 1 should be set to 0x3f8 and IRQ 4, while COM 2 should be set to 0x2f8 and IRQ 3. If these settings were changed, try resetting them to the defaults.

Now try autodetecting your modem again. No luck? Compadre, junk that modem, and get one that is Linux compatible.

My Modem's Detected Now! But I Cannot Connect!

If you have gotten KPPP to detect your modem but are still unable to connect, there are many additional problems that may be responsible. Happily, most of them are easy to solve. Once again, let us take it step by step.

TIP If you have an external modem, there are a series of lights on the modem that can help you diagnose most problems. Although the labels and number of lights vary from modem to modem, they normally include the indicators shown in Table 1.6. If the labels on your modem do not correspond, consult your documentation.

Table 1.6 **External Modem Lights**

Label	Function
AA	Auto Answer: if you have set up Linux as a Server, this shows that your modem is ready to receive a call.
CD	Carrier Detect: shows a clear signal between your computer and your modem. If this light is not on, check your connections.
RD	When this light flashes, your modem is Receiving Data. If your TD light is on and RD is off, your ISP is not answering.
TD	When this light flashes, your modem is Transmitting Data (often labeled SD).

PPPD Installation Problems

If you get a "PPPD is not properly installed" message when you start KPPP, change the permissions on the /usr/sbin/pppd file. This file manages your dial-up connection.

To change the permissions on pppd, you have to log in as the superuser or root user. If you are using your ordinary user account, log in as superuser by doing the following: open a terminal window, type **su** and press Enter, and type your password and press Enter. Now type **chmod u+s /usr/sbin/pppd** and press Enter.

Testing Your Modem with a Communications Program

Still not working? Let us watch the modem in action and make sure it is functioning correctly. To do so, you can use a communications program such as minicom, which is included with most Linux distributions. A communications program enables your computer to connect to non-Internet dial-up services, such as bulletin board systems (BBS). Here, you will use minicom just to see whether your modem will respond to minicom, get a dial tone, and connect successfully. If it does, it is a good bet that the problem lies in the information you have supplied to KPPP; chances are you made a typing mistake, or your ISP gave you the wrong information.

To run minicom, do the following:

1. Open a terminal window, and see whether minicom is installed on your system. To do so, type **whereis minicom** and press Enter. If it is installed in /usr/bin, you can start the program by typing minicom and pressing Enter.

    The program immediately attempts to access your modem. If all goes well, you will see the characters AT followed by an initialization string (commands that configure the modem), followed by the modem's OK response. If you do not see OK, you have configured the wrong port setting. Run KPPP again, and choose the correct one.

2. Try dialing the number of the line connected to your modem. If your modem has a speaker, you will get a busy signal, which lets you test whether your modem can get a dial tone and dial correctly. To dial your number, type **ATDT** followed by a space and your telephone number. Press Enter to start dialing. Once you have gotten a busy signal, press Ctrl + **A, H** to hang up.

    If you do not get a dial tone, make sure your modem is connected to a modular telephone outlet, and that both connections (the one on the modem end and the one plugged into the modular phone jack) are securely seated.

3. Press Ctrl + **A, Q** to shut down your modem and exit minicom.

If none of these measures work, your modem may not be compatible with Linux—many are not. Many reasonably good, Linux-compatible modems are available for bargain prices; it's better to replace your modem than to spend days in a courageous but possibly unsuccessful attempt to get your current modem working.

TIP Some modems will not work with the analog phone jacks provided on the side or back of digital telephone systems, such as those found in offices or hotels. This is a sign of an inexpensive, low-quality modem; consider replacing it rather than wasting time trying to get it to work.

Now you are ready to move on to Chapter 2, where you will configure Netscape Communicator on your Linux system. If you would like to learn more about the technical side of PPP connections with Linux, read the next section.

Looking Under the Hood

This section briefly introduces the technology that underlies PPP connections with Linux; in addition, it discusses some text-mode commands that you may wish to try. You do not need to have this information down cold to use Linux successfully; it is of interest only if you would like to learn more about how Linux works.

The PPP Network Interface (ppp0)

To connect your Linux system to the Internet, it is necessary to define a *network interface*. In brief, a network interface is a file that serves as an intermediary between a networking device, such as an Ethernet adapter or a modem, and the Linux kernel. When you connect to the Internet by means of a modem, the PPP software detects your modem and creates a network interface called ppp0. If your computer were equipped with more than one modem, the software would create additional interfaces (ppp1, ppp2, and so on).

The PPP Daemon

To implement PPP connections, Linux distributions make use of the pppd *daemon* (a daemon is a program that runs in the background, waiting to step into action when its services are needed). A pppd is not meant to be run manually; rather, it is launched by other programs. Among these is wvdial, a PPP dialer utility that dials the modem and negotiates the PPP connection with your ISP. Once wvdial achieves the connection, wvdial launches pppd, and you are connected.

Most user-friendly PPP utilities are little more than attractive-looking front ends for wvdial. (A *front end* is a user-friendly program that makes working with a text-mode program more pleasant.) In the following sections, you will learn that it is quite possible to connect to the Internet using wvdial alone. You may wish to try this approach if KPPP will not work for some reason that is not attributable to modem incompatibility.

Connecting with wvdial

If you would like to configure your PPP connection manually, you can do so by following these steps:

1. Run wvdialconf to detect your modem, determine its characteristics, and write the initial working copy of the wvdial configuration file, /etc/wvdial.conf. To run wvdialconf, open a terminal window and type **wvdialconf.**

2. Modify the wvdial configuration file (/etc/wvdial.conf) to dial your ISP and establish the connection. You can do this by running Midnight Commander's text utility; switch to superuser, type **mc**, and press Enter. Locate /etc/wvdial.conf and press F4 to edit the file.

The configuration file, /etc/wvdial.conf, has two or more sections. The first, Dialer Defaults, is generated automatically by wvdialconf. Do not alter the settings in this section. The second section, the name of which begins with

Dialer, specifies the settings for a given PPP connection, including the phone number, username, and password. You can create two or more such sections if you wish.

The following illustrates a typical wvdial configuration in /etc/wvdial.conf:

```
[Dialer Defaults]
Modem = /dev/ttyS1
Baud = 115200
Init1 = ATZ
Init2 = ATQ0 V1 E1 SO=0 &C1 &D2 S11=55
SetVolume = 1
Dial Command = ATDT


[Dialer MyConnection]
Username = suzanne
Password = ilw2mfc
Phone = 555-1212
Dial Prefix = 9,,
Area Code = 800
```

This configuration dials 9, waits two seconds, and then dials 800-555-1212. When the ISP responds, it supplies the username suzanne and the password ilw2mfc, and establishes the connection using the ISP's preferred authentication method.

Figuring Out Whether You Are Online: Ping

If you are trying to figure out whether you are really connected to the Internet, try this. Open a terminal window, type **ping** followed by a space and the IP address of your ISP's DNS server, and press Enter. This utility sends information to the specified server and requests a response. If the server responds, you will see the response on the screen. If there is no response, nothing happens—and you know that you are not connected. Check your settings with KPPP, and try connecting again.

Getting Information About Your Connection: ifconfig

A text mode called ifconfig can provide useful information about your Internet connection. To use ifconfig, open a terminal window, type **ifconfig,** and press Enter.

TIP If you see the message "No such file or directory," type **whereis ifconfig** and press Enter to find out where this utility is stored. If it is stored in /sbin, launch the command by typing **/sbin/ifconfig,** and press Enter.

If you are connected to the Internet with KPPP or wvdial, you will see several lines of information about the ppp0 interface, including the IP address your system is currently using.

Making Sure DNS Is Working Correctly: nslookup

Are you connecting successfully to the Internet, only to find that you cannot access Web sites? Chances are there is a problem with your Domain Name Server (DNS) setup. To find out, type **nslookup www.yahoo.com** and press Enter. If this utility replies with the numerical IP address of www.yahoo.com, DNS is working just fine. If not, there is a problem with your DNS setup. Check the IP addresses you typed in the DNS server dialog box, and try connecting again.

References and Further Reading

Lawyer, D. S. (2000). *Modem HOWTO*. Linux Documentation Project. Available online at www.linuxdoc.org/HOWTO/Modem-HOWTO.html.

Reijnen, P. (2000). *Linux Hardware Compatibility HOWTO*. Linux Documentation Project. Available online at www.linuxdoc.org/HOWTO/Hardware-HOWTO.html.

Wuebben, B. J. (2000). *The KPPP Handbook*. The KDE Project. Available online at www.kde.org/documentation/en/applications/kppp/index.html.

2

Using Internet Applications

Now that you are connected to the Internet, you are ready to use Internet applications, such as Netscape Communicator. Chances are you have already browsed the Web with Netscape. As you will quickly learn, though, you will need to do some configuration in order to get Netscape to work the way you expect—that is, as well as a browser works on a Windows or Macintosh system. For example, Netscape is not set up to display multimedia, such as movies and videos. In addition, you will need to configure Netscape to access your email.

This chapter introduces the Internet applications available on your system. It also shows you how to configure these applications, if necessary. The chapter does not attempt to teach you all the fundamentals of Internet use; if you are not familiar with the essentials of Web browsing, email and other Internet services, you should read a good general introduction to the Internet before proceeding with this chapter.

TIP If you are new to Netscape Communicator, check out Netscape Communicator (AP Professional), which covers the nearly identical Windows version.

Here is what you will find in this chapter:

- **Configuring Helper Applications.** Learn how to set up your system's default Web browser, Netscape Communicator, so that it can work with animations, movies, and sounds.
- **Configuring Netscape Communicator for Email Access.** Set up your Communicator package to access your email account.
- **Configuring Netscape Communicator for Newsgroup Access.** Set up your Communicator package to access Usenet newsgroups.
- **Accessing FTP Sites with File Manager.** Create virtual file systems for frequently accessed FTP sites; you will love this feature.
- **Exploring Additional Internet Applications.** Introduced are KFtp (a KDE-compatible FTP client), KXicq (an ICQ "buddy list" program), and KVIrc, a nifty KDE application for accessing Internet Relay Chat (IRC).

Configuring Netscape Helper Applications

Netscape Communicator is a full-featured suite of Internet applications that includes a browser (Netscape Navigator), email and newsgroups (Netscape Messenger), and Composer, a program that enables you to create Web pages. This section does not attempt to teach you how to use Netscape Communicator—that is a subject for a book in itself. Instead, it focuses on configuring the program for Internet use. In this section, you learn how to configure *helper applications*, which Navigator needs in order to display certain types of data.

Understanding Which Applications Navigator Needs

Netscape Navigator needs help to display data types that it does not recognize internally. If you configure the program as recommended in this section, Navigator will automatically start the correct helper application when you encounter the specified type of data (such as sound or a video). Table 2.1 lists the data types that you may encounter on the Internet, as well as the applications we recommend that you associate with these data types. For each application, you will find the recommended startup command (the command that Netscape passes to the application). This includes the command needed to start the application (such as esdplay), followed by recommended options, if any, and %s (a variable that automatically inserts the URL of the remote file you are accessing).

Table 2.1 Data Types and Recommended Application Settings

Data TypeApplication	Startup Command	%s Variable
AIFF Audio	Esound	esdplay %s
IEF Image	Electric Eyes	ee %s
MPEG Audio	Electric Eyes	mpg123 -b 4096 %s
MPEG Video	xanim	xanim +Zpe +q %s
MPEG2 Video	xanim	xanim +Zpe +q %s
PNG Image	Electric Eyes	ee %s
Portable Doc. Format	xpdf	xpdf %s
PostScript Document	gv gv %s	
PPM Image	Electric Eyes	ee %s
PGM Image	Electric Eyes	ee %s
PBM Image	Electric Eyes	ee %s
Real Audio	RealPlayer	raplayer %s
RGB Image	Electric Eyes	ee %s
SGI Video	xanim	xanim +Zpe +q %s
TIFF Image	Electric Eyes	ee %s
ULAW Audio	Esound	esdplay %s
WAV Audio	Esound	esdplay %s
Windows bitmap	Electric Eyes	ee %s
QuickTime Video	xanim	xanim +Zpe +q %s
X Pixmap	Electric Eyes	ee %s
X Pixmap	Electric Eyes	ee %s

TIP You must make sure that all the applications in Table 2.1 are correctly installed on your system before Navigator can make use of them. For more information on obtaining and installing software, see Chapter 12 of Linux Clearly Explained.

Associating Applications with Data Types

To configure Navigator to work with installed applications on your system, do the following:

1. First, open up Netscape Communicator. Click the Main Menu button, point to Red Hat, point to Internet, then click Netscape Communicator.

TIP In Corel Linux, click the Main Menu button, point to Applications, then click Netscape Navigator.

---

2. In Netscape Navigator, click Edit on the menu bar, and choose Preferences. You will see the Netscape Preferences dialog box.

3. In the Category list, click the arrow next to Navigator, if necessary to reveal the subcategories, and select Applications. You'll see the Applications page, shown in Figure 2.1.

4. Select the data type you want to change, and click Edit. You'll see the Application dialog box, shown in Figure 2.2.

5. In the Handled By area, check Application, and type the application's startup command in the text box.

6. Click OK until you see Netscape Navigator again.

TIP To test your helper application configuration, visit the "Ready-to-Go Solaris Helpers Page" (http://home1.swipnet.se/%7Ew-10694/helpers.html or http://www.ase.ee/moshkow/lat/ WEBMASTER/sol-helpers.txt#0). You will find links to small multimedia files throughout; click on these to test your helper applications.

Using Plug-Ins

Helper applications display data in a separate window. In contrast, *plug-ins* enable Netscape Navigator to display certain types of data *inline*—that is, within the Web page. Hundreds of plug-ins exist for the Windows and Macintosh versions of Netscape Navigator, but only a handful are available for Linux. Worse, installing them is not easy; unless the plug-in is available in an RPM file that is expressly designed for Red Hat Linux, you will need the command-line skills introduced in Part Five of Linux Clearly Explained.

The easiest place to find new plug-ins for Netscape Communicator is at the Netscape download site: http://www.netscape.com/plugins. As you review the available plug-ins, make sure that the plug-in you want is available for Linux.

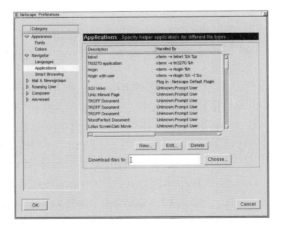

Figure 2.1 Select the data type from this list.

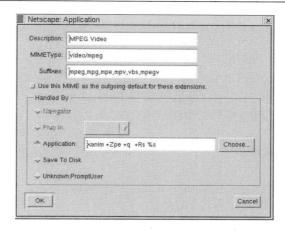

Figure 2.2 This is where you link a data type with an application.

The following is a sample of what is available:

- **Adobe Acrobat Reader.** (Adobe, www.adobe.com). Displays Portable Document Format (PDF) files within Web pages.
- **Glg Plug-in.** (Generic Logic, www.genlogic1.com). Displays real-time processes within Web pages. Navigate to "Glg Netscape Plugin" when you get to the General Logic Web site.
- **Plugger.** (Fredrik Hübinette, fredrik.hubbe.net/plugger.html). Organizes sound and video helper applications so that they play inline. Please note that the glibc2 RPM version available at this writing installs the needed file, called plugger.so, in an incorrect location (/usr/local/lib/netscape/plugins/); copy this file to the .netscape directory within your home directory. You will also need to configure Plugger to work with the various sound and video applications on your system; in order to do this, you will need to switch to root user and edit the file etc/pluggerrc. Examine the

file carefully to see where it mentions specific applications, and replace these application names with the ones installed on your system. Not for the faint of heart!

- **Macromedia Shockwave.** (Macromedia, www.macromedia.com). Plays Shockwave animations.
- **Real Audio.** (Real Networks, www.real.com). Plays real audio music and other broadcasts.
- **Xview.** (Fischer Computertechnik, www.fct.de). Allows you to use your browser to view different image types, including .tif, .bmp, .pcx. As you are downloading from a German language site, you need to know that "Firma" indicates where the name of your company goes, "englisch" is English, and you need to click "Abschicken" when you have filled out the form.

If you want to take a stab at obtaining and installing these plug-ins, be sure to read the instructions carefully—and set aside a day or two.

Configuring Netscape Messenger for E-Mail and Newsgroups

Netscape Messenger, the email component of Netscape Communicator, is a full-featured email program that compares favorably with Microsoft Outlook Express and Eudora, the leading packages in the Windows and Mac worlds. You can use Netscape Messenger to access mail from your service provider's POP or IMAP mail server. In the following sections, you will learn how to add your account information so that Messenger can access your mail.

Creating a Signature

You can create a signature (including your name, organizational affiliation, and optional contact information) that Messenger will add automatically to your outgoing messages. To do so, click the Main Menu button, point to Applications, and choose Text Editor. Type your signature information, and then click Save. Save the file using the name .signature (note the dot in front of the filename), and place this file in the top-level directory of your home directory.

Adding Your Account Information

When you add your account information to Messenger, it is necessary to do the following:

1. From the Edit menu in Netscape Communicator, choose Preferences. You will see the Preferences dialog box.

2. Click the arrow next to Mail & Newsgroups so you can see the subcategories.

3. Select Mail Servers. You will see the Mail Servers page as shown in Figure 2.3.

4. Click Add. You will see the General page as shown in Figure 2.4.

5. In the Server Name box, type the name of the server that handles your incoming mail (this server is also called the POP server, POP3 server, or IMAP server). For example, if you have a yahoo email address, your mail server is pop.mail.yahoo.com.

6. In the Server Type box, choose the server type (POP or IMAP).

7. In the User Name box, type the username you supply to log on to your email account. Usually, this is the first part of your email address (the part before the @ sign).

8. If you would like Messenger to remember your password, check this option. Don't check this option if others use your computer.

9. If you would like Messenger to check for new mail automatically at an interval you specify, select the Check for mail option, and type an interval in minutes (the default is 10).

10. Check Automatically download any new messages so that you will see your new messages automatically.

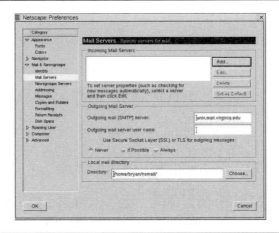

Figure 2.3 Use this dialog box to define your mail settings.

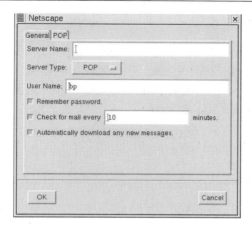

Figure 2.4 Enter general information about your account here.

11. If you are setting up a POP account, click the POP tab. If you would like to leave messages on the server so that you can access them from another computer, check Leave messages on server. If you would like Messenger to delete a message from the server when you delete it locally, check this option.

12. Click OK to confirm your incoming mail server settings. You will see the Mail Servers page again.

13. In the Outgoing Mail Server text box, type the name of the computer used for outgoing mail (also called SMTP server). Netscape automatically fills in default values for the other options, and these values are fine. The Outgoing Mail Server is defined by your Internet Service Provider.

14. In the Category list, select Identity. You will see the Identity page as shown in Figure 2.5. Supply your name, email address, and organization. State a reply-to address only if your reply address differs

from your regular email address. The location of the signature file should correspond to the file that you created in the previous section.

15. **Important:** In the Category list, click Formatting. You'll see the Formatting page. In the Message formatting area, be sure to check Use the plain text editor to compose messages. Don't use the HTML editor to compose messages; your messages will be unreadable by many recipients. You should send HTML-formatted mail only to those correspondents who have HTML-capable mail programs.

16. Click OK to confirm your mail settings.

To retrieve your mail, click Communicator on the menu bar, choose Messenger, and click the Get Mail button.

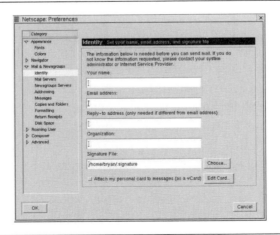

Figure 2.5 Supply your identity here.

Configuring Newsgroups

To configure Messenger to access the newsgroups your ISP makes available, follow these instructions:

1. From the Edit menu in Navigator or Messenger, choose Preferences. You will see the Preferences dialog box.

2. In the Category list, click the arrow next to Mail & Newsgroups, if necessary to display the subcategories, and select Newsgroups Servers. You will see the Newsgroups Servers page.

3. Click Add. You will see a dialog box that enables you to type the server name.

4. In the server text box, type the name of the server. If the server requires a name and password, check Always use name and password. If the server supports encrypted connections, check Support encrypted connections (SSL).

5. Click OK.

6. Click OK again to confirm your settings.

To access newsgroups, click Communicator on the Messenger or Navigator menus, and choose Newsgroups. You will see the Netscape Message Center. To download the list of newsgroups from your ISP, click Subscribe.

Accessing FTP Sites with File Manager

The File Transfer Protocol (FTP) is another of the Internet's most popular services. By means of *anonymous FTP*, individuals or organizations can make files freely available for public download. Anonymous FTP is one of the chief vehicles for distributing open source software. Other FTP servers require a username and password. If you plan to publish a Web page on your ISP's computers, you will need to learn how to use FTP for uploading files to a password-protected server.

You can use a separate program (such as KFtp) to access FTP servers, but you can also use the KDE File Manager. Configure the KDE File Manager from the Edit menu by choosing Show Tree.

What is so cool about using KDE File Manager for FTP is best understood by trying it. Once you have opened the FTP server's directory structure, you can use all the File Manager techniques you have already learned to work with files. For example, to download a file, you simply copy it to your home directory.

The following sections show you how to access FTP sites, starting with anonymous FTP servers. You will go on to learn how to access password-protected sites.

Accessing Anonymous FTP Sites

To access an anonymous FTP site with the KDE File Manager, do the following:

1.   Click the Main Menu button, point to System, then click File Manager.

2.   Enter the superuser password if required.

3.   From the edit menu, choose Show Tree.

4.   In the Location box, type the following URL: ftp:// followed by the Internet address of the FTP site (such as ftp.cdrom.com).

5.   Press Enter.

File Manager attempts to access the site, which may take a while. Once the site has been accessed, you will see files and directories from the ftp server in the right-hand side window.

TIP If you cannot reach an FTP site, there are two common solutions. First, check how you typed in the name of the site: spelling matters. Second, FTP sites often limit the number of users who can connect to it at the same time. You may just need to try again in a few minutes.

Accessing Password-Protected Sites

To access a password protected site, you embed your login name and password into the URL, as follows:

```
ftp://loginname:password@servername
```

For example, suppose you are accessing ftp.september. org; your user name is brenda and your password is 339jqq. You would type the following in File Manager's Location box:

```
ftp://brenda:339jqq@ftp.september.org
```

The connection works the same way. Depending on the permissions established at this server, you may be able to upload files as well as download them.

Exploring Additional Internet Applications

A number of promising KDE Internet utilities are currently under development. Check the KDE home page frequently (http://www.kde.org) for news about these and other KDE-compatible Internet utilities.

Here's an overview of some of the utilities planned for release with KDE 2.0:

- **KFtp.** You can use File Manager for occasional downloading or uploading from FTP sites. For extensive work with FTP, you will find it easier to use a utility, such as KFtp, that is designed expressly for FTP usage. Created by Eric Santonacci, KFtp is a network client that is fully compatible with KDE. When you access an FTP site with KFtp, you will see two file panels. On the left, you see your local files and directories; the right panel shows the remote server's files and directories. Downloading or uploading a file is as simple as selecting the file and clicking the download or upload arrow.

- **KXicq.** This program is an ICQ-compatible "buddy list" program that is fully integrated with the KDE desktop. A buddy list program enables you to tell when your friends or contacts are logged on to the Internet (and they, in turn, can tell when you are logged on). When you and a buddy are both online, you can send messages to each other by means of text chatting. You can use KXicq whether or not you have already signed up for ICQ. If you signed up for ICQ on another computer, jot down your ICQ number, your password, and other identifying information; KXicq will reestablish your connection to the ICQ network. If you have not already signed up, you can use KXicq to create a new ICQ membership.
- **KVIrc.** Internet Relay Chat (IRC) is a popular text-based chatting network, with hundreds of servers (and dozens of networks) in use throughout the world. KVIrc is a KDE compatible IRC client.

On the horizon are a KDE Office Suite, a full-featured email client, and much more. By the time you read this book, these projects may have produced preliminary versions (called *beta versions*) that are far enough along to try out on your system.

Looking Under the Hood

This section briefly discusses some text-mode utilities that may prove useful when you are exploring the Internet.

Interacting with Remote Systems: Telnet

The Telnet protocol defines a means of establishing a login session on a remote computer, just as if you were sitting at the computer's terminal and keyboard. To use

Telnet, use the Telnet utility installed by default with most Linux distributions.

To use Telnet, open a terminal window, type **telnet,** and press Enter. You will see a special prompt that lets you know you have entered the utility's interactive mode. In this mode you can use the commands listed in Table 2.2.

Table 2.2 Telnet Commands (interactive mode)

Command	Purpose
close	Close the session with the remote server, but without exiting telnet (see quit)
open *server*	Open a connection to the specified *server* (for example, open telnet.mydomain.com)
quit	Terminate the connection and exit the telnet utility
status	Show the current status of telnet

Using a Text-Only Browser: Lynx

If your main interest online lies in text rather than graphics, you may enjoy using Lynx, a text-only browser. Lynx does not display any of the pretty graphics that you see on the Web, so you are missing out on the Web's increasingly attractive visual appearance. But you are also missing out on the slow downloads and annoying animations.

Lynx is installed by default on most Linux distributions. To give Lynx a try, open a terminal window, type **lynx,** and press Enter. You will see a menu of available options at the bottom of the screen. To go to a Web page, press **g** (for Go), type the Web page address, and press Enter.

Table 2.3 summarizes the most useful Lynx commands that you can use when you are online with this utility.

Table 2.3 Lynx Commands

Command	Purpose
Ctrl + A	Go to the beginning of the current document
Ctrl + B	View the previous page of the document
Ctrl + D	Quit the browser unconditionally
Ctrl + E	Go to the end of the current document
Ctrl + F	View the next page of the document
Ctrl + H	Display stack of currently suspended documents
Ctrl + J	Go to the document given by the current link
Ctrl + K	View cookies
Ctrl + L	Refresh the screen
Ctrl + N	Go forward two lines
Ctrl + P	Go back two lines
Ctrl + R	Reload the current document
Ctrl + T	Toggle tracing of browser operations
Ctrl + V	Switch between two ways of parsing HTML
Ctrl + W	Refresh the screen to clear garbled text
d	Download the current link
Delete	Display stack of currently suspended documents

Down arrow	Move to next hyperlink down
e	Edit the current document
E	Edit the current link
End	Go to the end of the current document
f	Display file operations menu
F1	Display help
g	Go to the specified URL
G	Edit the current document's URL and go to the edited URL
h	Display help on using the browser
H	Show available options
Home	Go to the beginning of the current document
i	Display an index of potentially useful documents
j	Go to a target document or action
k	Display the current key bindings
K	Show keystroke mappings
l	List the links in the current document
m	Return to the first screen
n	Go to the next occurrence
o	Display option settings
p	Print the current document
PgDn	View the next page of the document
PgUp	View the previous page of the document

q	Quit the browser
Q	Force browser exit
r	Delete bookmark
Return	Follow the selected hyperlink
Right arrow	Follow the selected hyperlink
s	Search index
Space	View the next page of the document
t	Tag link for later action
Tab	Go to next link or text area
u	Go back to the previous document
Up arrow	Move to next hyperlink up
v	View bookmark list
V	List links visited during the current session
x	Force submission of link or form without the cache
z	Interrupt network connection

From Here

In the first two chapters, you learned to set up the elements of networking on your computer by setting up a dial-up connection to the Internet.

You are now ready to set up a smaller Linux network of two or more computers. In Part Two of this book, you will learn all that you need to connect and then share files and printers between different Linux computers.

Part Two

Building Your
Local Area Network (LAN)

3

Essential Networking Concepts

A *network* is a group of two or more computer systems that have been linked together by some kind of physical communications medium. In the first two chapters, you set up your modem to establish a link between your computer and your Internet service provider's computer. This simple network creates a big payoff. Your ISP's system serves as gateway to the Internet, the largest computer network in existence.

Physical Media

Most people think of computer networks in terms of cabling, but the physical medium is actually the least important part of a computer network. To be sure, some media place restrictions on the amount of data that can be transferred through a network, but even the simplest and least expensive cable—twisted pair, the type of cabling used for telephones—can transfer as much as 1.5 Mbps. Network signals can traverse any type of telecommunications medium, including telephone lines, coaxial cable, microwave relay systems, satellites, wireless (radio and infrared), and fiberoptic cable. Often, a single message travels over several different physical media before arriving at its destination.

The Internet connection that you created in Chapter 1 exemplifies the heterogeneity of network physical media. You connected to your ISP via a telephone line. From there, your computer's signals may have traversed a high-capacity digital telephone cable (called T1 or T3), fiber optic cables, or microwave relay systems.

Communications Standards (Protocols)

What makes a network function is not merely the physical connections, whether they are achieved through circuit switching or packet switching. Of fundamental importance are the standards that specify how the network functions. These standards are called *protocols*. Protocols are fixed, formalized standards that specify how two dissimilar network components can establish communication. Often, a given network's functionality requires dozens or even hundreds of protocols. For example, more than one hundred Internet protocols exist. The collection of protocols that defines a given network's functionality is called its *protocol suite*. Collectively, a protocol suite specifies the network's overall design, called the *network architecture*.

Data Routing Technologies

Networks funnel messages to the correct destination using two basic technologies, called circuit switching and packet switching.

Circuit Switching

In *circuit switching*, the network creates a physical, end-to-end circuit between the sending and receiving computers. This is the same technology used in telephone networks. It also can be used for computer data. Companies often lease *dedicated lines* from telecommunications providers. These lines give them a permanent, end-to-end connection that is created using the telecommunication company's switching network.

The major advantage of circuit switching lies in the high degree of security it provides. No other users have access to the connection. However, this type of connection is inefficient. Computer data traffic occurs in bursts, and sometimes there is no data transferred for a long time. The permanent, end-to-end connection typically makes inefficient use of the circuit.

Packet Switching

Packet switching works in a way that is radically different from the telephone system. In packet switching, an outgoing message is divided into data units of a fixed size, called *packets*. Each packet is numbered and addressed to the destination computer. The sending computer pushes the packets onto the network, where they are examined by *routers*. Routers are computer-based devices that examine each packet they detect. After reading the packet's address, the router consults a table of possible pathways to the packet's destination. If more than one path exists, the router sends the packet along the path that is most free from congestion.

Packet-switching networks are often called *connectionless* because, unlike switched networks, it is not necessary to have an active, direct electrical connection for two computers to communicate. For example, the Internet is a packet-switching network; you can send somebody an email message even if the destination computer is not operating. If the message does not get through, the software keeps trying to send it for a set period of time, after which it gives up.

Packet-switching networks are significantly more efficient than circuit switching networks. While en route, packets originating from one computer are commingled with those from many others, so the network is able to make full use of its data transfer capacity. However, packet-switching networks are inherently less secure than networks created with a private, end-to-end circuit. Intruders can use programs called *packet sniffers* to search for packets containing sensitive data, such as credit card numbers or passwords. To work with public packet-switching networks (for example, the Internet) safely, confidentiality safeguards such as encryption are needed.

Despite their disadvantages, packet-switching networks are by far the more widely used of the two basic networking technologies. Efforts have been made to develop circuit switching technologies (such as asynchronous transfer mode (ATM)) that can equal or exceed the efficiency of packet-switching networks, but the resulting technologies have not gained widespread acceptance.

When we are talking about networking, therefore, we are talking about packet switching.

Types of Packet-Switching Networks

Several different types of packet-switching networks exist. *Wide area networks* (WANs) provide direct, point-to-point data transfer services for businesses across hundreds and even thousands of miles. *Local area networks* (LANs) link anywhere from a handful to thousands of computers within a limited geographical area, such as a building or a group of buildings. *Metropolitan area networks* (MANs) resemble LANs, but they use high-speed, high-tech cables—crafted from light-transmitting fibers—to link an organization's offices throughout a regional area. The Internet is often called an *internetwork*, and for good reason. It is a network of linked networks, not just linked computer systems. In fact, the word "Internet" is a short version of internetwork.

As you have already learned, Linux is an excellent platform for gaining access to the Internet. It is equally capable for developing LANs, MANs, and WANs, as organizations everywhere are discovering. To get started with Linux networking, you should begin with your Internet connection, as you have already done. The next step, fully covered in this book, involves creating a local area network (LAN). Both MANs and WANs require exotic equipment and network administration skills that are far beyond the scope of this book. You will focus on LANs, and for good reason—that's where the major payoff is found, as the next section explains.

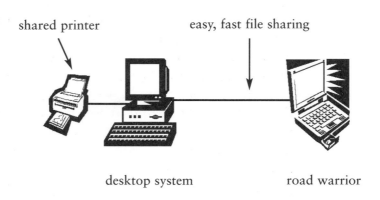

shared printer

easy, fast file sharing

desktop system

road warrior

Figure 3.1 A simple, two-person network can make excellent sense.

Why Create a Local Area Network (LAN)?

Just a decade ago, LANs were relatively rare; considerable expertise and expense were required to set up and administer them. Today, LAN networking is experiencing the kind of explosive growth that made personal computers and the Internet household words. Everywhere, organizations of all types, including schools, churches, nonprofit agencies, small businesses, community government offices, and more, are installing LANs to connect their computers. One of the fastest-growing sectors of LAN development is home networking, in which all of the computers in a house are linked so that they can share a single Internet connection. In computer-savvy areas such as Washington, DC, Boston, and San Francisco, homes that are prewired for LAN connectivity are getting premium prices in the housing market.

What is all the excitement about? The advantages of LAN networking are well described by one word: *synergy*. Synergy refers to a gain that is greater than merely summing up all of the parts. Ethernet inventor and LAN networking pioneer Robert Metcalfe puts the point this way. Networks, Metcalfe says, are like telephones, in the sense that both become more valuable the more people hook up. A telephone system with only two subscribers lets people connect only two ways (each person can call the other). But a telephone system with four subscribers lets people connect twelve different ways (each person can call three others).

How Is the Network Hooked Up? (LAN Topologies)

Local area networks vary in their *topology*, the method used to connect the computers physically. The next section introduces star, bus, and ring topologies, all of which are supported by Linux.

Star Networks

The most common network topology is the *star network,* in which each computer is connected via a cable to a central device, called a *hub.* The major disadvantage of a star network lies in the amount of wiring that is needed to connect each computer to the hub. The major advantage is that individual machines can be disconnected and reconnected without disturbing the network's functioning. Star networks are by far the most popular network topology.

Bus Networks and Ring Networks

A *bus network* connects computers by means of a straight-line cable, in which the networked computers are strung out in a daisy chain from one end to the other. A *ring network* is much the same, except that the two ends of the bus are connected to form a circle. Although bus networks require less wiring than star networks, it is not possible to disconnect one of the systems without disrupting network service. The same is true of ring networks. For this reason, bus and ring networks are much less popular than star networks.

Who Is in Charge? (LAN Network Relationships)

Networks vary in size and scope from a simple, two-computer connection to the Godzilla of networking, the globe-spanning Internet. Whatever the size of your network, you can set up three basic relationships in a network: timesharing networks, peer-to-peer networks, and client/server networks. Linux supports all three types of network relationships.

Timesharing Systems

Developed back in the days when computers were fabulously expensive, *timesharing systems* enable two or more users to gain access to a single, large computer, called a *mainframe*. This type of network was made possible by a key innovation in computer operating systems, called *timesharing*. With timesharing, access to the computer's central processing unit (CPU) is shared out among all those who are logged in to the network, so that each individual has the impression of having sole access to the computer.

Timesharing systems are highly centralized and tightly controlled by the personnel who run the mainframe. Users do not have their own computers; instead, they use *terminals*. A terminal does not have its own computer processing circuitry, memory, or storage, beyond that which is required to communicate with the mainframe. Multiuser networks are still used when it is desirable to keep all computing resources in one, central location.

During the 1970s and 1980s, the large mainframe computer makers underestimated the market for smaller timesharing systems. Manufacturers such as Digital Electronic Corporation (DEC), Hewlett-Packard (HP), and Sun Microsystems entered the market with *minicomputers,* which are junior versions of mainframes intended for medium-sized businesses and divisions within large corporations. Like mainframes, minicomputers use timesharing to enable two or more users to access the CPU simultaneously by means of remote terminals.

Minicomputer manufacturers equipped their computers with their own versions of the Unix operating system. Originated at AT&T's Bell Laboratories in the 1970s, Unix is a multiuser operating system.

Because Linux was originally a version of Unix for Intel-based personal computers, it shows its Unix heritage. Like Unix, Linux is a multiuser, timesharing operating system that enables two or more users to access the CPU simultaneously. Although few Linux users access Linux by means of remote, standalone terminals, the terminal concept is deeply intertwined with the way Linux works. On Linux, every session you begin takes place in one of several *virtual terminals*, seven of which are available by default with most Linux distributions.

TIP To explore the virtual terminals on your system, press Ctrl + Alt + F1 to view the first virtual terminal, Ctrl + Alt + F2 to view the second one, and so on. Press Ctrl + Alt + F7 to return to the current terminal.

Although it is possible to use Linux and remote terminals to emulate a timesharing system with Linux, few network designers would go this route now that inexpensive PCs are available. As the next section explains, PCs enable network designs that give much more freedom to the user. However, the timesharing system's high degree of central control does have its advantages. Internal security is excellent because users' access is tightly controlled from the central computer. In addition, the central computer's system administrator can control which applications are available.

Peer-to-Peer Networks

Timesharing systems are like dictatorships, in which the central computer's system administrator has total control over users' access privileges and software selection. In contrast, peer-to-peer networks are well described as democracies that verge on outright anarchy.

Composed of linked personal computers, a peer-to-peer network is a network of equals. On a peer-to-peer network, each computer's user decides which, if any, files or directories are to be shared with other users.

Peer-to-peer networks originated (along with a great many additional key innovations) at Xerox Corporation's Palo Alto Research Center (PARC) in the 1970s. The PARC is a research institute where academics work individually and in groups. They need their own, powerful computers, and they also need to communicate, share, and collaborate. Within PARC's overall framework of research goals, they are free to pursue their interests as they see fit. As the originators of peer-to-peer networking themselves recognize, this type of networking reflects the organizational culture of PARC. A peer-to-peer network gives each user a powerful, private computer. Each user decides which files and directories, if any, are shared. There is no central control.

The PARC designers built peer-to-peer networking into the ill-fated but pioneering computer system they designed, the Xerox Star. The concept reached the marketplace with the Macintosh, which emulated many of the Star's features, including built-in peer-to-peer networking. Every Macintosh comes with peer-to-peer networking capabilities built in. Today, peer-to-peer networking hardware and software is widely available for any type of personal computer.

Classic, peer-to-peer networking is well illustrated by the Macintosh's native LocalTalk network. LocalTalk is a proprietary Apple networking standard that defines a simple, peer-to-peer network that can connect a few to a few dozen Macintoshes. Physically, the connections require a LocalTalk adapter, which enables the Macs to be connected in a bus network topology. Once the computers are connected, each user opens the Macintosh File Sharing utility to determine which drives and directories are to be shared with other users. On each system, the Chooser utility enables users to open the shared resources made available on other user's computers. Similar capabilities are implemented in Microsoft Windows 95/98 by means of the Network Neighborhood utility.

Peer-to-peer networks are easy to set up. They are also easy to administer, but this remains true only as long as the network remains small. In general, a peer-to-peer network that links more than a dozen or so computers is likely to become chaotic. Security risks could develop because no one single person is watching out for the network as a whole.

Linux does not natively support peer-to-peer networking in the simple, transparent way that Mac OS and Microsoft Windows 95/98 do. However, Linux can run networking software, called Samba, that gives it these capabilities. Samba is a Linux implementation of the native Windows 95/98 peer-to-peer networking system. You will learn more about Samba later in this book.

Client/Server Networks

The history of networking reads much like the history of France in the eighteenth century: a despotic regime, followed by an experiment in democracy that degenerates into anarchy. Between these two extremes are *client/server networks*, which represent a middle ground between timesharing systems and peer-to-peer networks. Most LANs that connect more than a dozen or so computers are client/server networks.

On a client/server network, each workstation is a full-fledged computer, with its own processing circuitry, memory, storage, and software. In this sense, the workstation is like a personal computer, in which the user can control application selection. However, the network is integrated by a *server*, also called a *dedicated server* or *file server*.

Administered by the person who bears responsibility for the network as a whole, the *network administrator,* the server contains shared file storage and applications that are accessible to everyone on the network. The server also makes expensive peripherals such as network printers and scanners available to network users.

In terms of software, client/server networks make use of programs that are divided into two parts, a *client* part and a *server* part. The client portion of the program runs on users' workstations. It contains code that enables it to access the *server,* the portion of the program that makes a certain type of data available. Internet applications make use of the client versus server distinction. A Web browser is a client for the World Wide Web, one of several Internet services. Browsers contact Web servers, which make Web data available via the network.

Client/server terminology is somewhat confusing because it refers to two different levels, hardware and software. At the hardware level, client/server networks often use powerful computers called file servers, which are dedicated to the purpose of making files and applications available to network users. At the hardware level, server programs are installed on the file server. However, they may also be installed on users' workstations. In principle, any computer in a client/server network can take on the server role. In practice, the best performance is achieved when a file server is set aside so that it can focus on server duties.

How Big Is It? (Small, Medium, and Large LANs)

The simplest LAN is a two-computer network. As the next section explains, such a network can make excellent sense, even when both machines are used by only one person! Medium-sized LANs, called small group networks, link a few to about a dozen users. The largest LANs can link as many as several thousand workstations in a complex, internally segmented network.

The Basic Two-Computer Network

The simplest network consists of two computers. Is it worth the effort to network just two computer systems? Here are just some of the advantages:

- **Shared Access to an Expensive Printer.** With a network, you need just one printer. The savings you realize will more than pay for the networking hardware.
- **Easy File Exchange.** If you need to transfer files from one computer to the other, the network makes this task so easy that it is like copying the file from one directory to another.
- **Internet Sharing.** To connect two separate computers to the Internet at the same time, you will need two modems, two telephone lines, and two Internet accounts. With a network, all the computers can share a single Internet connection.
- **Transparent Access for Multiple Users.** Suppose two people use the two-computer network. When the two systems are networked, a user can use either of the computers and have full access to all of that user's files and applications.

A basic, two-computer network can make sense even when the two computers are used by only one person. For example, many professional people have a notebook computer and a desktop computer. You can easily set up a network that enables the notebook computer to be plugged in when it is not on the road. After the notebook computer connects to the network, you can easily transfer files between the two systems.

Two-computer networks are almost always set up in a peer-to-peer relationship. A peer-to-peer network lets you work from either computer. Although any local area network needs to be protected from external intruders, a basic, two-computer network is generally used by only one person or two closely related people or close co-workers, so internal security is not an issue.

Small Group Networks

Small group networks typically include anywhere from a few to a dozen or so users, and they are typically implemented using peer-to-peer network technologies. The following examples show the potential of small group networks.

- **Families.** Increasing numbers of families have at least one computer per person. A network allows them to connect their computers, pool common resources, and share an Internet connection while protecting their private files from prying eyes. If one of the computers functions as a server as well as a workstation, it is possible to set up a family Web page, a family email system, or even a family newsgroup.
- **Small Businesses.** Networks offer many advantages to small businesses. Servers can provide employees with useful resources such as generic versions of contracts, employee regulations, and forms for data entry. Shared applications can cut down software costs. Users can share expensive peripherals, such as

color laser printers, scanners, and fax machines. An internal email system keeps everyone in close touch.

- **Classrooms.** Schools everywhere are discovering the advantages of networking within the classroom. With a small, classroom-based network, schools can introduce what are arguably the most important computer concepts of all, the concepts of networking. A classroom-based network offers the potential to develop exercises that are collaborative in nature rather than individualistic and isolating.

Like any LAN connected to the Internet, small group networks need protection from external intruders. Depending on the context, internal security may present some challenges, too. In a small business, for example, the business owner may not want employees to see confidential files, such as performance evaluations.

Although most small group networks use peer-to-peer networking, growing numbers of them incorporate a server. Linux runs so efficiently that a disused, older Pentium or even a 486 machine can be set aside to provide centralized file sharing, file storage for backup files, shared printer access, and other server functions. Alternatively, one of the user's workstations can be configured to function as a server as well as a workstation. This approach does not work well on larger networks, where the server needs to be dedicated to its networking tasks so that it can perform these tasks as speedily as possible.

What keeps many families, small businesses, and schools from implementing small group networks is the heterogeneity of their hardware. Most personal computers are acquired without any thought given to how they will be networked. For example, a family may have one or two

Macintoshes and one or two Microsoft Windows 98 systems. Macintosh and Windows systems cannot "talk" to each other on a network without adding expensive, commercial software to both systems.

A major Linux advantage for small group networks is that Linux can easily integrate heterogeneous hardware into the network. A Linux networking package called netatalk enables Macintosh users to access shared directories and shared printers on Linux systems. Samba, introduced earlier in this chapter, enables Windows and Linux users to set up peer-to-peer networking that provides easy, transparent file transfer between both platforms. When a Linux directory that is accessible to Macintosh users is shared with Windows users by means of Samba, file transfer becomes possible between Macintosh and Windows users.

Large-Scale LANs

When the number of networked systems exceeds a dozen or more, peer-to-peer networking can become sufficiently chaotic that the network needs a guiding hand. Technologically, such guidance is provided by a powerful system that has been set aside for server duties. Organizationally, such guidance stems from a *network administrator,* a person whose role includes supervising the network, dealing with users, safeguarding the network's security, backup of mission-critical data, and much more. For really large networks (those with hundreds or even thousands of linked systems), network administration duties require one or more full-time employees.

Large-scale client/server networks are characterized by segmentation as well as bureaucratization. In a corporate network with thousands of employees, the network could become overwhelmingly complex and confusing if it were not segmented into smaller, more manageable sections. Network segmentation is accomplished by dividing the network into two or more *subnets*. In brief, a subnet is a section of the network that is set off for use by a group of workers, such as members of a design team or all the employees within a department.

In a large-scale, client/server network, security is an overriding concern. Disgruntled employees could sabotage mission-critical tasks. Sometimes, employees steal confidential data, such as plans for forthcoming products, and try to sell this data to competitors in exchange for a lucrative job offer. Among the major responsibilities of network administrators is the duty to make sure the network itself, as well as the confidential data it contains, is safe from internal as well as external attack.

Networks are a balance of security and access. The most secure network consists of computers that are cut off from all others. But this level of security keeps you from sharing your work.

Looking Under the Hood

To gain a deeper understanding of networking concepts, you would be wise to learn a bit about the concept of network layers. This section explains the essential concepts of layers, introduces the OSI Reference Model, and discusses the model's seven layers.

Why Define Network Layers?

In the earliest computer networks, one complex protocol governed all aspects of the network, including the way applications communicated and the way data signals traveled through the network's physical medium. However, this approach proved unworkable. A new application or physical medium could not be introduced without forcing revision of all the network software. As a result, network designers quickly learned to use a "divide and conquer" approach. The result was a conception of network *layers,* in which the various functions of a network are divided into separate categories or levels, each with its own protocols.

The OSI Reference Model

The most influential concept of network layering stems from the Open Systems Interconnection (OSI) Reference Model, an abstract network architecture designed by an international standards committee. This model, called the OSI Reference Model, originated during the 1970s and has strongly influenced network design ever since.

The OSI Reference Model is not a complete specification for a functioning network; rather, it is a set of design concepts. The most fundamental of these concepts is the notion that network designers should break the network down into manageable pieces, called layers. When an actual network is designed, engineers can then concentrate on getting the layer to do its job correctly, rather than having to worry about other layers. For example, one of the layers in the OSI Reference Model is called the application layer. Engineers working on this layer concern themselves with the protocols needed to establish communication between the client part of the application and the server part. They do not need to worry about the other layers, which take care of getting the client's request to the server (which may be located on a computer halfway around the globe, or in the office next door).

The Protocol Stack Concept

To understand how layers work in the OSI Reference Model, it is helpful to conceptualize a network as consisting of just two computers which are linked by physical network media. On each computer, one can think of the various layers as if they were like a layer cake, with a "stack" of horizontal slices. At the top of this stack, called a *protocol stack,* are layers concerned with accepting input from the user and establishing connections with servers. At the middle layer of the stack are protocols that are devoted to packaging the outgoing data for transmission on the network. At the lowest level of the stack are layers that are concerned with relaying the packaged data to the network's physical medium.

As the preceding suggests, outgoing data travels "down" the protocol stack until it reaches the network's physical medium. At the receiving computer, the data travels "up" the stack in a reverse of this process. At the lowest level, the lower layers retrieve the incoming data from the network's physical medium. They then pass the incoming data "up" to the middle layers, which "unwrap" the data from the packages in which it has been sent. The middle layers then pass the incoming data to the upper layer, where it is made available to the application for which the data is intended.

Working with the protocol stack concept, network designers can focus their energies on one layer at a time.

They specify protocols for each layer that perform two functions. First, these protocols govern the way that data is "handed down" or "handed up" to neighboring layers in the stack. Second, these protocols govern the way that the layer interacts with its corresponding layer on the receiving computer. At the core of the protocol stack concept is the notion that network designers can and should forget about the details of other layers.

The proof of this concept's success is the Internet. Although the Internet does not precisely conform to the OSI Reference Model's layer specifications, in that it specifies fewer layers, it does indeed use the protocol stack concept. This is the key to the Internet's great versatility and its success worldwide. It does not matter what type of computer an Internet application runs on; Web browsers have been developed for just about every type of computer in common use. All that matters is that the Web browser originates messages that can be correctly read, and responded to, by a Web server on the Internet. Similarly, data that has been packaged by the middle and lower levels of the Internet can travel over virtually any type of network medium ever invented. To get the Internet working with a brand new network medium, designers need only concern themselves with the task of getting the packaged Internet data to travel on the new physical medium; the rest of the layers need no modification in order to work with the new medium, once the new lower level protocols have been defined.

Layers in the OSI Reference Model

The OSI Reference Model defines a total of seven network layers, divided into two levels (upper and lower). In general, the upper level consists of protocols that the user is aware of, or of which the user could be aware. The lower level consists of protocols that are invisible to the user.

At the upper level are the following three layers:

- **Application Layer.** The application layer defines the communication standards needed for clients of a certain type, such as an email client, to communicate with their corresponding servers. Also defined at this layer are protocols that pass outgoing data "down" to the next layer.
- **Presentation Layer.** The presentation layer is not concerned with presenting data to the user, as might be thought. Rather, this layer defines a number of protocols that can be used to define the way outgoing data is presented to the network as a whole. For example, protocols at this layer define how data should be compressed or encrypted before it is sent out over the network. Such tasks could be handled by applications, but it is better to handle them "beneath" the application layer so that all of the applications can take advantage of the same, shared standards. A major shortcoming of the Internet protocol suite is that it does not define a separate presentation layer. Although efforts are under way to define this layer for the Internet, most compression and encryption tasks are handled at the application layer. The result is a profusion of incompatible compression and encryption standards, precisely the situation that the layer concept is designed to prevent.
- **Session Layer.** This layer establishes a connection between the sending computer and a similar service running on the destination computer. When the connection is established, the session layer handles the dialog between the sending and the receiving computer.

At the lower layer of the OSI Reference Model are found the following four layers:

- **Transport Layer.** At this layer, outgoing data is broken up into packets. A corresponding layer on the receiving end accepts the packets, unwraps them, and reassembles the data so that it has meaning to the next layer up.
- **Network Layer.** At this layer, the outgoing data packets are addressed so that they will arrive at the correct destination. A corresponding layer on the receiving computer reads the addresses to make sure that they are intended for that computer.
- **Data Link Layer.** At this layer, the outgoing, addressed packets are transferred to the physical medium. At the receiving computer, the incoming packets are taken from the physical medium and passed "up" to the transport layer.
- **Physical Layer.** This layer governs the transmission of data packets over a physical medium of a certain type, such as coaxial cable, fiberoptic cable, satellite systems, radiowaves, high-bandwidth digital telephone cables, or microwave systems.

Where Linux Fits In

As you have learned in this chapter, there are many different types of computer networks. However, by far the largest percentage of new networks are local area networks (LAN) that use a bus topology, packet-switching protocols, and a peer-to-peer or client/server design.

In such networks, Linux possesses a decisive advantage. That is because TCP/IP, the collective name for the Internet protocol suite, is built into Linux as its native networking architecture. Installed by default with most Linux distributions, TCP/IP is ready to go when you have started your system. As you learned in Chapter 1, connecting a Linux system to the Internet is as simple as telling Linux, in effect, which type of physical medium you are using (such as a modem and telephone line), and figuring out which applications you want to run. In other words, you make choices at the data link layer and the application layer—and everything else is completely automatic.

Linux has another advantage, as well. TCP/IP is based on open, public, nonproprietary standards that are defined by international standards committees. In contrast, vendor-specific (proprietary) network protocols, such as Apple Computer's AppleTalk or Microsoft's native networking protocols, are controlled by for-profit companies. These companies can and will alter the underlying protocols if they believe that doing so will increase the returns they are able to give to their stockholders. The result could be that you are stuck with applications and equipment that will not function correctly unless you are willing to pay for an expensive software upgrade. By choosing Linux as the basis for your computer network, you protect yourself from the marketing antics of for-profit computer companies.

The next chapter turns to TCP/IP, the native networking technology of the Linux operating system. You will learn how TCP/IP works, and how it is implemented in Linux. You will also learn some additional ways in which TCP/IP varies from the OSI Reference Model.

References and Further Reading

Tanenbaum, A. S. (1996). *Computer Networks*. Upper Saddle River, NJ: Prentice-Hall, Inc.

4

Selecting and Installing Network Hardware

If you are planning to implement an inexpensive, reliable local area network (LAN), there is only one game in town—a 10-Mbps or 100-Mbps Ethernet. Although Linux works with many other network technologies, the Linux kernel is designed to detect and configure most Ethernet adapters automatically. Creating a simple Ethernet network is almost as simple as installing Ethernet adapters in all the computers you want to network, stringing Ethernet cables to the Ethernet hub, and turning everything on. (There is more to network configuration, to be sure, but this part is surprisingly easy, too.)

Because 10/100-Mbps Ethernets are the easiest type of networking hardware to install and configure, this chapter (and those that follow) focus on Ethernet LANs. This chapter begins by introducing Ethernet networking. Next, you will learn about a variety of ways you can hook up computers in an Ethernet network, beginning with a simple connection that involves a special cable linking two computers. Subsequently, you will learn how to select and install an Ethernet adapter, and make sure it is working properly.

Introducing the Ethernet

Originally developed in the 1970s by Bob Metcalfe and other researchers at Xerox Corporation's Palo Alto Research Center (PARC), the various versions of Ethernet are used by approximately 80% of all LANs. Metcalfe chose the name "Ethernet" in ironic homage to disproven, nineteenth-century theories of a "luminiferous Aether," through which light particles and electricity were believed to propagate.

Although many other LAN technologies exist, Ethernet is an excellent choice for most users. It provides users with a good balance between speed, reliability, expense, and ease of installation. The equipment to create a 10baseT Ethernet for five PCs can cost as little as $200.

Ethernet Standards

Ethernet standards are now the responsibility of international standards organizations. Current Ethernets conform to standard 802.3 of the Institute of Electrical and Electronic Engineers (IEEE). However, the IEEE 802.3 standard has not proven universally popular. In particular, the Internet protocols (TCP/IP) expect Ethernets to conform to the older, proprietary standards created by Xerox. In general, most Ethernet hardware can work with both standards.

Ethernet Protocols

As you learned in Chapter 3, computer networks are profitably analyzed using layer classifications supplied by the OSI Reference Model. The Ethernet's role becomes clear when you realize that Ethernet protocols operate at the very lowest layers of the protocol stack, the data link layer, and the physical layer. The data link layer, as explained in Chapter 2, governs the means by which data encapsulated in packets is transferred to the physical network medium. The physical layer governs the transmission of data on the physical medium itself.

Protocol Independence

Because the Ethernet is concerned only with the lowest levels of the protocol stack, it can work with many different networking protocols that operate at higher levels. Any of the following will work smoothly with an Ethernet:

- **AppleTalk.** This Apple Computer protocol provides the network routing and addressing functions for all Macintosh networks, whether they use LocalTalk, Ethernet, or token-ring networks at lower layers.
- **IPX/SPX.** These are the network and transport layer protocols used for Novell NetWare networks.
- **NetBIOS/NetBEUI.** The NetBIOS/NetBEUI protocols (NetBEUI is pronounced "net-booey"), jointly created by Novell and Microsoft, provide the foundation for Microsoft Windows 95/98/NT networks.

The most important NetBEUI protocol, called *server message blocks* (SMB), defines the packet format for NetBEUI networks.

- **TCP/IP.** This is the name of the Internet protocol suite. Like AppleTalk, TCP/IP can be used with a variety of lower-level protocols, such as Ethernet.

The ability of the Ethernet to work with any of these protocols (and others not mentioned here) is called *protocol independence*. In other words, the Ethernet protocols are independent of any of the forementioned protocols. The degree of independence is so great that, in fact, you can run more than one of these protocols simultaneously on an Ethernet without worrying about them conflicting with each other. It is quite commonplace to run TCP/IP, NetBEUI, and AppleTalk on the same Ethernet so that Linux, Microsoft Windows, and Mac OS systems can share network resources.

Ethernet Versions

Although early versions of Ethernet used coaxial cable in bus networks, the most popular versions today are Ethernet star networks that use hubs and UTP (*unshielded twisted pair* wire). Two versions are available: 10baseT (10 Mbps) and Fast Ethernet (100 Mbps, also called 100baseT). A new version, called Gigabit Ethernet, enables data transfer at 1000 Mbps (1 Gbps).

- **10Base2.** 10-Mbps Ethernet using thin coaxial cable; also called *Thin Ethernet*. Limited to 185 m of unrepeated cable.
- **10Base5.** 10-Mbps Ethernet using thick coaxial cable. Limited to 500 m of unrepeated cable.

- **10BaseF.** 10-Mbps Ethernet using fiber optic cable. Enables a maximum of 2 km of unrepeated cable.
- **10BaseT.** 10-Mbps Ethernet using Level 3 or higher UTP (unshielded twisted-pair cable). Limited to 150 m of unrepeated cable.
- **100BaseTX.** 100-Mbps Ethernet using Level 5 (also called Cat-5) UTP (unshielded twisted-pair cable). Limited to 100 m of unrepeated cable.

How Ethernets Work

In any network, the key question is how data gets onto the network in the first place, and how it gets delivered to the right place. In the Ethernet, these questions are answered, respectively, by two protocols, called *Carrier Sense Multiple Access/Collision Detection* (CSMA/CD) and *MAC addresses.*

CSMA/CD

When a workstation originates data, there is danger another workstation will attempt to do so at exactly the same time. The result is a *collision,* which destroys the data from both workstations. To prevent collisions, the Ethernet uses a technique called Carrier Sense Multiple Access/Collision Detection (CSMA/CD).

The basic principle of CSMA/CD is "listen before speaking." Workstations do not transmit data if the network is busy; they wait until the network is free. Even so, there is a chance that two workstations will begin transmitting simultaneously. The result is a collision. With CSMA/CD, the workstation can detect when a collision has occurred. After a collision is detected, the workstation waits for a period of time that is determined by a randomization algorithm, and then attempts to retransmit the message. The theory is that, due to the randomization factor, the two workstations involved in the collision will not begin retransmitting at the same time.

Careful studies show that CSMA/CD is an effective measure against collisions and ensures that properly designed Ethernets will transfer data at or close to their rated capacity. A properly designed network does not exceed the maximum number of workstations per collision domain.

MAC Addresses

To make sure data is delivered to the right place, Ethernet devices are assigned a fixed address, called the *MAC address* (MAC is short for *Media Access Control.*). These MAC addresses are assigned by the device's manufacturer and are unique to the device.

Ethernet Hardware

To build an Ethernet, you will need some or all of the basic hardware building blocks, which include transceivers, Ethernet adapters, hubs, repeaters, bridges, routers, and switches. Simple Ethernets don't require all of this equipment, but you will need cables, Ethernet adapters for each computer, and a hub.

Cables

Both 10BaseT and 100BaseTX Internets use unshielded twisted pair (UTP) cables with RJ-45 connectors at either end. These connectors look very much like modular telephone jacks (RJ-11 jacks), but they are bigger. The UTP cables are rated according to their quality (levels 1 through 5). The 10BaseT networks require Level 3 cables (also called Category 3 or Cat-3). The 100BaseTX networks require Level 5 cables (also called Category 5 or Cat-5).

TIP You can buy ready-to-use Ethernet cables in a variety of lengths up to 100 feet. If you are planning to wire new construction, consider purchasing the cable in bulk; you can also buy snap-on RJ-45 plug kits that enable you to attach the plugs without soldering.

Transceivers

Also called a *Medium Access Unit* (MAU), a *transceiver* is an electronic device that enables the computer to connect to the Ethernet's physical media. Transceivers are included on PC Ethernet cards. Although Macintoshes come with built-in Ethernet support, some older Macs require an external transceiver to connect to Ethernet cabling.

Ethernet Adapters

An Ethernet adapter is a type of *network interface card* (NIC) designed to fit into a PC's expansion slot. On the adapter's backplane, you will generally find two connectors, a *BNC connector* for coaxial cable and an *RJ-45* connector for UTP cables. Ethernet adapters are available for a variety of expansion busses, including ISA and PCI, the two most common bus architectures found in PCs. For notebook computers, Ethernet adapters are available for PC Card slots (also known as PCMCIA slots). Although Ethernet adapters are also available for Universal Serial Bus (USB) ports, this format is not yet fully supported by the Linux kernel; it is best to avoid it until full support is announced and you have upgraded to the latest kernel version.

TIP Widely available are Ethernet adapters capable of working with 10BaseT and 100BaseTX networks. These adapters automatically sense the type of network to which they are connected, and adjust data transfer rates accordingly. Even if you plan to begin with a 10-Mbps network (10BaseT), it is a wise investment to pay the small additional amount required to get a hybrid 10/100-Mbps adapter.

Hubs

A *hub* is a central wiring device used in star topology Ethernets (10BaseT and 100BaseT). Containing RJ-45 receptacles for several workstations, the hub serves to repeat or mirror the network's signals so that all workstations receive an exact copy of these signals. The hub is not merely an electronic "mirror"; it also contains circuitry that regenerates and synchronizes the network's signals, ensuring a high degree of reliability.

Hubs come with a fixed number of ports, but most hubs also include an *uplink port* that enables them to connect to another hub.

You'll notice that hubs typically have several light-emitting diode (LED) lights. Here's what they mean:

- **Power.** Lights up when your hub is connected to power.
- **Collision.** Lights up when more than one computer is sending information simultaneously. The signals from each computer are actually interfering with each other inside your hub. Ethernet adapters are designed to try again after a collision, so this is not

normally a problem. But if this light is on constantly, the speed of your network may suffer; you may need to consider a faster or more complex network.

- **Individual Connections.** Each connection that you make between a hub and a computer also has an individual light. This light is on when you have a solid connection. This light flashes when data passes between that computer and the hub.

Repeaters

A *repeater* is a simple device that receives Ethernet data from one *segment* of an Ethernet (a portion of the network that is physically bounded by a hub, repeater, bridge, router, switch, or line termination). It then amplifies the signals and repeats them at full strength for a new network segment. Repeaters are used to extend an Ethernet beyond the maximum unrepeated cable length.

Repeaters are simple devices that do nothing but extend the maximum length of Ethernet physical media. The result is a lengthier network, but all of the attached workstations are part of a *shared Ethernet,* a single, virtual network in which all the computers are contending for network access. In other words, all of the workstations are part of the same *collision domain.* If you connect too many workstations to the network, performance degrades.

TIP How many workstations is "too many?" Experience with real-world Ethernets suggests that the number is far below the rated capacity of 10BaseT and 100BaseTX networks (1024 workstations). The real-world limit varies according to the network's use; for example, if you are using the network to give every user access to the Internet, network traffic will be significantly higher than it would be without an Internet connection. As a rule of thumb, try not to exceed 64 workstations per collision domain—and cut that number in half if you are providing Internet connections.

Note that a hub is essentially a repeater with some added electronics. Star networks are really bus networks in which each workstation is connected to its own, one-cable segment. The hub functions as a repeater to unite all the segments into a single collision domain.

Bridges

Like a repeater, a *bridge* connects two Ethernet segments. However, the bridge contains electronics that enable it to "learn" the MAC addresses of all the workstations in each segment. When the bridge receives signals from the first segment, it examines the signals and determines where the signals are coming from. If the signals are from a workstation in the first segment, the bridge does not pass them on to the second segment.

The effect of connecting segments with a bridge is a dramatic reduction in the number of potential collisions, since workstations on separate segments do not have to contend with all of the other segments' signals. In other words, a bridge isolates network segments so that each of them is, for most purposes, a separate collision domain. For this reason, bridges enable Ethernets to be extended with less degradation of the network's performance.

Routers

Like repeaters and bridges, *routers* connect two Ethernet segments. They include the functions of bridges; that is, they examine the MAC addresses of data packets and forward the packet only if it needs to go on to the next segment. However, routers also operate at a higher layer of the protocol stack. For this reason, they can determine whether a packet is addressed to a destination that is not on any segment of the local Ethernet. They can forward packets to wide area networks (WANs), including the public Internet.

A router is needed to connect an Ethernet to the Internet. However, it is not necessary to purchase an expensive, standalone router for this purpose. You can set up a Linux system to function as a router that connects your Ethernet to the public Internet, as explained later in this book.

Switches

Switches are advanced, expensive devices that solve the media access contention problems of Ethernets by establishing, in effect, a direct physical connection—a circuit—between two communicating workstations. Because switches enable workstations to communicate in *full duplex mode,* in which the workstations can send and receive data at the same time, they effectively double the network's bandwidth (20 Mbps for 10BaseT, and 200 Mbps for 100BaseT).

Designing Your Ethernet

If creating a local area network seems like rocket science, read on, because you are in for a pleasant surprise. Today's Ethernet hardware is almost ridiculously easy to install and configure. Creating a network is, in most cases, as simple as hooking up all the hardware and turning on the power.

This section walks you through the network design considerations involved for small and larger networks, beginning with a few pointers on cabling.

Essentials of Good Cabling Practice

Star networks have many advantages over bus networks, but there is one disadvantage that you will notice right away: they are cable-intensive. Each workstation requires its own cable run to the hub, adding to the overall "vermicelli effect"—the profusion of wires running all over your office. Devote some thought now (rather than later) to how you can minimize the confusion and perils caused by all these wires.

- **Keep Cables Off the Floor.** You do not want to trip, of course, but you could also do a lot of damage—at the extreme, you could rip the network card out of its slot and cause physical damage to the motherboard. It is easiest to route cables along the baseboard, where the wall meets the floor.
- **Consider In-Wall Wiring.** In new construction, you can string Cat-5 cable to your heart's content, as long as you do so before the drywallers arrive. In existing construction, an electrician can install cables in existing walls. Faceplates with RJ-45 connectors are available from network hardware supply companies.
- **Keep Cables Away From Machinery.** Avoid anything with a motor, such as refrigerators and washing machines. The electrical fields they generate can affect the performance of your network.
- **Avoid Power Cables.** Although the Ethernet specification warns against running cables near electrical power cables, experience suggests that this is not a major concern for 10BaseT and 100BaseTX networks, which have robust error correction. If you have to route your network cable near a power cord, try to make the cable and power cord cross at right angles.

- **Avoid Sharp Bends.** If you bend your cables too severely, the wires inside the cable can thin out or even break. Thinner wires can carry fewer data. A good rule of thumb for UTP cable is a 2-in (50-mm) bend radius.

The Minimalist Ethernet

If you're planning to connect just a few computers, such as a notebook and a desktop system, you can create your network with an Ethernet adapter for each workstation, Ethernet cables, and an inexpensive hub with five or eight ports. Although you may hear that it is possible to connect two computers directly with a *crossover cable*, thus dispensing with the hub, you cannot do this with 10BaseT or 100BaseTX Ethernets—at least, not without risking errors and unreliable data transfers.

TIP Consider purchasing an "Ethernet in a box" kit, which contains network interface cards, cables, and a hub. Because all the components come from the same manufacturer, it is reasonable to expect that they will function together flawlessly. Still, you should compare the price to "bargain basement" Ethernet equipment. Above all, make sure the Ethernet adapters are compatible with Linux (see the section on Making Sure Your Hardware is Linux-Compatible on page 106).

More Complex Networks

If you have more computers than your hub can handle, or if your network is slowing down, you may need to consider specialized equipment. You can use any of the following components to increase your network's capacity.

- **Additional Hubs.** As you learned earlier in this chapter, you can "daisy chain" hubs through their uplink ports. However, note that the additional hubs act as repeaters. They keep all of the connected workstations within one collision domain. If network performance degrades unacceptably, you may have tried to connect too many workstations to this domain.
- **Bridges.** If you have plenty of ports but network performance is poor, divide your Ethernet network into two or more collision domains by means of a bridge.
- **Router.** To connect your network to the Internet, you will need a router. As previously mentioned, this does not have to be a separate, physical device; a Linux system can be set up to function as a router so that an Internet connection can be shared out over a network.

Making Sure Your Hardware Is Linux-Compatible

When you set up a network, make sure that all of the equipment you are using is compatible with your choice of networks. Of concern here is the network interface card (NIC); once you have got the Ethernet adapter working, Linux can work with any Ethernet-compatible network repeater, bridge, router, or switch.

Compatibility Levels

Red Hat and others extensively test hardware for compatibility. Red Hat rates individual components according to the following scheme:

- **Tier 1 Compatibility.** Linux can detect and use these components, which are known to install and work reliably on Linux systems.
- **Tier 2 Compatibility.** Although Linux should be able to detect and use these components, they are known to have some quirks that cause some users problems. Such problems can normally be resolved by doing a bit of system tweaking. If this is your situation, pay special attention to the sections that help you determine the right IRQ, I/O, and DMA for your card.
- **Tier 3 Compatibility.** Linux can work successfully with many of these components. However, the drivers may be buggy or experimental, or the components may cause problems that are difficult or impossible to resolve. If you have one of these cards, look for Linux drivers from the manufacturer's Web site.
- **Incompatible Hardware** These components do not work with Red Hat Linux.

Although Red Hat's ratings are specific to the Red Hat distribution, Red Hat's compatibility with Ethernet adapters is almost exclusively determined by the capabilities of the Linux kernel included in a specific Red Hat distribution. If you are using a different distribution that uses the same kernel version, chances are that its hardware compatibility is the same as that of Red Hat Linux.

You can find the latest version of this Red Hat specific network hardware compatibility list at http://www.redhat.com/support/hardware.

Remember, unless you see your network card on the Incompatible list, it may still work at least as well as a Tier 2 or Tier 3 card. Check your network card manufacturer's Web site; many will help you get your network card working with Linux.

TIP You can find similar lists for other Linux distributions at their Web sites, for example, http://www.caldera.com/support or http://www.suse.com. You can also review the generic list of compatible network cards in Section 5 of the Ethernet-HOWTO at http://www.linuxdoc.org/HOWTO/Ethernet-HOWTO-5.html. This is a good list that includes a number of hints for making specific cards work for you.

Tips for Choosing a Compatible Ethernet Adapter

In general, you are in good shape with recent PCI and PCMCIA adapters made by 3Com, Linksys, and Intel. The following tips may also prove useful.

- Ethernet adapters based on the DEC "Tulip" chip work well with Linux. This chip is widely used in many inexpensive, "no-name" adapters, including SMC EtherPower 10 PCI, SMC EtherPower 10/100 PCI, Allied Telesis LA100PCI-T, Lite-On Communications LNE100TX, Kingston EtherX CP 10-/100TX PCI, and Netgear FA-310-TX.
- For Red Hat Linux 6.2, Tier 1 compatibility adapters include the following 3Com adapters: 3Com EtherLink III, EtherLink PCI III/XL, 3c59x, 3c900, 3c905, and 3c579.
- Most NE2000-compatible adapters will work with Linux, but they may require some tweaking.

- The Intel PCI EtherExpressPro 100-Mbps adapters are a good choice, but note that the EtherExpress Pro/10 PCI is incompatible with Linux.
- Xircom Ethernet adapters are not compatible with Linux.

Installing Your Network Card

Now that you have selected a compatible Ethernet adapter, it's time to install it in your computer. Follow these steps.

1. Take appropriate precautions with your computer. Before installing your card, turn off your computer, ground yourself, check whether your card is ISA or PCI, do not use a magnetic screwdriver, and be careful. If you need more information, review the sections in Chapter 1 on installing internal modems.

2. Carefully press the adapter into the expansion slot, and make sure the card is fully inserted.

3. Screw the adapter into place. Do not skip this step!

4. Plug the network cable into the RJ-45 receptacle on the adapter's backplane.

5. Start Linux, and observe the startup messages. If you see a message concerning eth0, you are in luck: the Linux kernel has detected the adapter and configured your system to work with this adapter automatically.

TIP If the messages flew by too fast for you to read, open a terminal window, switch to superuser, type **dmesg I less**, and press Enter.

If the kernel failed to configure your adapter correctly, check the following:

- Is your network adapter compatible with Linux? Do not waste time trying to get an incompatible adapter to work. If your time is worth anything, it is cheaper to buy a new one that is fully compatible with Linux.
- Is the adapter fully inserted into your computer?
- Does the connection light on the adapter's backplane (as well as the corresponding light on the hub) indicate that a good connection has been made? Both lights should be on.

Still having problems? If you are determined to get this adapter to work, you'll have to configure the Linux kernel *module* that drives the adapter. For more information, see the next section.

Configuring Module Parameters

Today's Linux kernels support a wide variety of peripheral devices using *loadable kernel modules* (or just *modules* for short). In brief, modules are kernel components that are designed to do a specific job, such as supporting a specific brand and model of Ethernet adapter. As the term implies, modules are modular; they are standalone components that can be added to the running kernel, or removed from the running kernel, without harming the kernel's functionality in any way.

The modules for Ethernet make certain assumptions about default settings, such as the adapter's I/O port and IRQ setting. If the kernel failed to detect your Ethernet card when you started your system, it is possible that the default settings have been changed by means of physical modifications to the card (such as changing the jumpers for I/O, DMA or IRQ settings. Sometimes the Linux kernel just plain fails to detect PCI Plug and Play adapters. You can try to get the card working by specifying module parameters, as the following section explains.

Introducing Module Parameters

If the Linux kernel failed to detect your Ethernet adapter when you started your system, chances are that you will need to specify *module parameters* manually. In brief, module parameters are load-time statements that customize the module's operation. For Ethernet adapters, they consist of hardware settings, such as interrupt request (IRQ), input-output (I/O) addresses, and direct memory access (DMA) channels, which the module cannot automatically determine.

Determining the Correct Settings

If you are planning to use a module that requires information about hardware settings such as these, you will need to determine the correct settings before you can use the module. To do so, check the adapter's documentation. If you are installing a non-Plug-and-Play device, you should also look at the adapter's jumpers, if any, to see which configuration settings have been chosen.

Learning the Module Parameter Syntax

It is not enough to know the correct settings; you must also know how to type the module parameters. The format varies for each module, so you will need documentation. To obtain the documentation needed to specify module parameters correctly, look for the module's name in /usr/src/linux/Documentation/networking.

Here is an example of module parameters in action. To load the 3Com 3c501, you can specify the I/O address and the IRQ. By default, the 3c501 module assumes that the adapter is using I/O base address 0x280 and IRQ 5; if the card is set to use a different I/O address or IRQ, you will need to specify the module parameters manually. You do this by using the modprobe command, generally found in the /sbin directory. For this adapter, the correct modprobe syntax looks like this:

```
modprobe 3c501x io=0x340 irq=10
```

This command tells the modprobe utility to load the 3c401 module into the kernel, and configures the module to use I/O base address 0x340 and IRQ 7.

Specifying Module Configurations

If you plan to load a particular module frequently, you will want to take advantage of modprobe's ability to work with the /etc/conf.modules configuration file (also called /etc/modules.conf). In brief, this configuration file enables you to specify an *alias* for the module. It also enables you to specify the module parameters needed to load the module successfully.

Here is an example of a module configuration file for the 3Com 3c501 adapter mentioned here:

```
alias eth0 3c501x
options 3c501x io=0x340 irq=7
```

Note that the alias defines the first Ethernet network interface (eth0) so that it is linked to the 3c501 module. The second line specifies the module parameters for this module. (For an introduction to network interfaces, see the Under the Hood Section in Chapter 1.)

With this addition to your module configuration file, the kernel should be able to detect your Ethernet adapter when you next start your system.

Looking Under the Hood

You can use standard Linux utilities to learn how well your Ethernet adapter is performing.

To view the current status of your adapter and view statistics concerning the adapter's operation, switch to superuser, type **cat /proc/net/dev,** and press Enter. You will see a wealth of statistics about the adapter's performance, including the number of bytes received and transmitted, the number of collisions, and the number of errors. If the number of collisions is 25% or more of the number of bytes transmitted, consider dividing your network into segments, as explained earlier in this chapter.

You can use the ping utility to determine how speedily given workstations on your LAN receive and return data. To see how fast your network is operating, type **ping** followed by the address of one of your network's workstations, and press Enter. To see how speedily 192.168. 100.33 responds, for example, you would type **ping 192.168.100.33** and press Enter. Press Ctrl + C to stop pinging the workstation; you will see minimum, maximum, and average roundtrip times. On a 10 Mbps (10BaseT) Ethernet, you should see roundtrip times ranging from 0.5 (very good) to 2.5 (OK) µs; significantly larger trip times may indicate that your network is overloaded.

References and Further Reading

Eckhoff, M. (1998). Token Ring mini-HOWTO. Linux Documentation Project. Available online at www.linuxdoc.org/HOWTO/mini/Token-Ring.html.

Gortmaker, P. (1999). Ethernet HOWTO. Linux Documentation Project. Available online at www.linuxdoc.org/HOWTO/Ethernet-HOWTO.html.

McCauley, P. n.d. Data Communications Cabling FAQ. Available online at http://www.faqs.org/faqs/LAN/cabling-faq.

Red Hat, Inc. (2000). Red Hat, Inc. Hardware Compatibility List for Intel/6.1. Available online at http://www.redhat.com/support/hardware.

Reijnen, P. (2000). Linux Hardware Compatibility HOWTO. Linux Documentation Project. Available online at www.linuxdoc.org/HOWTO/Hardware-HOWTO.html.

Spurgeon, C. (2000). Ethernet FAQ. Available online at http://wwwhost.ots.utexas.edu/ethernet/faq.html.

Spurgeon, C. (2000). Ethernet: The Definitive Guide. Petaluma, CA: O'Reilly and Associates.

5

Getting Started with TCP/IP

The technical name given to the protocol suite that underlies the public Internet, TCP/IP, is by far the most widely used networking protocol suite in the world. TCP/IP is also widely used to govern the network layer of communications in virtually every type of local area network, including LANs. In addition, it is the native networking technology of the Linux operating system. For all of these reasons, it is important to understand the essential concepts of TCP/IP, and what is more, how they are realized in the Linux environment.

This chapter introduces TCP/IP, covering all the concepts that you will need to set up and administer TCP/IP networking with your Linux system. You will also learn how to configure your local area network (LAN) to use TCP/IP.

Introducing TCP/IP

This section briefly introduces the Internet protocols (TCP/IP), beginning with a brief review of the Internet's history. You will learn why TCP/IP has been so phenomenonally successful, and why Linux is a very wise choice as the basis for creating your own TCP/IP network.

A Brief History of the Internet

The TCP/IP protocol suite is the result of public investment in science and technology. In 1969, the U.S. Defense Department's Advanced Research Projects Industry (ARPA, later known as DARPA) took the leadership in funding research to build an experimental packet-switching network, the first of its kind. The early network, called ARPANET, linked a number of research centers and universities. Although the early ARPANET did not use the Internet protocols, it served as the testbed for TCP/IP development. (The ARPANET protocols were subsequently adopted by the private sector in the form of X.25 public data networks, which are still in widespread use.)

In the early 1980s, the Internet protocols were under rapid development; by 1983, ARPANET migrated to the Internet protocols, and the first Internet was born. Subsequently, ARPA funded a project to implement the Internet protocols in the Berkeley Unix distribution (BSD Unix). With the release of BSD 4.2 in the early 1980s, the fortunes of Unix and TCP/IP became closely intertwined.

Since colleges and universities were among the most enthusiastic adopters of BSD Unix, the Internet's growth during the 1980s was primarily among educational institutions; the network was not known to the general public and it was not used for commercial purposes. In 1985, the National Science Foundation (NSF) took over administration of the Internet and constructed a new, transcontinental backbone network, called NSFNet. NSF's funding was predicated on acceptable use policies that prevented commercial use of the network.

In less than a decade, the Internet was transformed from a little-known, obscure network in use primarily by academics into what must be seen as an emergent public medium, comparable in its probable social penetration to newspapers, radio, and television. The vestiges of the past fell away during the 1990s. In the year 1990, the ARPANET went off-line; in 1995, NSF withdrew its subsidy of the Internet backbone, removing the barriers to commercialization of the Internet. At the same time, the network grew at an almost unbelievable pace, doubling in size each year. The Internet now reaches more than half of all U.S. households.

The Internet and Internets

The Internet's rapid growth has made the term "Internet" a household word, but this word is often misunderstood. The huge, public Internet (with a capital "I") is what most people mean when they use the term *Internet*. However, it is possible to create a network based on the TCP/IP protocols that is not connected to the wider, public Internet. The term *internet* is used to describe such networks. You may also encounter the term *intranet*. An intranet is a private, internal network that resembles the public Internet in that services such as the Web, FTP, and e-mail are available. Companies create intranets to create internal information systems capable of linking employees worldwide.

In this chapter, you will learn how to create your own, private internet. You can connect your *internet* to the *Internet*, as you will see, but it is important to keep these two terms separate.

Factors in the Internet's Success

The Internet's rapid growth and widespread public adoption are caused by many factors, including cultural and economic ones. But the TCP/IP protocols are surely among the most important contributors to the Internet's phenomenal success. In brief, the TCP/IP protocols offer advantages that remain unsurpassed by any competing networking standards.

- **Platform Independence.** The TCP/IP protocols are *open protocols*, which means that they are public, nonproprietary standards that are developed independent of any hardware or software company's interests. This means that the Internet can connect all types of computers and use all types of network physical media. To put this another way, the TCP/IP protocols are *platform-independent*.
- **Effective Standards.** Because the TCP/IP protocols are controlled by effective standardization authorities, network hardware and software providers do not have to worry that their products will work with any TCP/IP-compatible network. This fact has encouraged hardware and software companies to invest in the Internet's future.

- **Network Hardware Independence.** As you will see in the next section, the TCP/IP protocols do not define the lowest layers in the OSI Reference Model, discussed in the previous chapter. As a result, TCP/IP can work with virtually any physical network hardware or network medium ever invented, and it will work with future network technologies.

The Internet's impressive growth is threatened by software firms that hope to "embrace and extend" TCP/IP, so that customers will become dependent on the firms' products. In itself, this is an excellent reason to implement TCP/IP networks using Linux and open source TCP/IP software, such as the Apache Web server. Linux and Apache implement standards-conformant versions of TCP/IP.

Understanding Internet Layers

As you learned in Chapter 3, it is useful to conceptualize networks in terms of separate layers, each of which has its own protocols. The OSI Reference Model defines seven layers. In Chapter 4, you learned that the Ethernet, the most commonly used technology for TCP/IP local area networks, operates at the physical and data link layers. In this section, you will learn how layers manifest in the TCP/IP environment. As you will see, TCP/IP layers do not map precisely to their OSI Reference Model equivalents.

Layers in TCP/IP

TCP/IP distinguishes four layers instead of the seven identified in the OSI Reference Model. Although there is some disagreement over just how the levels should be distinguished and named, they are generally described as follows:

- **Application Layer.** This layer corresponds to the Application, Presentation, and part of the Session layer in the OSI Reference Model. This layer consists of client applications and servers. Protocols at the Application Layer include the File Transfer Protocol (FTP), the Hypertext Transfer Protocol (HTTP), the Simple Mail Transfer Protocol (SMTP), Domain Name Service (DNS), and Network Filesystem (NFS).

- **Host-to-Host Transport Layer.** This layer corresponds to portions of the Session and Transport layers in the OSI model. It provides end-to-end data services. The two most important protocols at this layer are the Transmission Control Protocol (TCP), which establishes a reliable, connection-oriented link between two hosts on the Internet, and the User Datagram Protocol (UDP), which provides a data delivery service that does not require an active connection.

- **Internet Layer.** This layer corresponds to the lower portion of the Transport layer in the OSI model. It wraps data in packets and handles addressing and routing. The most important protocol at this layer is the Internet Protocol (IP). This protocol defines the structure of Internet packets (called *datagrams*), specifies the form of Internet addresses, and moves data from TCP or UDP to the Network Access layer.

- **Network Access Layer.** This layer corresponds to the Network Access layer in the OSI model. It consists of routines for delivering the data to physical networks. An example of a Network Access Layer protocol is the Address Resolution Protocol (ARP), which maps

IP addresses to Ethernet MAP addresses. Another example is the Point-to-Point Protocol (PPP), which enables TCP/IP to access modem connections.

Comparing the OSI Model and TCP/IP

The differences between the OSI model's seven-layer scheme and TCP/IP's four-layer scheme have advantages as well as disadvantages.

One advantage of TCP/IP is that it is not overspecified with respect to physical network technologies. The TCP/IP does not define the Data Link and Physical layers of the OSI model in any way. This is one of the strengths of TCP/IP. Because these layers are not defined, TCP/IP can work, in principle, with any type of physical network ever devised (and those that have yet to be devised).

A disadvantage of TCP/IP is that the TCP/IP Application layer subsumes layers that, in the OSI model, are differentiated. As a result, individual applications must provide services such as encryption or compression that should be uniformly available to all applications.

What This All Means for Linux Users

One of the greatest advantages of Linux is that a typical Linux distribution installs nearly everything that is needed to create TCP/IP networks. Most Linux distributions include a suite of high-quality servers and clients that function at TCP/IP's Application layer, including the Apache web server, the wu-ftp FTP server, powerful mail client and server applications, and much more. In addition, the Host-to-Host Transport and Internet layers are woven into the very fabric of the Linux kernel, which provides native support for TCP/IP. In addition, Linux distributions come with all the software needed to connect a Linux system to a variety of physical network media, including Ethernets, modems, and many more.

To get the most out of TCP/IP in the Linux context, you will find it helpful to understand some basic concepts. In the following sections, you will learn the concepts necessary to administer TCP/IP networking in this and the chapters to follow.

Internet Addresses (IP Addresses)

Every device that is fully connected to the Internet is called a host, and each such device must have a unique Internet address, called an *IP address*. An IP address is a four-byte number, called a *dotted quad*, that is written using decimal equivalents, with each number separated by a dot (as in the following example: 192.168.100.44).

Each IP address begins with a portion that is shared by all the hosts within a network; this section is called the *network portion*. The remaining portion of the IP address identifies unique hosts within the network. This portion is called the *host portion*.

Internet addresses are divided into classes for administrative purposes. Table 5.1 describes these classes.

Table 5.1 Internet Addresses

Class	Description
A	Very large networks that can accommodate millions of hosts. Addresses begin with a number less than 128.
B	Large networks that can accommodate thousands of hosts. Addresses begin with

	a number from 128 through 191.
C	Small networks for homes, schools, and offices that can accommodate 254 hosts. Addresses begin with a number greater than 191.

When TCP/IP was developed in the 1970s, there were around 100 organizations connected to the ARPANET. There are over four billion possible IP addresses, which seemed to be more than enough. The IP addresses were assigned to every computer on the network, as well as the routers that managed the traffic between networks. However, the system of addresses classes (Classes A, B, and C) wastes many addresses that would otherwise be available. For example, many Class A and Class B networks do not use anything close to the number of addresses allocated to them. Moreover, Class C networks are in short supply.

Although the technical details are not of concern here, an interim solution has been devised to this problem. However, the Internet will soon need to migrate to the next generation Internet protocols, called IPv6 (IP version 6). The current version of the IP protocols, in use throughout the Internet and implemented on Linux, is IPv4.

Special-Use IP Addresses

Some IP addresses are reserved for special uses. In all network classes, host number 0 is reserved for the network address, while host number 255 is reserved for the broadcast address. In addition, the following addresses are reserved:

- 127.0.0.1—This address, called the *loopback address*, is reserved so that a host can address itself.

- 10.0.0.0—This network address is reserved for private, internal networks that can accommodate millions of hosts.

- 172.16.0.0—This network address is reserved for private, internal networks that can accommodate thousands of hosts.

- 192.168.0.0—This network address is reserved for private, internal networks that can accommodate up to 254 hosts.

You cannot use any of these private addresses to connect to the Internet. However, you can use some of these addresses for your own local network, connected indirectly to the Internet. In the next sections, you will learn how to set up a group of addresses on your private internal network. Subsequently, you will also learn to use an active Internet IP address to give access to all computers on your network.

Netmasks and Network Addresses

As you have learned, IP addresses are divided into two parts—the network portion and the host portion. The network part of the address is on the left and the host part is on the right.

Where does the network portion end, and where does the host portion begin? To determine this, you need to know the *netmask*. The netmask is another four-byte number; like an IP address, it is written with four decimal numbers, separated by dots. However, the netmask can contain only two numbers; 0 and 255. The number 255 is used to specify those portions of the address that make up the network portion, while the 0 is used to specify the portions of the address that make up the host portion. If the netmask is 255.255.255.0 and the IP address is 192.168.100.44, the network portion is 192.168.100, while the host portion is the last of the four numbers in the address. Additionally, the network address is the lowest possible address available for a host in the network; in the example here, the network address is 192.168.100.0.

Broadcast Address

In addition to the addresses already mentioned, a given network has a broadcast address. This is the address that is monitored by every workstation on the network. By convention, the broadcast address is typically the network address with a final decimal value of 255. For the network with an address of 192.168.100.0, the broadcast address is 192.168.100.255.

Gateway Address

If your computer is connected to a local area network with access to the external Internet, or another private network, you will need to know about yet another type of IP address, the *gateway address*. The gateway address is the IP address of the device that provides access to external networks. For example, suppose your local area network is connected to an ISDN adapter and router, which enables all the computers on your network to access the external Internet. The IP address of this device is 192.168.100.7. This is the gateway address for your network. To access the external Internet, you will need to configure each machine on the network so that it knows the gateway address. You will learn how to do this in Chapter 10.

Domain Name Service (DNS) and Domain Names

As the previous section explained, every host connected to a TCP/IP network has its own, unique IP address. However, people find that it is difficult to work with IP addresses. Moreover, a given machine's address may change if it is connected to a different network. In the early days of TCP/IP, the network had to be maintained by manually adding all IP address changes to files stored on every network host. Obviously, this approach is inefficient and soon became unworkable. The domain name service (DNS) solves this problem by providing an automated means of mapping people-friendly domain names (such as www.yahoo.com) to specific IP addresses.

The domain name service is a worldwide service that involves the use of servers at many levels. If you are creating a small private network, you can revert to the early days of TCP/IP and implement your internal domain name service by means of tables kept on each computer. The file that contains this information is called /etc/hosts. You can also run a DNS server on your internal network, should the task of keeping every computer's /etc/hosts file up-to-date become too tedious. Discussed in this chapter is the technique used to configure /etc/hosts for a small internal network.

Creating a Simple TCP/IP Network

In this section, you will learn how to create an internet—that is, a small, internal network that uses the TCP/IP protocols. Don't concern yourself yet with connnecting this network to the wider, public Internet; that will be the job for Chapter 10.

Basic TCP/IP Configuration

To create your private, internal Internet, you can use one of the address groups that is available for this purpose, such as those beginning with 192.168. This is a Class C address for private networks. You can use it to create a network with up to 254 hosts.

To assign IP addresses to the computers on your network, begin by installing Ethernet cards in all of them. Connect each of the machines to a hub. Once you have connected the computers physically, follow these steps to assign IP addresses to each of the machines:

1. Log in as the root user.

2. Use your Linux distribution's network configuration utility to assign the following items.

    Hostname. Give each computer a distinctive name. Some people like to use Sesame Street characters (Bert, Ernie, Elmo, etc.), others like Star Wars characters (Luke, Yoda, Darth, etc.). Use your imagination—but pick names that are easy to remember and spell.

    Domain. Use the same domain name of your own devising for each machine, such as skywalker.org. It does not matter which name you choose; all that matters is that you type it exactly the same way each time you configure a computer.

    IP address. Give each machine a unique address. Start with 192.168.1.1. The next machine is 192.168.1.2, and so on. Note that you are assigning this address to the network interface—

that is, the Ethernet adapter, so be sure to link this address with the Ethernet card's interface name (eth0). Most of the network configuration utilities enable you to do this.

Netmask. As you are creating a Class C network, this is 255.255.255.0. Most Internet configuration utilities will deduce this automatically from the IP address you entered, but in some cases you may need to supply it manually.

You may be prompted to supply additional information, such as a default search domain and primary and secondary nameservers, but just leave these blank.

3. Save the configuration.

4. Use a text editor to open /etc/hosts. You will find that the network configuration utility you used in steps 2 and 3 has added the current host's IP address, a domain name, and an alias, as in the following:

```
127.0.0.1   localhost.localdomain   localhost
192.168.1.1 luke.skywalker.orgluke
```

5. To this list, add the IP addresses, domain names, and aliases of all the other machines in your network. After you do so, the /etc/hosts file on all the machines will look something like this:

```
127.0.0.1   localhost.localdomain   localhost
192.168.1.1 luke.skywalker.orgluke
192.168.1.2 leia.skywalker.orgleia
192.168.1.3 han.skywalker.orghan
```

```
192.168.1.4 r2d2.skywalker.orgr2d2
```

6.   Restart all of the computers.

Testing Your Network

Now that you have set up your network and created your connection to the Internet, it's time to test your connections with the ifconfig and ping commands.

To make sure you have configured your network interfaces properly, open a terminal window, type **ifconfig**, and press Enter. You should see something like the following:

```
eth0     Link encap:Ethernet   HWaddr
         00:A0:CC:22:6E:58
         inet addr:192.168.100.10
         Bcast:192.168.100.255   Mask:255.255.255.0
         UP BROADCAST RUNNING MULTICAST   MTU:1500
         Metric:1
         RX packets:436817 errors:2640 dropped:0
         overruns:0 frame:3899
         TX packets:315205 errors:0 dropped:0
         overruns:0 carrier:0
         collisions:57537 txqueuelen:100
         Interrupt:11 Base address:0xe400


lo       Link encap:Local Loopback
         inet addr:127.0.0.1  Mask:255.0.0.0
         UP LOOPBACK RUNNING   MTU:3924   Metric:1
         RX packets:774 errors:0 dropped:0 over-
         runs:0 frame:0
         TX packets:774 errors:0 dropped:0 over-
         runs:0 carrier:0
         collisions:0 txqueuelen:0
```

Do not worry about what all this verbiage means. If you see network interfaces for eth0 (your Ethernet adapter) and lo (the loopback interface), you are set. If not, run your distribution's Internet configuration again, and restart your system.

If all went well when you used ifconfig, try ping to see whether you contact additional hosts with ping. Short for the Packet Internet Groper utility, the ping command tests whether you can send network data to various computers. Open up a command line interface, type **ping 127.0.0.1,** and press Enter. If the command succeeds, you will see something like the following:

```
64 bytes from 127.0.0.1: icmp_seq=0 ttl=255
time=0.5 ms
```

Stop this process manually by pressing Ctrl + C.

Now try pinging the current host's IP address. If it is 192.168.1.1, type **ping 192.168.1.1** and press Enter. If this command does not succeed, there is something wrong with the network interface. Run your Linux distribution's network configuration utility again, and associate the eth0 interface with the correct IP address. Reboot your system, and try again.

Next, try pinging another host on the network. If one of these machines has the address 192.168.1.4, type **ping 192.168.1.4** and press Enter. If you see the message "Network is unreachable," check your network connections, and make sure the hub is plugged in. If the machine does not respond, go to the machine and check its configuration.

Looking Under the Hood

This chapter has mentioned a few of the essential configuration files that determine the way Linux works with TCP/IP. This section introduces all of the important TCP/IP configuration files and indicates the role they play in your Linux system's configuration.

letc/sysconfig

In most Linux distributions, network interfaces are defined by scripts placed in the /etc/sysconfig/network-scripts directory. For example, the following script (called ifcfg-eth0) defines the network interface for eth0 (the first detected Ethernet card). It does so by specifying the boot protocol (the options are static, bootp, or dhcp), the broadcast address, the adapter's IP address, the default netmask, the network address, and the startup option ("yes" means that the interface is automatically activated when your system is booted):

```
DEVICE=eth0
BOOTPROTO=static
BROADCAST=192.168.100.255
IPADDR=192.168.100.10
NETMASK=255.255.255.0
NETWORK=192.168.100.0
ONBOOT=yes
```

Although you can edit such scripts manually, your best course of action lies in using your Linux distribution's default network configuration utility to define basic network interfaces.

/etc/sysconfig/network

The most basic TCP/IP configuration file, /etc/sysconfig/network, enables TCP/IP networking and defines basic networking settings. (Note that this file may be located in a directory other than /etc/sysconfig on some Linux distributions.) A typical /etc/sysconfig/network file contains the following:

```
NETWORKING=yes
FORWARD_IPV4=no
HOSTNAME=lothlorien.mydomain.org
GATEWAY=192.168.100.7
GATEWAYDEV=
```

This first line in this file specifies that TCP/IP networking is enabled, but the second turns IP forwarding off; these settings are appropriate for a single-user workstation that is connected to a LAN or the external Internet. The HOSTNAME line specifies the name of this computer, as it is defined for TCP/IP purposes. The GATEWAY line contains the IP address of the gateway device, if any, that is used to access the external Internet. (This line is not needed if you are accessing the Internet by means of a modem.)

/etc/hosts

One of several essential TCP/IP configuration files, /etc/hosts indicates the IP addresses of the computer's loopback interface and that of the default network interface. A typical /etc/hosts file looks like the following:

```
127.0.0.1      localhost.localdomain   localhost
192.168.100.10 lothlorien.mydomain.org lothlorien
```

For each line, the first column indicates the IP address (such as 127.0.0.1). The second indicates the fully qualified domain name (FQDN) of the host that is being defined (for the loopback interface, localhost.localdomain is the default). The third column indicates aliases that can be used to refer to this host.

/etc/HOSTNAME

This file should contain your computer's fully qualified domain name (FQDN), which should match the entry in /etc/hosts. For example, if /etc/hosts assigns lothlorien.mydomain.org to the machine located at 192.168.100.10, /etc/HOSTNAME must contain lothlorien.mydomain.org.

/etc/host.conf

Another essential TCP/IP configuration file, /etc/host.conf defines the order in which TCP/IP attempts to resolve domain names. In domain name resolution, the TCP/IP software tries to find the numerical IP address equivalent of a fully qualified domain name, such as www.yahoo.com, or an alias, such as rivendell. A typical /etc/host.conf file contains the following, which will suffice for most systems:

```
order hosts,bind
multi on
```

These lines tell the TCP/IP software to check the /etc/hosts file first. If the needed information is not available there, the software uses the domain name service (DNS). In addition, the software retrieves all the available addresses for the requested host, not just the first one that is encountered.

/etc/resolv.conf

If your network will access the external Internet, or if you are connecting to a local area network that is running a domain name service, you need to tell your system the address of a domain name server. To do so, add the needed information to /etc/resolv.conf. For example, suppose you are connecting to the Internet by dialing your Internet service provider (ISP). Your ISP tells you that you should configure your system to access a primary name-server (206.205.42.2) and a secondary nameserver (206.205.42.254). You are also told that your search domain, the domain TCP/IP uses to look for assistance in resolving IP addresses, is cstone.net. Your /etc/resolve.conf file will look like this:

```
domain cstone.net
search cstone.net
nameserver 206.205.42.2
nameserver 206.205.42.254
```

/etc/hosts.allow and /etc/hosts.deny

To help prevent unauthorized intrusions into your system, you should configure the file called /etc/hosts.allow so that only the hosts connected to your internal network, if any, are allowed to access TCP/IP services on your computer. You can do so by modifying /etc/hosts.allow and /etc/hosts.deny as explained in this section.

The file called /etc/hosts.allow lists the names of hosts that are allowed to access TCP/IP services on your com-

puter. If you are connecting to a local area network in
which all the other users are trustworthy, you can make
your computer available to all the hosts on the network
by typing the first three values of the network's IP
address, followed by a period, as in the following
example:

```
192.168.100.
```

Any of the machines connected to this network can access
TCP/IP services on your computer. When you define
/etc/hosts.allow, do not forget to grant access to the localhost. To do so, type a space after the abbreviated network
adress, a colon, another space, and 127. as in the following example:

```
128.168.100. : 127.
```

The file called /etc/hosts.deny lists the hosts that are
specifically denied access to TCP/IP services running on
your computer. The safest way to configure this file is to
type the following:

```
ALL:ALL
```

This configuration denies access to all hosts, except those
specifically granted permission in /etc/hosts.allow.

References and Further Reading

Hunt, Carig. (1992). *TCP/IP Network Administration,* 2nd. ed. Petaluma, CA: O'Reilly Publishers.

Kirsch, Olaf. (1996). *The Linux Network Administrator's Guide.* Linux Documentation Project. Available online at http://www.linuxdoc.org/guides.html.

Loshin, Peter. (1999). *TCP/IP Clearly Explained,* 2nd. ed. San Francisco: Morgan Kaufmann Publishers.

6

Understanding User Accounts, Ownership, and Permissions

Thus far, you have installed network hardware (Chapter 4) and created a simple TCP/IP-based network (Chapter 5). You are anxious to get into the cool stuff—sharing files and printers with other Linux machines, and bringing Windows and Macintosh systems into the network—but please, hold your horses! It is essential that you have a crystal-clear understanding of user accounts in the network context as well as file ownership and permissions before you proceed.

Why bring up these admittedly rather tedious subjects when there is so much excitement around the corner? It is simple: Many, if not *most*, of the networking problems you will experience are caused by discrepant user accounts, file ownership messes, and incorrect permissions. The sooner you fully and clearly understand what user account, file ownership, and file permissions are all about in the Linux context, the happier will be your networking experience.

Creating User Accounts for Smooth Networking

Because Linux is a multiuser operating system, it is important that some files are accessible to every user, while others—particularly configuration and password files—are accessible only to the system administrator. In addition, users need to be given full access to their own files, while such access should be restricted or prevented entirely for other users. When you are dealing with user accounts on the network, there is a further complication. *For each user who will share files on the network, you must create identical user accounts on each machine.*

Why Identical User Accounts Are Necessary

You are creating the network in all likelihood so that you can access your own files on a remote machine. For example, suppose you have hooked up your notebook computer to the network, and you want to transfer files between your notebook and the desktop system. However, this will not work unless the two systems are set up with *identical* user accounts—and I mean *identical*. To make full use of all the networking capabilities discussed in this book, both machines must define your user account so that *all* of the following are identical:

- User name;
- Numeric user ID;
- Primary group; and
- Password.

Suppose you create a user account for your use on your notebook computer. The user name is suzanne, the numeric ID associated with this account is 501, the primary group membership is wheel, and the password is yai2bfw. On the desktop computer, you create what you think is the same user account—the user name is suzanne (with a lowercase "s"), the group is wheel, and the password is yai2bfw. However, you did not notice that the user utility gave this account a different numeric ID (500). Guess what? The Network File System (NFS), discussed in the next chapter, will not work.

The reason why NFS will not work is simple: it will not be able to connect to a second computer unless all of these user account characteristics are the same on both machines. There is no way to supply a different user name or password or group membership or numerical user ID. Period! As you will see, Samba (Windows networking) is somewhat more forgiving, as is netatalk (AppleTalk networking). However, both of these protocols may behave strangely if the user accounts vary, and sometimes they will not connect at all.

So you will have to go around to every machine on your network and create identical accounts for *every* user. This is something of a pain, admittedly. That is why larger networks have tools such as the Network Information Service (NIS), which enables network administrators (among other things) to manage user accounts centrally. However, NIS is beyond the scope of this book, and it is overkill anyway for a small network with only a few machines.

Creating Valid User Accounts for Networking

To create valid user accounts for network use, you can use a user configuration utility, such as LinuxConf. If you use such a utility, make sure you assign all the required account information (user name, numerical user ID, primary group membership, and password). You can also use text-mode utilities, such as useradd.

To use the useradd utility, log in as the root user or switch to superuser. You should use the command with the following options:

- **-u *uid*.** Creates the user with the specified numerical user ID.
- **-g *group*.** Creates the user with the specified primary group.
- **-p *password*.** Creates the user with the specified password.

The useradd command creates a new user account, including a new home directory for the new user (unless your system has been configured to skip creating home directories by default).

TIP To determine whether your system creates users' home directories by default, when you run useradd, examine /etc/login.defs. If you see the line CREATE_HOME yes, useradd will automatically create a new home directory for each new user and will copy to this directory all the files found in /etc/skel.

Understanding File Ownership and Permissions

Linux is a multiuser system, so it needs a way to keep users from raiding each other's files. It is not enough to set them apart in separate directories. To make it clear just who belongs to what, Linux defines the following attributes for each file:

- **File ownership.** A file is owned by the person who creates it. When you create a file in your home directory, you are the owner, and you automatically have permission to read and alter this file. However, your rights to read or alter files outside your home directory may be restricted.
- **Permissions.** A file's *permissions* specify just who can do what with the file. For a given type of user, permissions specify whether the user can read the file, write to the file (including deleting the file), or execute the file (if it is an executable file).

The following sections explain these concepts in more detail; subsequently, you will learn how to adjust file ownership and permissions with File Manager.

Types of File Owners

Linux defines the following categories of file owners:

- **User.** The user who owns the file. Normally, this is the person who created the file, but the root user (system administrator) can change file ownership.
- **Group.** When you create user accounts, you can place two or more users into a *group*. Groups are very useful when two or more people need to work on the same file or within the same directory.

- **Others.** This category includes all other users *except* the user and group.

Types of Permissions

For each type of file owner, you can define the following permissions:

- **Read.** Determines whether a given category of users can read a file.
- **Write.** Determines whether a given category of users can alter a file (including deleting the file).
- **Execute.** Determines whether a given category of users can launch (execute) a program or script. Applied to directories, this term is equivalent to directory access.
- **Set User ID (SUID)** and **Set Group ID (GUID).** These permissions specify that a program will start with the permissions available to the owner (SUID) or the group owner (GUID) of the file. It is very convenient to change the permissions of certain networking utilities so that they run with SUID permission; this enables you to run them from ordinary user accounts. For example, **smbmount** and **smbumount** (see Chapter 8) must be run unless their SUID bit is set (this is done with the command **chmod u+s /usr/sbin/smbmount** and **chmod u+s /usr/sbin/smbumount**). However, you should be aware that using the SUID or GUID setting exposes your system to certain security risks. It is best to avoid SUID and GUID unless you are sure your network is secure and you really want the convenience.

Viewing and Changing Ownership and Permisions

To get networking to work smoothly, you must make sure that all the files in every user's directory have the correct ownership—including primary group ownership–and that permissions are set correctly. The following section reviews essential skills for viewing and changing file ownership and permissions.

Reading File Permission Information

When you view a file directory with ls -l, you will see the current permissions for each file expressed in an oddly, such as the following example:

```
r w x r - x - - x
```

Here is how to understand what this means. These are *positional* expressions in which the location of each character means something. The nine symbols are in groups of three:

```
Owner         Group             Other
r  w  x       r  w  x           r  w  x
```

If any of the permissions has not been granted, you see a hyphen instead of the symbol. For example, consider this example:

```
r w - r w - r - -
```

Here is the table again; note where the hyphens are placed:

```
Owner          Group              Other
r   w   -      r   w   -          r   -   -
```

In other words, the owner and the owner's group have read and write permissions (but not execute), while all others have only read permission.

See Table 6.1 for a guide to the permissions you commonly see in file directories.

Table 6.1 Understanding Permissions Indicated in Directories

Directory listing	Symbolic mode	Numeric mode
r w - - - - - -	u=rw,g=,o=	600
r w - r - - - -	u=rw,g=r,o=r	644
r w - r w - r w -	u=rw,g=rw,o=rw	666
r w x - - - - -	u=rwx,g=,o=	700
r w x - - x - - -	u=rwx,g=x,o=	710
r w x - - x - - x	u=rwx,g=x,o=x	711
r w x r - x - - x	u=rwx,g=rx,o=x	751
r w x r - x r - x	u=rwx,g=rx,o=rx	755
r w x r w x r w x	u=rwx,g=rwx,o=rwx	777

Changing File Ownership with chown

To change the ownership of files or directories, use the chown command. To use chown, type **chown** followed by a space, the user or group name, and the name of the file or directory. The following is an example:

```
chown bryan mydoc.txt
```

A very neat option is -R, which changes ownership recursively. This option enables you to change file ownership throughout a directory and all the subdirectories it contains. An example is as follows:

```
chown -R bryan /home/bryan
```

TIP If you have messed up file ownership in your home directory by saving files there while you are logged in as root user, you can use the recursive (-R) option just mentioned to restore the correct file ownership throughout your home directory. Do not kill these processes; doing so could damage data or bring your system down.

Changing a File's Permissions with chmod

To alter a file's permissions, use the chmod command. To use the chmod command, you need to learn a few abbreviations. Use the following to indicate permission types:

- **r (read).** Indicates read-only permission (the file can not be altered or deleted).
- **w (write).** Indicates write permission (the file *can* be altered or deleted).
- **x (execute).** For program files, indicates execute permissions (the program is available).

Use the following to indicate types of owners:

- **u (user).** Normally, this is the user who created the file. Using chown, you can specify a different file owner.
- **g (group).** Additional users who are members of the owner's group.
- **o (others).** All other users *except* the user and group.
- **a (all).** Any user of the system, including user, group, and others.

When you use chmod, you change the file's current permissions. You can change the current permissions in the following ways:

- **+ (add).** Adds the specified permission to whatever permissions currently exist for the file. If a file currently has read and write permissions, and you add an execute permission, the file now has read, write, and execute permissions.
- **- (remove).** Takes away the specified permission from whatever permissions currently exist for the file. If a file currently has read and write permissions, and you take away an execute permission, the file now has only the read and write permissions.
- **= (equals).** Erases all current permissions and assigns the specified permissions for the file. If you specify a read permission for a file that formally had all permissions (read, write, and execute), the file is now restricted to read-only access.

Using chmod

When you use the chmod command to change file permissions, you first type **chmod** and press the space bar. Then you type the user category, the operation, and the permission. Finally, you type the filename or directory name.

An example:

```
chmod +w recipes.txt
```

This command says, in effect, "add the write permission to recipes.txt for all users no matter what other permissions might exist for the file."

In the following are some additional examples:

- **chmod -x /usr/sbin/pppd.** "Take away execute permissions for the pppd program from all users except the file owner and members of the file owner's group."
- **chmod +x /home/everyone.** "Enable any user to access this directory."
- **chmod =r /usr/docs/minitab.ps.** "Erase whatever permissions currently exist for this file, and enable any user to read this file (but not to alter it)."

You can combine user categories and permissions, as the following examples indicate:

- **chmod uo+rwx /usr/sbin/pppd.** Sets full permissions (read, write, and execute) for the user and the user's group.
- **chmod u+rwx,o=r /usr/bin/myprogram.** Note the use of the comma to separate the two expressions (do not include a space). Sets full permissions for the owner, but limits the owner's group to read-only permission.
- **chmod u+rwx,o= /usr/bin/myprogram.** Note that there is nothing after "o=". This specifies that owners have *no* permissions at all. They cannot read, write, or execute the file.

Using Numeric Permission Modes

In the previous sections, you have learned how to set permissions using the *symbolic* mode. In this mode, you use symbols for user categories, operations, and permissions. Sometimes, you will encounter manuals that give you specific chmod commands that use the *numeric* mode. The numeric mode requires a bit of math to understand it fully, but there is a quick, easy way to grasp the gist of it.

The trick is to begin with the assumption that the read permission = 4, the write permission = 2, the execute permission = 1, and no permissions = 0. Then use a table such as Table 6.2 to add up the permissions for each category.

Table 6.2 Explanation of Mode 664

Permission	Owner	Group	Other
Read	4	4	4
Write	2	2	0
Execute	0	0	0
TOTAL	6	6	4

Thus chmod 664 is the same as chmod ug=rw,o=r.

TIP Although numeric mode permissions are harder to understand, they're easier to type—which is exactly why Linux users love them. In practice, there are a few numeric permissions that get used so frequently that you memorize them (such as chmod 664).

Another example of a table that is often used to set permissions for Web pages is given in Table 6.3.

Table 6.3 Explanation of Mode 755

Permission	Owner	Group	Other
Read	4	4	4
Write	2	0	0
Execute	1	1	1
TOTAL	7	5	5

This is the same as:

```
chmod o=rwx,g=rx,o=rx
```

In other words, this command gives the owner full permission to read and write the page, as well as to execute any active content (such as scripts) that may be present on the page. Members of the owner's group, as well as all other users, are given rights to read the page *and* to execute any content it may contain, but *not* to write (alter) the page.

The following table shows another example, chmod 711.

Table 6.4 Explanation of Mode 711

Permission	Owner	Group	Other
Read	4	0	0
Write	2	0	0
Execute	1	1	1
TOTAL	**7**	**1**	**1**

This permission gives full privileges to the file owner, but restricts everyone else to executing the file (which is a script or a program). This permission is commonly used when you install a file and want to make it available to everyone in the system.

Using Common Permission Modes

You do not really want to work out a table every time you encounter (or want to use) a numeric file permission. For reference purposes, Table 6.5 lists the ones that are commonly used. Often, you will type one of these permission modes in response to detailed program configuration instructions; you can refer to this table to see what the numeric file permission means.

Table 6.5 Commonly Used Numeric File Permissions

Permission	Symbolic mode equivalent
600	u=rw,g=,o=
644	u=rw,g=r,o=r
666	u=rw,g=rw,o=rw
700	u=rwx,g=,o=
710	u=rwx,g=x,o=
711	u=rwx,g=x,o=x
750	u=rwx,g=rx,o=x
755	u=rwx,g=rx,o=rx
777	u=rwx,g=rwx,o=rwx

Understanding Default Permissions

When you create a new file or directory, Linux assigns default permissions to it. If you would like to find out what these permissions are, type **umask** and press Enter. You will see a number, such as 022.

To find out what this number means, subtract it from 666 (read/write permissions for owner, group, and other)— but note that this is not the sort of subtraction you learned in grade school. For each digit, if the subtraction results in a quantity less than zero, put zero. Suppose the umask is 027:

$$
\begin{array}{r}
666 \\
-\ \underline{027} \\
640
\end{array}
$$

The numeric mode value 640 corresponds to read/write permission for the owner, read permission for the owner's group, and no permissions for others. Equivalents are:

```
r w - r - - - -
u=rw,g=r,o=
```

For directories, you subtract the umask value from 777:

$$
\begin{array}{r}
777 \\
- \underline{027} \\
750
\end{array}
$$

In symbolic mode, the directory permission 750 is the same as:

```
r w x r - x - - -
u=rwx,g=rx,o=
```

Table 6.6 provides a list of typical umask values and their equivalents.

Table 6.6 Understanding Permissions Indicated in Directories

Umask	For files	For directories
077	600 (r w - - - - - -)	700 (r w x - - - - -)
067	600 (r w - - - - - -)	710 (r w x - - x - -)
066	600 (r w - - - - - -)	711 (r w x - - x - - x)
027	640 (r w - r - - - -)	750 (r w x r - x r - x)
022	644 (r w - r - - r - -)	755 (r w x r - x r - x)
000	666 (r w - r w - r w -)	777 (r w x r w x r w x)

Looking Under the Hood

To deal with user accounts, file ownership, and permissions, you will make frequent use of the utilities discussed in this section. Here is some additional information on the options available with these commands.

chmod

This command changes the permissions settings of the filename to the mode. Here is the basic command syntax:

```
chmod [ option ] mode filename
```

To specify the *mode*, you can use symbolic or numeric modes. The *filename* can be a single file, a shell pattern (using wildcards), or a directory. If you are using the symbolic mode, you use the following operators to specify actions:

+   Add the specified permission to the existing permissions

=   Set the permission to the specified level, erasing all existing permissions

-   Remove the specified permission from the existing permissions

Table 6.7 lists the options you can use with this command.

Table 6.7 Command Options (chmod)

Option	Description
-c, --changes	Display messages only when changes are made
-f, --silent, --quiet	Hide messages
-v, --verbose	Display messages concerning all processed files
-R	Change permissions in the current directory and all associated subdirectories
--help	Display available options
--version	Display version number

chgrp

This command changes the ownership of the specified file to the specified group. It comes in handy when you have discovered that some of the files in a user's directory have the wrong group membership—a problem that can cause networking glitches.

Here is the command syntax:

```
chgrp [ option ] group filename
```

To specify the group owner, you can supply group names or ID numbers.

Table 6.8 lists the options you can use.

Table 6.8 Command Options (chgrp)

Option	Description
-c, --changes	Display messages only when changes are made
-f, --silent	Hide messages
-h	Change symbolic links, not the file to which symbolic links point
--help	Display available options
-R	Change ownership in the current directory and all associated subdirectories
-v, --verbose	Display messages concerning all processed files
--version	Display version number

chown

This command changes the ownership of the specified file to the specified user. To change the group ownership at the same time, type a period after the user name and type the group name or ID (with no intervening spaces). To specify owners or groups, you can supply user or group names or ID numbers.

Here is the command syntax:

```
chown [ option ] user [ . group ] filename
```

Table 6.9 lists the options you can use with this command.

Table 6.9 Command Options (chown)

Option	Description
-c, --changes	Display messages only when changes are made
-f, --silent	Hide messages
-h	Change symbolic links, not the file to which symbolic links point.
--help	Display available options
-R	Change ownership in the current directory and all associated subdirectories
-v, --verbose	Display messages concerning all processed files
--version	Display version number

useradd

Creates a new user (or updates an existing user) with the specified user-name. When you create a new user account, this command automatically configures the appropriate system files, creates a new home directory for the user (named /home/user-name), and copies the files found in /etc/skel. Here is the command syntax:

```
useradd [ option ] user-name
```

The options you can use with this command are listed in Table 6.10.

Table 6.10 Command Options (useradd)

Option	Description
-c *comment*	Insert the specified comment in the user's profile
-d *directory*	Create the user's home directory with the specified directory name, instead of the default (/home/user-name)
-e *date*	Expire the account on the specified date (The date is specified in the format YYYY_MM-DD.)
-f *days*	Disable the account after the password has been inactive for the specified number of days.
-g *group*	Add the user to the specified initial login group
-G *group*	Add the user to the specified supplementary group. To add the user to more than one group, type group names in a comma-separated list.
-m	If this option is not configured by default in /etc/login.defs, create the user's home directory and copy to this directory the files found in /etc/skel
-M	Skip creating the home directory, even if automatic home creation is enabled by default in /etc/login.defs
-n	Skip creating a group with the same name as the new user
-r	Create a system account with a numerical user ID lower than the minimum number for user account IDs specified in /etc/login.defs
-p *password*	Use the specified password. If you omit

	this option, useradd will create the account, but will not enable it
-s *shell*	Assign the user the specified shell by default. If you omit this option, the account users the system-wide default shell
-u *uid*	Create the account with the specified numerical user ID (uid)

References and Further Reading

Frampton, Steve. (1999). *Linux System Administration Made Easy*. Linux Documentation Project. Available online at http://www.linuxdoc.org/guides.html.

Frisch, Aileen. (1995). *Essential System Administration*. Petaluma, CA: O'Reilly & Associates.

7

Configuring and Using NFS

You have gone through a lot of trouble to set up a network. You have wired your home or office, you have set up and configured network software, and you have reviewed basic concepts of file ownership and permissions. Now you are ready to reap the rewards.

In this chapter, you will learn to share files and printers between Linux computers with the Network File System (NFS). Although you can use NFS with Microsoft Windows and Apple Macintosh computers, these other operating systems need special software to read files through NFS. In later chapters, you will learn to extend the benefits of networking to these computers with applications similar to NFS, known as Samba and AppleTalk.

Introducing the Network File System (NFS)

The Network File System (NFS) is the native local area networking protocol not only of Linux, but all Unix-like operating systems. If you have never used NFS before, however, you may find the basic concepts unfamiliar. The following is a brief introduction to these concepts.

Servers and Clients

Similar to all the Internet services discussed in this book, NFS consists of two complementary software packages—the server and the client. The NFS server exports certain directories to the network. Using the NFS client, qualified users can then mount these exported directories to their filesystems.

Here is an example. Suppose Suzanne is using her notebook computer, but she stores all of her important files on Lothlorien, a desktop system with a huge hard drive. Lothlorien is running an NFS server, and this server exports Suzanne's directory from Lothlorien so that it is available on the network. Using her notebook computer and the NFS client software, Suzanne mounts her Lothlorien directory so that it appears to be part of her notebook computer's filesystem.

As this example suggests, NFS seems to be designed around a client/server model (see Chapter 4). However, it is possible to use NFS to implement peer-to-peer networking as well. The trick lies in installing NFS server and client software on every computer on the network. Users can decide for themselves which directories and files they want to make available to other users on the network.

Typical NFS Applications

As you have just learned, NFS enables users of Unix and Linux workstations to mount one or more remote directories, so that these remote directories appear to become part of the local filesystem. You can use this capability in the following ways:

- **Automating data backups.** Using utilities such as **cron** and **tar,** you can easily create automated backup procedures that copy all of a user's new or modified files to a backup directory on the remote server.
- **Reducing storage requirements on client systems.** Rather than installing read-only resources such as fonts and documentation on every system, you can make these available to everyone by sharing the directories on the server that contain these resources.
- **Providing a central location for applications.** Rather than installing StarOffice on every computer on the network, you can install it on the server, and make the StarOffice directory available to all network users. You can do the same with other applications. This application reduces maintenance tasks significantly. For example, suppose a new version of StarOffice is introduced. By installing the new version on the server, you automatically upgrade everyone's copy. The alternative? Install the new version repeatedly on everyone's computer. Note that this use of NFS is another way to reduce storage requirements on client systems.
- **Sharing expensive printers.** Rather than equipping each system with its own computer, you can purchase

just one high-end printer that is accessible to everyone via the network.

Shortcomings of NFS

Although NFS is useful and convenient, it has certain drawbacks that you should be aware of. These drawbacks include the following:

- **Security.** Intruders know how to use NFS to gain root access to improperly configured networks. If some of your network's client systems are located in insecure locations, or if you plan to connect your network to the Internet, you should take precautions to safeguard your network against the better-known attack methods. In particular, do not connect to the Internet without implementing IP masquerading, discussed in Chapter 10.
- **Fault Tolerance.** No network protocol handles a severed server connection with anything approaching grace, but NFS is particularly weak in this area. If a network connection goes down, you may have difficulty restoring network services until you reboot all the machines.
- **Linux-Specific Problems.** To improve NFS performance, much of the NFS code is now directly incorporated into the Linux kernel (version 2.2 and later). Although this is a positive development from a performance angle, it means that virtually all of the NFS documentation available on the Internet is out of date and cannot be used to implement NFS on your network. In addition, all the NFS daemons had to be rewritten to accommodate the kernel changes. Inevitably, when software is updated, new bugs are introduced that take some time to iron out.

> **TIP** Do not try to implement NFS without making sure that you are running the latest version of your Linux distribution and the latest version of the NFS daemons. Be sure to check your Linux distribution's home page for software updates. If you are having trouble getting NFS to work, you may be using an older, flawed version of one of the NFS daemons or utilities.

Preparing to Use NFS

To use NFS, begin by implementing security safeguards. This is not only a good idea, it is necessary to get the NFS daemons working properly. Next, make sure the necessary server and client *daemons* (background processes) are running on all the machines on your network. You then determine which directories you want to share. Finally, make sure that the directories to be shared have the appropriate ownership and permissions.

> **TIP** Before proceeding, make sure you fully understand the user account, ownership, and permissions concepts introduced in the previous chapter. If you have trouble getting NFS to work, chances are that the problem is in one of these areas.

Securing Your System

To use NFS safely, you'll need to take a few steps to secure your system. In the following, you will modify the /etc/hosts.allow and /etc/hosts.deny files so that you are protected against a whole series of possible attacks. This protection is not bulletproof, to be sure, but it will eliminate a number of tricks that the script kiddies have been pulling for years.

1. Open a terminal window, and switch to superuser (type su followed by your password).

2. Use your favorite text editor to open /etc/hosts.deny

3. On a blank line, type portmap: ALL

4. Save the file.

5. Open /etc/hosts.allow

6. On a blank line, type portmap: followed by a space, the IP address of the client machine, a forward slash mark, and the netmask of the client machine. For a Class C network, which is what you are probably using, the default netmask is 255.255.255.0. If you are not sure what the client's netmask is, go to the client, open a terminal window, type ifconfig, and press Enter. Look for the IP address and netmask under the Ethernet network interface (eth0, unless the machine has more than one Ethernet card). Here is an example of a valid entry in /etc/hosts.allow:

    ```
    portmap: 192.168.100.10/255.255.255.0
    ```

    If you would like to make the exported directories available to all the machines on your network, you can use a wildcard, as in the following example:

    ```
    portmap: 192.168.100.*/255.255.255.0
    ```

7. Save the file.

Making Sure NFS Is Installed

To work with NFS, you will need the following daemons (memory-resident programs) running on both servers and clients:

- **portmap.** Accepts remote requests for information and guides these requests to the appropriate port.
- **rpc.mountd.** This daemon enables the system to mount and unmount remote NFS directories.
- **nfsd** This is the NFS server daemon proper.
- **rpc.lockd.** This daemon handles file locking on the server. Clients request file locks so that they can use the files without other users overwriting them.
- **rpc.statd.** This daemon monitors locking processes and resets locks after a crash.

Configuring Your System to Start NFS Automatically

You should configure all the machines on your network so that they start these daemons at the beginning of each session. On Red Hat systems, you do this with the /usr/sbin/setup utility, a text-mode utility that enables you to specify which system services you want to run. Red Hat launches daemons by means of startup scripts located in the /etc/rc.d/init.d directory. Most Linux distributions use the same technique or a close variation of it.

On Red Hat and Red Hat–derived systems (such as Mandrake), make sure that your system is running the following services: netfs (the NFS mount daemon); nfs (the NFS server daemon); nfslock; portmap; and rstatd. (Note: If none of these options are available on the Setup program menu, you need to install the RPM packages for these services.) Other distributions provide varying means to specify which services run automatically at startup;

check your distribution documentation to find out which utility to run.

Making Sure the NFS Daemons Are Running

To make sure you are running the needed utilities, you can run the startup scripts with the status option. Here is how to do this:

1. Switch to the directory where network scripts are stored. On Red Hat and kindred systems, this directory is /etc/rc.d/init.d.

2. Type ./portmap status and press Enter. You should see a message stating that portmap is running. If not, type ./portmap startup and press Enter.

3. Now type ./nfs status and press Enter. You should see a message informing you that rpc.mountd and nfsd are running. If not, type ./nfs start and press Enter.

4. Got everything running? Just to make sure, type /usr/sbin/rpcinfo -p and press Enter. You should see a list of all the running daemons, including their version numbers and the protocol they are using.

If you see an error message such as "can't contact portmapper," "Connection refused," or "PROG NOT REGISTERED," then portmap is not running, or your /etc/hosts.deny and /etc/hosts.allow files are not properly configured. Check your configuration; then restart your system and try the aforementioned steps again.

Setting Up Directories for Sharing

You should now devote some thought to which directories you want to share. Note the following:

- **NFS shares an entire directory and all associated subdirectories at a time.** In other words, if you share /home/suzanne, the share will include all the files in /home/suzanne, /home/suzanne/documents, /home/suzanne/poetry, and /home/suzanne/private-journal. However, note that this point does *not* apply to subdirectories that are mounted on a different disk or partition than the parent directory. If /home/suzanne/documents is on a different partition, then it is not exported along with the other subdirectories of /home/suzanne. You must export this directory separately.

- **The exported directory's ownership and permissions determine just who gets to see it (and what they can do once they've seen it).** You'll need to make sure the ownership and permission setting are correct for the directory's intended uses. For example, /home/suzanne could be exported with permissions that make the directory invisible to members of Suzanne's group and to all other users.

You can control access to shared directories by using one of the following permission settings:

- **A specific user, and no others.** The directory must be owned by the user who will access it remotely. To deny access to others in the user's group as well as to other users, the permissions must be set so that the user alone has read and read/write access to this directory. To set the shared directory's permissions so that the user is the only person who can see, read, and alter the files, switch to superuser, type **chmod u=rwx,g=,o=** followed by the name of the directory, and press Enter.

- **All the members of a group.** The directory must be owned by the group that will access it remotely. The permissions must be set so that the file can be read by group members. If desired, you can set the permissions so that all members of the group have read/write access (use **chmod u=rwx,g=rwx,o=rx** followed by the name of the directory). If you want to hide the directory from people who are not members of the group, change the permissions so that others have no access (use **chmod u=rwx,g=rwx,o=** followed by the name of the directory).

- **Everyone.** To make a directory accessible to all users, set the permissions so that everyone has full read access (use **chmod u=rx,g=rx,o=rx** followed by the name of the directory). You can also give everyone read/write access, but this probably is not a very good idea unless you are creating a very small network that will be used by one or two people and you have boundless faith in the inherent goodness of human nature and the exceptional competence of your co-users.

Setting Up Exports

To make shared directories available to remote clients, you need to export them. This is a two-step process. First, you will list the directories to be exported in an important configuration file, called /etc/exports. Then you will use the exportfs command, which makes the exported directories available to clients on the network.

You need to follow these steps only once. After you have configured /etc/exports, the server will automatically export the dirctories each time you start your system. If you wish, you can restart your system instead of using exportfs.

To configure /etc/exports and export shared directories, do the following:

1. Open a terminal window, and switch to superuser (type su followed by your password);

2. Use your favorite text editor to open /etc/exports;

3. On a blank line, type the name of the directory you want to export, followed by a space, and the IP address of the client or clients to which you want to make the directory available. After the IP address, place the export options you want within parentheses. Here's an example:

```
/home/suzanne 192.168.100.33(rw)
/mnt/cdrom 192.168.100.*(ro)
```

In this example, I am exporting /home/suzanne to Suzanne's computer (192.168.100.33), and I am specifying that this directory should be exported with read-write permissions (rw). I am also exporting the server's CD-ROM drive (/mnt/cdrom) to all the clients on my network, with read-only permission. With this configuration, I can keep the Linux distribution disk in my CD-ROM drive so that it is always available, should anyone need to grab additional files.

TIP Be careful as you set up the /etc/exports file. You need a space after the shared directory, each computer name permission (rw), and the "#." Do not put a space between the computer name and its permissions, or Linux will try to find a computer named "(rw)."

---

4. Important: Before NFS can make use of the modifications you have made, you must use the exportfs utility to update the exported directory database /var/lib/nfs/xtab. This database is needed by the remote mounting daemons; if it is not accurate, clients will not be able to mount the exported directories. To synchronize /etc/exports with the database, type exportfs -rv and press Enter.

When you have completed these steps successfully, your server is making the exported directories available to clients on the network. In the next section, you move to the clients, and you learn how to mount the remote directories that the server is making available.

Mounting Remote Directories

To mount remote directories that an NFS server is making available, you need to do the following. First, make sure the directories are actually available by running the **showmount** command. Next, decide how you want to mount the remote directories. If you would like to do so only when the remote directories are needed, you can mount them manually by using the mount command. If you would like the directories to be mounted automatically every time you start your system, you need to add an entry to /etc/fstab. The following sections detail these procedures.

Determining Whether the Remote Directories Are Available

At one of the client machines, switch to superuser, if necessary, and type the following command:

```
/usr/sbin/showmount —exports server
```

Here, *server* is the IP address of the computer that is running the NFS server. Here is an example of a valid showmount command:

```
/usr/sbin/showmount —exports 192.168.100.34
```

If you set up your /etc/hosts file correctly (see Chapter 5) so that all the hosts on your network are listed with IP addresses and aliases, you can type the alias instead of the IP address, as in the following example:

```
/usr/sbin/showmount —exports lothlorien
```

If you see the message "RPC: Program not registered," it means that showmount was not able to find the server, or that the server is not running the NFS daemons. Re-check your installation, and try again.

A successful command shows something like the following:

```
Export list for lothlorien:
/home/mike        frodo.mydomain.org
/home/bryan            rivendell.mydomain.org
/usr/doc              (everyone)
/usr/share/fonts(everyone)
```

The export lists shows the available directories. It also shows which machines may access them. The /home/mike directory is available only to frodo.mydomain.org. The /home/bryan directory is available only to rivendell.

mydomain.org. However, /usr/docs and /usr/share/fonts are available to all the computers on the network.

Mounting Remote Directories Manually

If you would like to mount remote directories on an as-needed basis, you can do so with the mount command. This command requires superuser status. To use mount, you will need to specify the mount point. The mount point is a directory on your local system. After you mount the remote directory, the remote directory's contents will appear within the mount point directory, as if these contents were part of your local filesystem.

Suppose I am using my notebook computer, called rivendell, and I want to connect to my home directory on the remote computer, called lothlorien. The following example specifies the remote directory to be mounted (/home/bryan, on lothlorien) as well as the mount point (/home/bryan/lothlorien, on rivendell):

```
mount -w lothlorien:/home/bryan
/home/bryan/lothlorien
```

This command mounts the lothlorien directory /home/bryan to the client system, using the mount point /home/bryan/lothlorien. The –w switch gives users write privileges (but only if you set up the rw option in the server's /etc/exports file.

When you are finished using the remote directory, you can unmount it using the **umount** command. Switch to superuser, type umount followed by mount point's name, and press Enter. The following command unmounts the mount point directory called /home/bryan/lothlorien:

```
umount /home/bryan/lothlorien
```

Note that it is not necessary to tell umount the name of the server or the remote directory.

Mounting Remote Directories Automatically

If you would like your client to mount the remote directory automatically each time the system starts, you can add the mount information to /etc/fstab. You should do this only if the following are true:

- **The server runs 24/7.** If you shut down the server, TCP/IP service on the clients will be interrupted and you may have to reboot the clients to get them working again.
- **The client is permanently connected to the network.** Do not configure a notebook computer to load remote shares automatically.

To add the information to /etc/fstab correctly, you must carefully observe the following syntax:

server:directory mount-point `nfs` *options*

Here, *server* refers to the alias or IP address of the remote server, while *directory* refers to the name of the remote directory that is being shared. *Mount-point* is the name of the local directory, where the remote directory will be mounted. This directory must already exist; if it does not, create it using **mkdir**.

For *options,* you can choose from the options listed in Table 7.1.

Table 7.1 NFS Mounting Options in /etc/fstab

Option	Description
ro	Mount the remote directory read-only
rw	Mount the remote directory read-write
user	Permit ordinary users to mount the filesystem, as long as the remote filesystem is configured with the correct permissions
soft	Allow the connection to time out if the server does not respond. The default is hard, in which the client keeps trying to connect until it succeeds. Although this setting would appear to solve the problems caused by a server crash or network service interruptions, you should avoid using it because it prevents the network from confirming file writes; some applications cannot handle this and will crash
rsize=n	Specify a read block size of n bytes. Try 8192 (rsize=8192) for good performance
wsize=n	Specify the write block size in bytes. Try 8192 for good performance (wsize= 8192)

The following /etc/fstab entry mounts /home/bryan on lothlorien to the mount point /home/bryan/lothlorien. It specifies that the directory should be mounted read/write. In addition, ordinary users can mount the directory (user), the client is told to stop trying if the server does not respond (soft), and the read and write block sizes are set to 8192 blocks (rsize=8192,wsize=8192):

```
lothlorien:/home/bryan /home/bryan/lothlorien
nfs rw,user,soft,rsize=8192,wsize-8192 0 0
```

To mount remote directories automatically, follow these steps:

1. Switch to superuser, or log in as the root user.

2. Launch a text editor, and open /etc/fstab.

3. On a separate line, add the remote mounting information, following the format specified in the foregoing. Be sure to omit spaces in the comma-separated list of options. Do not forget to type the filesystem type (nfs) between the mount point and the options.

4. Save the file.

To mount the remote directories, you can restart your system. Alternatively, you could restart the mount daemon; on Red Hat systems, switch to superuser, type **/etc/rc.d/init.d/netfs restart**, and press Enter.

Sharing Printers

Suppose one of the computers on your network is connected to a laser printer by means of a parallel port connection. It is very easy to make this printer available to every user on the network.

To share a printer across your network, do the following:

1. Make sure the printer is working properly on the machine to which it is connected. (This is not the place to go into the details of how to get your

printer working with your Linux system; consult your Linux distribution's documentation for the details.) In what follows, it is assumed that you have installed your printer using the default print spool (lp).

2. Make sure that every user who will access this printer has an account on the machine to which the computer is connected. The account must be identical to that on the user's system.

3. On the computer that is attached to the printer, open a terminal window, and switch to superuser.

4. Start a text editor. Create a new file. In this file, type the aliases of all the machines that will be able to access this printer. Suppose you are creating the file on lothlorien, and you want to give the computers named frodo, strider, and sauron access to this printer. Type the following:

```
frodo
strider
sauron
```

5. Save the file and exit.

6. Now go to the first client computer that will access this computer.

7. Use the printer configuration utility that came with your Linux distribution to define a new printer. If you are using Red Hat or a Red Hat-derived distribution, you can use the printtool utility for this purpose. To run printtool, switch to superuser, type **/usr/sbin/printtool**, and press Enter. You will

see the Red Hat Linux Print System Manager, shown in Figure 7.1. If you are using some other Linux distribution, consult your documentation to determine how to launch the printer configuration utility.

8. Click Add to create a new printer profile. You will see the Add a Printer Entry dialog box.

9. Click Remove Unix (lpd) Queue, and click OK. You will see the Edit Remote Unix (lpd) Queue Entry dialog box shown in Figure 7.2.

10. In the Names area, type one or more names for the printer, separated by vertical bar characters. You can use the proposed name, if the utility inserted one.

11. In the Spool directory area, accept the proposed directory name.

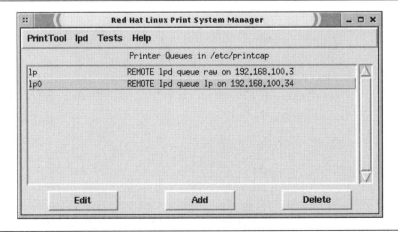

Figure 7.1 Set up a network printer using a configuration tool.

12. In the Remote Host area, type the IP address of the computer to which the printer is connected.

13. In the Remote Queue area, type the name of the default printer queue on the computer to which the printer is connected (type **lp** unless you've altered the default configuration).

14. Click Input Filter, and select the computer type from the list. Choose PostScript Printer if your printer is not on the list, but it works with Post-Script. Click OK to exit the input filters list.

15. Click OK to confirm the network printer settings.

16. Click Tests on the menu bar, and choose Print Post-Script test page. Check to make sure that the printer indeed printed the page.

17. Repeat the preceding steps on all the client machines on your network.

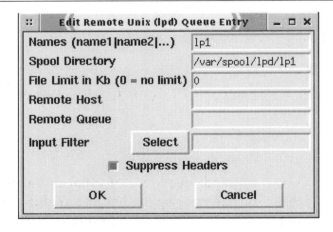

Figure 7.2 Specify network printer settings in this dialog box.

Should you need to configure the printer manually, you will need to make changes to the file called /etc/printcap on each of the client systems. Here is an example of a valid /etc/printcap entry that defines a remote printer named lp (with the aliases "grumpy" or "deskjet"):

```
lp|grumpy|deskjet:\
:sd=/var/spool/lpd/lp:\
:mx=#0\
:sh\
:rm=192.168.100.34\
:rp=lp:\
:if=/var/spool/lpd/lp/filter:
```

This is not the place to go into the details of /etc/printcap files, but this entry specifies the local spool directory (:sd=/var/spool/lpd/lp), sets no limit on the size of files to be printed (:mx=#0), suppresses header printing (:sh), indicates the location of the remote printer on the network (:rm=192.168.100.34), specifies the name of the remote printer queue (:rp=lp:), and indicates the location of the printer filter for this printer (:if=/var/spool/lpd/lp/filter:).

Looking Under the Hood

This section briefly discusses a couple of text-mode utilities that will come in very handy when you are working with NFS.

rpcinfo

This command displays information about NFS, and helps you determine whether the required daemons are running properly. Here is the syntax:

```
rpcinfo -p [ host ]
```

For *host,* type the IP address or the alias of the server. If you leave *host* blank, you will see information about the daemons running on the current system.

showmount

This command displays the mounts available on the specified *server.* Here is the syntax:

```
showmount [ option ] server
```

The most often used option is -e, which displays the server's export list. See Table 7.2 for a complete list of options available with this command.

Table 7.2. Command Options (rpcinfo)

Option	Description
-a,--all	List both the client hostname and mounted directory in host:dir format
-d, --directories	List only mounted directories
-e, --exports	Show the NFS server's export list
-h, --help	Show available options
-v, --version	Display the version number

References and Further Reading

Langfeldt, N. (1999). *NFS HOWTO*. Linux Documentation Project. Available online at http://www.linuxdoc.org.

Welsh, M., Matthias, K. D. and Kaufman, L. (1999). *Running Linux*, Petaluma, CA: O'Reilly & Associates.

8

Configuring and Using Samba

Samba is the name of a suite of Linux applications that enable Linux computers to provide Microsoft Windows networking services. The most immediate appeal of Samba is in its ability to enable transparent, reliable file and printer sharing between Linux and Microsoft Windows systems. However, Samba works just fine on a Linux-only network, and, as you'll see, it has some important advantages over NFS, which was discussed in the previous chapter.

This chapter introduces Samba, walks you through the Samba installation and configuration process, and shows you how to include Microsoft Windows systems in your Linux network.

Introducing Server Message Blocks (SMB)

Often called *Windows networking*, the protocols that underlie the capabilities of current Windows operating systems conform to a series of industry standard protocols initially developed by IBM, Intel, and other firms. Two strands of collaborative development created today's Windows networking: IBM-led efforts to implement the NetBIOS network interface, and a Windows-Intel effort to define a high-level networking protocol called *Server Message Blocks* (SMB).

NetBIOS

Network Basic Input-Output System (NetBIOS) stems from an IBM-led effort during the 1980s to develop LAN networking protocols for personal computers. In brief, NetBIOS is a LAN networking protocol that defines an addressing scheme to identify network workstations. In addition, NetBIOS defines an *application programming interface* (API) that enables applications to work on the network.

Because NetBIOS is little more than a network interface for applications, it is not a complete networking protocol. Efforts to create a complete NetBIOS implementation have created three prominent "flavors" of NetBIOS:

- **NetBEUI.** NetBIOS Extended User Interface (NetBEUI), is an implementation of NetBIOS for IBM's LanManager networks.

- **NetBIOS/IPX.** This is a version of NetBIOS developed by Novell for Novell networks.
- **NetBIOS/TCP/IP.** This is a version of NetBIOS that is designed to work with TCP/IP networking. Samba uses the TCP/IP "flavor" of NetBIOS.

When implemented in any of the preceding "flavors," NetBIOS accomplishes the functions of the network and transport layers in the OSI Reference Model (see Chapter 4).

Server Message Blocks (SMB)

The second strand of Windows networking development involved a collaboration between Microsoft and Intel. The result was the Server Message Blocks (SMB) protocol suite. In brief, SMB runs "on top" of any of the three NetBIOS "flavors." In OSI terminology, it functions at a high level—namely, the session and presentation layers. What it accomplishes can be simply stated: SMB tries to make it possible for users to perform *on the network* any file-management operation they would perform on their PC.

Microsoft is busy at work extending SMB. The company now calls the protocol *Common Internet File System* (CIFS). However, the company's CIFS implementation is still downwardly compatible with SMB. The most recent versions of Samba work with Microsoft Windows 2000. Exactly how long Microsoft will retain this compatibility is anyone's guess.

How SMB Differs from NFS

SMB's lofty goal, that is, transparently implementing a network version of the user's local file system, requires a much more complex and much more capable protocol than NFS. As you learned in the previous chapter, NFS is capable of providing file-sharing services, but it provides no assistance with user authentication, printer sharing, file sharing, or name resolution (mapping computer names to numerical addresses); SMB provides all of these services, and does so in a distinctive way. The following sections introduce concepts that are essential to understanding how SMB blends these services.

Workgroups

A workgroup is an entirely arbitrary collection of computers on the network. A given network can contain one or more workgroups. To assign Windows computers to a workgroup, you type the workgroup name in the Identification area of the Network control panel.

When a given Windows machine is assigned to a workgroup, the Network Neighborhood window shows only those resources that are available within the workgroup. Other network resources, if any, are grouped under the Entire Network icon.

Shares

In SMB networking, any resource that is made available to other users is called a *share*. Users decide which resources on their computer are shared with others. They can also choose between the mode of authentication used to access shares on their systems, as the following section explains.

User- and Share-level Authentication

Users can choose between the following two authentication modes to control access to shares:

- **Share-level authentication.** In this mode, a user shares a given resource (such as a directory, disk, or printer), and makes it available to anyone in the user's workgroup who possesses the correct password. The share is visible to anyone logged onto the network. In this mode, security is poor, because anyone who possesses the correct password can access the share.
- **User-level authentication.** In this mode, access to shares is restricted by username as well as by password. Users can determine which users have access to shared resources.

For security reasons, it is best to use user-level authentication.

Workstation Names

In SMB networking, the name space is *flat,* which means that every computer must have its own unique name. In addition, each share has a name. The following describes the naming conventions used in SMB networks to name specific shares:

```
\\workstation\share
```

For example, the following describes the name of a shared printer (speedy) on the computer named Lothlorien:

```
\\lothlorien\speedy
```

TIP When you are working with Samba utilities on the Linux command line, you cannot use the backslash symbol, which is interpreted by the shell as a line continuation symbol. Use forward slash marks instead, as in the following example: smbmount //rivendell/documents.

Browsing

In SMB networking, the concept of *browsing* differs from the concept of Web browsing. In brief, browsing is a process by which a networked computer discovers the names of other computers on the network. When a computer logs onto the network, it advertises itself by saying, in effect, "Hi! I'm \\lothlorien," and the name of this machine is added to a list of active machines. By detecting these messages, called *broadcasts,* an SMB client can eventually discover all the available machines on the network.

The list of active machines is maintained by the *local master browser,* which is one of the computers on the network. The computer that becomes the local master browser does so by means of an *election,* in which the various machines decide which of them should carry out this role. The election is decided by means of rules that give preference to Windows computers. The election process is automatic.

Name Resolution

Although an SMB client can discover other networked machines by browsing, this technique is inefficient. To provide a more efficient means of listing available comptuers on a network, Microsoft developed the Windows Internet Name Service (WINS). When you enable a WINS server on your network, the WINS server determines which machines are available, and creates a master list. Clients can be configured to get the list of machine names and addresses from the WINS server.

Windows Domains

The workgroup concept works well for small, peer-to-peer networks. In a larger network of a dozen machines or more, users may need to remember several different passwords to access all the resources to which they are granted access. To solve this problem, Microsoft introduced the concept of a *Windows NT domain*. In brief, Windows NT domains solve the problem of multiple passwords by providing network logins. With a network login, a user can log onto the network just once, and gain access to all of available resources without supplying additional passwords.

TIP A Windows NT domain is not the same thing as an Internet domain, so do not confuse them. A Windows NT domain is an arbitrary construct and has nothing to do with the Internet domain name system.

To implement a Windows NT domain, your network needs a *domain controller*. A domain controller is a computer that is running appropriately configured SMB server software. Because this software was formerly available only by purchasing and installing Microsoft Windows NT, Microsoft chose to call these domains Windows NT domains. However, Samba can function as a domain controller for Windows 95/98 clients (but not, at this writing, for NT Workstation clients). For this reason, Samba users prefer to speak of Windows domains rather than Windows NT domains.

Introducing Samba

The Linux implementation of SMB, called Samba, has its origins in Australian programmer Andrew Tridgell's desire to mount disk space from a Unix server on his PC. In the early 1990s, Tridgell wrote the first version of Samba and released it on the Internet. Interest was slow to develop initially, but today Samba is a flourishing open source development project, attracting contributions from programmers worldwide. Samba's home page is located at http://www.samba.org.

The Samba version available at this writing (2.0.7) can do all of the following:

- Enable a Linux user to share resources (directories and printers) with Windows users.
- Enable a Windows user to access shared resources on a Linux system.
- Emulate Windows NT Server's WINS capabilities for name resolution.
- Emulate Windows NT Server's role as a primary domain controller for Windows 95/98 network logins.

The Samba team is working to add additional functionality to Samba. For more information on the latest Samba capabilities, visit the Samba home page at http://www.samba.org.

When you're running Samba on your system, the following two daemons are operative:

- **nmbd.** This is the NetBIOS daemon that handles name resolution.

- **smbd.** This is the Samba dameon that handles file and printer sharing.

Planning Your Samba Strategy

This chapter assumes that you are setting up Samba for a small peer-to-peer network in which one or more Windows users can access shared resources (home directories and printers) on a Linux system that is running a Samba server. To set up Samba networking in this way, you will do the following:

1. Create Linux accounts for all the Windows users who will access shared resources on the Linux system.

2. Decide whether to use plain text or encrypted passwords.

3. Determine how you want to handle name resolution issues.

Obtaining and Installing Samba

If you installed Linux with all the available server options, Samba may be running on your system already. To find out, open a terminal window, type ps aux | grep mbd, and press Enter. This command looks through the applications running on your system for the character string "mbd." If Samba is running, you will see something like the following:

```
599   ?       S      0:00   nmbd -D
1649  ?       S      0:00   smbd -D
```

You need to have both nmbd and smbd running for Samba to work on your network.

If Samba is not already installed on your system, consider using a compiled (binary) version of Samba that is designed to work with your Linux distribution. Of course, you could compile Samba from source code, but you would need to do considerable configuration before you compile, and you will need detailed, expert knowledge of your Linux distribution in order to succeed.

Make sure you get the latest version of Samba. Each new version of Samba fixes bugs, and some of them involve serious security holes. If you are hooking up Windows 2000 workstations to your network, you need Samba 2.0.7 or later. This is the first Samba version to work smoothly with Windows 2000. Never use a version earlier than 1.9.17p2; previous versions had a serious security flaw that enabled intruders to gain root access to the server.

To get up-to-date binaries, do one of the following:

• Check the Samba home page (http://www.samba.org) to see whether there is a binary version of the current stable Samba distribution that is designed to work with your Linux distribution. Currently available are packages for Slackware (version not specified), SuSE (5.1, 5.2, 5.3, 6.0, and 6.1), TurboLinux (6.0), and Red Hat (5.2, 6.0, 6.1, 6.2).

• If the Samba home page does not have a binary that is compatible with your Linux distribution, check your Linux distribution home page. Check the update or errata page to see whether there is an updated version of Samba available for the specific version of Linux that you are running. If not, you can install Samba from your Linux distribution CD-ROM, or download Samba from your Linux distribution FTP site.

Once you've downloaded and installed the Samba binaries, check to make sure that your system is configured to start the Samba daemons (smbd and nmbd) at system start-up. Most of the binary distributions are configured to perform the necessary system modifications automatically, but you should check to make sure. On Red Hat systems, for example, you can use a text-mode setup tool (/usr/sbin/setup) to select the system services you want to start when you power up. Check your distribution documentation to find out how to select start-up services, if you are not sure.

Creating Linux Accounts for Windows Users

To get Samba to work correctly, you need to set up accounts on the Linux server that duplicate the username and password that users supply to the Windows network login dialog box.

Why do you need to set up these accounts? Windows clients provide no logical way to supply a username when a Windows user makes a Samba connection. Instead, the Windows client sends the username that the user supplied in the Windows Networking login dialog box, which appears at the start of a Windows session. Unless you want to configure all your Samba services to be accessible to guest users, which would create a security hole, you need to set up Linux accounts in which the username parallels the one that the Windows client is submitting. While you are at it, create these accounts with exactly the same password that Windows users supply in the Windows Networking login box. If the user's Linux password is the same as the same user's password on the Windows client, users can access their Samba resources without supplying a password.

To set up the user accounts, you can use the useradd utility or your Linux distribution user configuration utility (such as LinuxConf on Red Hat and Red Hat-derived systems). To set up an account for Suzanne with the password yai2bfw, log in as superuser, type useradd –p yai2bfw suzanne, and press Enter. By default, this command creates a home directory (here, /usr/suzanne); if the command fails to do this, it means the value CREATE_HOME is turned off in /etc/login.defs. To change this behavior, edit /etc/login.defs. If CREATE_HOME is set to no, change it to yes; if the value does not appear, type CREATE_HOME yes and save the file, and run useradd again.

Deciding Whether to Use Encrypted Passwords

Next, you will need to consider whether you want to use plain text or encrypted passwords. If you want to use plain text passwords, you will need to modify the Windows clients; if you want to use encrypted passwords, you will need to modify your Samba installation, as explained in the next section.

For the best security, you should use encrypted passwords. By default, Samba uses plain text passwords, which means that passwords are sent as ordinary text over the network. These passwords could be detected by an intruder and used to gain access to confidential resources. This is not a problem in a small network in which all users are reasonably trustworthy. Still, it is not a bad idea to use encrypted passwords, even on a small network. As you have just learned, the most convenient way to configure Samba passwords is in using exactly the same usernames and passwords for the user's Linux and Windows accounts. The downside is in what might happen if someone uses a packet sniffer to detect user passwords: they will get access to all of the user's accounts, including their Linux accounts, and from there it is not very difficult to get into the rest of the server. In a large network connected to the Internet, or in a private network in which some workstations are placed in insecure locations, you must use encrypted passwords.

If you decide to use plain text passwords, you will need to modify Windows 95 (Service Pack 2 and later), Windows 98, and Windows NT/2000 to disable the default password setting (encrypted passwords only). This involves changing one of the settings in the Windows registry and rebooting the system. Remember, if you opt for plain text passwords, you will need to modify all the Windows clients to work with plain text passwords, and you will have to remember to do so when somebody brings a new Windows client online. To find out how to modify the registry in various incarnations of Windows, see the Samba FAQ (http://us3.samba.org/samba/docs/FAQ/#28).

Setting Up Name Resolution Services

To make sure the computers on your network can locate each other, you will need to implement some type of name resolution service. A name resolution service translates between alphanumeric machine names (such as \\lothlo-rien) and IP addresses (such as 192.168.100.10). To implement name resolution services for SMB networking, you can choose between the following options:

- **Manually configuring each client.** This option is suitable for very small networks only. You will need to create files on each client, as well as the server, that list all the machines on the network. The disadvantage of this technique comes into focus when you add a new machine to the network. You will have to update all these files manually.
- **Configuring Samba to function as a WINS server.** It is very easy to configure Samba to act as a WINS server for SMB name resolution. This is the recommended option, even for small network.

Configuring Name Resolution Services Manually

To implement name resolution without running a WINS server, you will need to provide a file on each computer that lists the numerical IP address and domain name of all the computers on the network. On the Linux systems, you do this by adding entries to /etc/hosts (see Table 8.1); the entries use a three-column format beginning with the numerical IP address, the fully qualified domain name (FQDN), and aliases, if any. On the Windows systems, you must create and save a file called c:\windows\HOSTS that contains exactly the same information.

Table 8.1 Sample /etc/hosts and c:\windows\HOSTS Files

127.0.0.1	localhost.localdomain	localhost
192.168.100.10	frodo.mydomain.org	frodo
192.168.100.33	bag-end.mydomain.org	bag-end
192.168.100.34	strider.mydomain.org	strider

Configuring a WINS Server

If you decide to handle name resolution by means of a WINS server, you will still need to add the IP addresses, hostnames, and aliases of all the machines on your network to the /etc/hosts file on the Samba server. To implement the WINS server with Samba, you will need to activate one of the Samba configuration options, which are discussed later in this chapter.

Configuring Windows Clients

Turning to the Windows clients, this step shows you how to configure these clients so that they can work with your Samba server. Before proceeding, make sure the Windows systems can "see" each other in the Network Neighborhood window; if not, you will need to make sure all the needed networking support is installed, including the Client for Microsoft Networks.

Follow these steps to configure the Windows 95/98/NT client to access your Linux network:

1. Go to the first Windows client that you would like to connect to your network.

2. In the Windows Control Panel, double-click Network. You will see the Network dialog box, shown in Figure 8.1.

3. Click the Identification tab.

4. In the Computer Name box, type a name for this computer (you are limited to 15 characters).

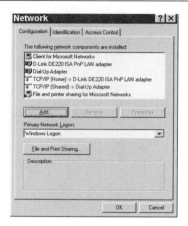

Figure 8.1 Use this control panel to configure the Windows clients.

5. In the Workgroup box, type a workgroup name, or simply use the default (WORKGROUP).

6. In the Computer Description box, type a brief description that identifies the computer's main user and location (such as "Suzanne's PC—Room 106").

7. Click the Access Control tab.

8. Choose Share-level access control. You cannot use user-level control unless you have configured Samba to make the master user list available, which is beyond the scope of this article.

9. Click the Configuration tab.

10. Select TCP/IP, and click Properties. If there is more than one TCP/IP option, select the one associated with your network card, and click Properties.

Figure 8.2 Specify an IP address here.

11. In the TCP/IP dialog box, click the IP Address tab, if necessary. You will see the IP Address page (see Figure 8.2). Do one of the following:

If your LAN is running a DHCP server, enable Obtain an IP Address Automatically;

or

Click Specify an IP address. In the IP Address box, type a static IP address for this system. Chances are that you have set up your network using one of the Class C network numbers that are available for private network use, such as networks using addresses beginning with 192.168.1.0. You'll also need to supply the subnet mask (for a Class C network, it's 255.255.255.0).

12. Click the WINS Resolution tab, and do one of the following:

If you plan to configure Samba to emulate a WINS server, enable WINS resolution;

or

If you plan to use manual host resolution, disable WINS resolution.

13. Click the Gateway tab. Here, you enter the IP address of the computer or router that provides access to the public Internet. In the New Gateway box, type the IP address of the computer or router that is used to link your network to the Internet, and click Add.

    Be sure to enter exactly the same gateway address on all the Windows systems. If your network is not connected to the Internet, leave this box blank.

14. Click the DNS Configuration tab.

15. Click Enable DNS.

16. In the Host box, type a host name that uniquely identifies this computer.

17. In the Domain box, type your network's domain name. If you have set up a private internal network, you can use any domain name you like (such as mydomain.org), but make sure you use the same domain name for all of the computers on your network.

18. In the DNS Server Search Order area, do one of the following:

If you've set up a DNS server on your LAN, type the primary and secondary DNS addresses here;

or

If your LAN lacks a DNS server but is connected to the Internet, type your ISP's primary and secondary DNS addresses here;

or

If your network is not connected to the Internet and you are not running DNS, give the Samba server's address as the primary DNS server. As this machine is not running a server, Windows will not get the information it needs, but this failure will force it to look at the c:\windows\HOSTS file you created in the previous section.

19. Click the Bindings tab. Check Client for Microsoft Networks. If you would like to make this system's resources available to other workstations on the network, including Linux workstations running Samba, check File and Printer Sharing.

20. Click the NetBIOS tab, and make sure NetBIOS is enabled. If it is not there is a problem with the TCP/IP installation; you should repeat the installation and start over.

21. Click OK. If Windows needed any additional software, you will be in for a round of rebooting before you can take the next step.

22. In the Network control panel's main page, select Client for Microsoft Networks and click Proper-

ties. Uncheck Log On To Windows NT Domain, if necessary. In the Network Logon Area, check Quick Logon or Logon and Restore Network Connections; either option is acceptable. Quick Logon does not restore network drive mapping, in which a user's network drive is mapped to a local system drive letter.

23. Click OK to confirm the Client for Microsoft Networks settings.

24. In the Network control panel's main page, click the File and Print Sharing button.

25. In the File and Print Sharing dialog box, check the access options that the user wants (the user can share files, local printers, or both).

26. Click OK to confirm the file and print-sharing options.

27. Click OK to confirm the Windows networking settings. You will need to restart your system.

28. Repeat the preceding steps for the rest of the Windows boxes on your network, if any.

Configuring Samba: An Overview

Samba relies on a single, text-based configuration file, called /etc/smb.conf. Most versions of Samba come with a sample configuration file that is very well documented by means of comments placed in the file. (Samba ignores any line that begins with a semicolon or hash mark.) You can get Samba working in short order by using a text editor to make a few changes to this file. If /etc/smb.conf doesn't exist, or is blank for some reason, you can type in the necessary information from the examples supplied in this section.

The Samba configuration file is divided into two major sections, that is, the [global] section and a subsequent portion that defines specific shares (resources made available over the network). The [global] section contains settings that affect Samba's overall operation. The shares section defines resources on the local system, called shares, that are accessible to qualified users via network connections.

Creating a Basic Samba Configuration

To get a basic Samba configuration running, follow these steps:

1. Log in as root user or superuser, start a text editor, and open /etc/smb.conf.

2. In the [global] section, find the workgroup setting. Change the default name (WORKGROUP), if necessary, to the setting you typed in each Windows workstation's Identification dialog box. Here is an example:

   ```
   workgroup = MAGICAL
   ```

3. Locate the line that begins with "server string," and uncomment the line, if necessary. Type the name that will identify this server in the Network Neighborhood window on Windows systems, such as server string = Lothlorien (note that the name cannot exceed 15 characters). This name need not

match the system's hostname as it is defined for TCP/IP purposes. Here's an example:

```
server string = Samba server
```

4. Now find the line that starts with "hosts allow." This setting is very important for security reasons; it specifies which hosts can access the Samba resources. The alternative is to leave the machine open to anyone who manages to gain access to the network. You can type the IP address of one machine, a comma-separated list of IP addresses, or a pattern (for example, 192.168.100. matches any computer that has an IP address starting with these numbers). Here is an example:

```
hosts allow = 192.168.100.
```

5. Look for the line that starts with "hosts deny." If the line exists, uncomment it, and change it so that it reads hosts deny = all. If the line doesn't exist, type hosts deny = all. Here is how the line should look:

```
hosts deny = all
```

6. Look for the line that starts with "security." Uncomment this line, if necessary, and make sure it reads as follows:

```
security = user
```

7. Now look for the line that begins "encrypt passwords." Uncomment the line, if necessary, and do one of the following:

If you decided to use plain text passwords, change this line to encrypt passwords=no, and make sure the next line (smb passwd file) is commented out;

or

If you decided to use encrypted passwords, change this line to encrypted passwords=yes, and remove the comment from the next line (smb passwd file = /etc/smbpasswd). See the next section, "Configuring Encrypted Passwords," for essential information on getting encrypted passwords to work; you will need to follow the steps in this section to get Samba working.

8. Look for the line that starts with "wins support." Uncomment this line and the next one, if necessary, and make sure they read as follows:

```
wins support = yes
name resolve order = wins hosts bcast
```

9. In the [global] section, locate the line that begins with "printcap name." If you want to make all the local printers available to Windows users, uncomment this line and the next, if necessary, or add them if they are not in the file:

```
printcap name = /etc/printcap

load printers = yes
```

10. Look for the line that begins with [homes]. Uncomment the following options (or add them, if they are not present):

```
comment = Home Directories

browseable = no

writable = yes

available = yes

public = no
```

These options automatically give users the ability to access their home directories on the Samba server.

11. Save /etc/smb.conf, and exit the text editor.

12. Restart Samba. To do so, type /etc/init.d/rc.d/smb restart and press Enter.

Configuring Encrypted Passwords

To use encrypted passwords with Samba, you will need to modify your Samba system to work with the encrypted passwords the Windows clients will send. The Windows password encryption format is not compatible with the default password encryption system used on Linux systems. As a result, you will need to create an additional password file for Samba users, one that conforms to the Windows format.

1. Important: Log in as root user or superuser.

2. Create a directory to store the encrypted password file by typing mkdir /usr/local/samba/private and pressing Enter.

3. Important: Change the permissions on this directory so that it is invisible to all users except root. To do so, type chmod 500 /usr/local/samba/private and press Enter.

   Now you will extract the Linux passwords from /etc/passwd, the default password file on Linux systems, and write them to a new file named /usr/local/samba/private/smbpasswd. You will do so with the mksmbpasswd.sh script, which is provided with Samba.

4. Find out where the script is installed by typing mksmbpasswd.sh and pressing Enter. If the script is not on the default path, be sure to include the pathname in the next step's command.

5. Launch the script using the following command: cat /etc/passwd | mksmbpasswd.sh > /usr/local /samba/private/smbpasswd.

6. Open /usr/local/samba/private/smbpasswd with a text editor. As you will see, each user's password is defined on a single (rather lengthy) line; enlarge the window's size, if necessary, so that you can see the whole line. Now delete all the entries except the ones for the users to whom you are granting access. In particular, be sure to delete root, cron, and daemon!

7. Save the file, and exit the text editor.

8. The file you have just created contains usernames, but the password fields are blank. You must now define passwords for each of your users. Be sure to use the same password that these users supply

when they log onto Windows using the Windows Networking dialog box, which appears when Windows starts. To use smbpasswd, type smbpasswd followed by a space and the user's name; you will be prompted to type and repeat the user's password.

Testing Your Samba Configuration

Now go to one of the Windows boxes, log on with the user's Windows networking username and password, double-click Network Neighborhood, and determine whether the Samba server shows up. If so, try opening the user's home directory.

If the Samba server does not show up in the Network Neighborhood window, try the following:

- **Passwords.** If you chose encrypted or plain text passwords, check your work to make sure you configure Windows or the Samba server correctly.

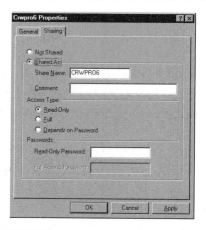

Figure 8.3 Choose Windows sharing options in this dialog box.

- **Typos.** Open the configuration file and make sure you typed everything correctly.
- **Testing your installation.** On the Samba server, type **testparm /etc/smb.conf** and press Enter. This diagnostic problem will detect certain flaws in the Samba configuration file.

Sharing Windows Resources

To enable resource sharing from a Windows client, do the following:

1. Click Start, point to Programs, and then click Windows (or NT) Explorer.

2. Right-click on the folder that you want to share, and click Sharing (see Figure 8.3).

As you can see in Figure 8.3, you can set up read-only or full (writes allowed) sharing on any specific folder. There are several options:

- **Not Shared.** If you choose Not Shared, others on your network will not be able to see, read, or write to or from this folder.
- **Shared As.** Enable this option to share this resource.
- **Share name.** When you browse the shared folders from other computers on your network, this is what you will see.
- **Comment.** Similar to the description options when you set up Linux or Windows computers, a comment such as "Project 2002" allows you to briefly describe what you are sharing.
- **Access Type.** Read-Only access allows Linux users to read what you share. Full access allows them to write

to the directory that you are sharing. Depends on password sets up two levels of sharing, for which you will need two different passwords.

- **Passwords.** The password that you set for the specified level of sharing.

Once your setup is complete, click Apply or OK to implement it. You can share directly connected printers in a similar fashion. Click Start, point to Settings, then click Printers. Right-click the printer that you want to share and then click Sharing.

Mounting Shares Automatically

Now that you have got your basic Samba installation working, you will want to configure the Windows systems, and possibly the Linux system, to load shares automatically.

Mapping Linux Shares to a Windows Network Drive

On the Windows clients, you can mount the user's Linux share automatically by opening the Network Neighborhood window, right-clicking the share you want to mount, and choosing Map to Network Drive. In the Map to Network Drive dialog box, select a drive letter, and check Reconnect at Logon. Click OK to confirm the network drive.

Mounting Windows Shares to a Linux Directory

If you're using the Samba server as a workstation, you may wish to access your shares on your Windows system.

To mount and unmount your Windows shares on your Linux workstation, you can use the utilities supplied with

Samba (smbmount and smbumount). You will want to make these utilities accessible to ordinary users by turning the SUID (set user ID) bit on for both of these utilities. Note that this procedure entails a security risk if you are configuring a workstation on a wide-open network, such as a university network, but it should not pose unacceptable risks in a small private network.

To modify smbmount and smbumount so that you can access these utilities from your ordinary user account, do the following:

1. Open a terminal window and log in as superuser.

2. Type **chmod u+s /usr/sbin/smbmount,** and press Enter.

3. Type **chmod u+s /usr/sbin/smbumount,** and press Enter.

Next, you will need to know the exact name of the share you want to mount. To do so, type smbclient –L followed by two slashes and the name of the computer that contains your Windows share (such as //lothlorien). You will be asked to supply your password. When you have done so successfully, you will see a list of the available shares. From this list, identify the share that you want to mount, such as //lothlorien/suzanne.

Before you can mount the Windows share on your Linux system, you will need to create a mount directory. It is convenient to place this directory within your home directory, where it is easily accessible.

To create the mount directory:

1. Log off the superuser account (type exit and press Enter).

2. In your home directory, create a directory that you will use to mount the share. To create /home/ suzanne/lothlorien, for example, you would type mkdir /home/suzanne/rivendell and press Enter.

Now that you have created the mount directory, you can use smbmount to mount the share to this directory. To do so, follow these steps:

1. Log in to your ordinary user account, and open a terminal window.

2. Type smbmount followed by the share's name (such as //lothlorien/suzanne) and the name of the mount point (such as /home/suzanne/lothlorien), and press Enter. Note that the mount point, that is, a directory, must exist in order for this command to succeed. The following is an example: smb- mount //lothlorien/suzanne /home/suzanne/lothlo- rien.

3. You will be prompted to supply this user's pass- word. Do so, and press Enter.

If you would like to unmount the share, simply type smbumount followed by the name of the mount point (for example, smbumount /home/suzanne/lothlorien).

To mount this share automatically every time you log in, add the smbmount command to .bash_profile in your home directory.

References and Further Reading

Auer, K. and J. Allison. (1998). *Manual page for smb.conf(5)*. The Samba Team. Available online at http://www.samba.org.

Eckstein, R., Collier-Brown, D. and Kelley, P. (1999). *Using Samba*, Petaluma, CA: O'Reilly and Associates.

Wood, D. (1999). *SMB HOWTO*. Linux Documentation Project. Available online at http://www.linuxdoc.org.

9

Configuring and Using AppleTalk

AppleTalk is Apple Computer's protocol suite for local area networking. Similar to NFS and SMB, it is a higher-level protocol suite that is designed to run "on top" of more basic networking protocols and physical media, including Ethernets, FDDI (fiber optic) networks, token-ring networks, and Apple's proprietary, low-speed LocalTalk networks. On an Ethernet, AppleTalk coexists peacefully with other middle-level protocols, including TCP/IP and SMB, the Windows networking protocol that is supported by Samba.

The Linux kernel natively supports AppleTalk networking. To connect Macintoshes to a Linux network,

215

you will need to install and configure netatalk, a package that transforms a Linux workstation into an AppleTalk server. In the same way that Samba enables a Linux system to appear within Windows users Network Neighborhood, netatalk enables Linux systems to appear as a connection option within the Macintosh Chooser.

TIP Netatalk enables Macintosh users to access shared resources on Linux systems. However, there is no free software that enables Linux users to access resources on Macintosh systems. A package that formerly made this type of connection possible, afpfs, is not compatible with recent Linux kernels; for information on updates, see http://www.panix.com/~dfoster/afpfs.

Although netatalk is a working package that can be used successfully to network with Macintoshes, you should be aware of the following:

- In contrast to Samba, netatalk development is sporadic and poorly coordinated.
- Documentation is skimpy or, worse, incorrect. For example, the main netatalk distribution site located at the University of Michigan does not indicate that the netatalk code obtainable from this site does not work with Linux. In order to get netatalk to work with Linux, you need netatalk with Adrian Sun's extensions (netatalk+asun).
- Although netatalk enables Macintosh users to access shared resources on Linux systems, Linux users cannot access Macintosh files or directories. However, they can access Macintosh printers.

Despite these deficiencies, netatalk is worth installing and configuring; currently, the package works reasonably well for making Linux directories available to Macintosh users. Printer configuration is possible, but the software is sufficiently buggy that it is not recommended; for example, a known bug causes certain printers to become comatose after finishing a print job, which means the printer has to be restarted after a print run. Accordingly, this chapter focuses on making Linux directories available to Macintosh users.

Introducing AppleTalk

The AppleTalk protocol suite contains the following protocols:

- **Datagram Delivery Protocol (DDP).** This protocol governs the "wrapping" of AppleTalk data into packets for network transmission. The protocol is natively supported by the Linux kernel, but you will need to make sure that this support is enabled (see "Configuring Your System for Macintosh Networking," later in this chapter.
- **Routing Table Maintenance Protocol (RTMP).** This protocol defines the way an AppleTalk propagates routing tables so that all networked machines know where the other machines are located.
- **Name Binding Protocol (NBP).** This protocol specifies hostname resolution within AppleTalk networks.
- **Zone Information Protocol (ZIP).** This protocol supports separate AppleTalk zones, or virtual subnetworks, within an AppleTalk network. The zones show up in the Chooser, a Macintosh utility that is used to connect to the network.
- **AppleTalk Echo Protocol (AEP).** This protocol enables a network service similar to ping. It is sup-

ported by the aecho utility, which is part of the netatalk package.

- **AppleTalk Transaction Protocol (ATP).** This protocol defines AppleTalk services that require reliable exchanges of data between the client and server.
- **Printer Access Protocol (PAP).** This protocol provides access to network printers.
- **AppleTalk Session Protocol (ASP).** This protocol defines the means to open, maintain, and close transactions during a session.
- **AppleTalk Filing Protocol (AFP).** Designed to run "on top" of ASP, this protocol enables Macintosh users to access data files on a shared server.

As the preceding indicates, AppleTalk is a comprehensive suite of protocols that is comparable to SMB in its breadth (see Chapter 8). It implements file sharing and printer sharing. For authentication, AppleTalk relies on the user names and passwords available on the server.

Introducing Netatalk

Netatalk+asun consists of a number of separate daemons and utilities that collectively implement all of the AppleTalk protocols. The most important of these are as follows:

- **atalkd.** This daemon implements RTMP, NBP, ZIP, and AEP; NBP, ATP, and ASP are implemented as libraries;
- **papd.** This daemon implements PAP;
- **psf.** This utility is a PostScript printer filter for lpd, which enables lpd to work with PAP; and

- **afpd.** This daemon implements the Apple Filing Protocol so that Mac users can access files on Unix and Linux systems.

System Configuration Essentials

To integrate Macs into your Linux network, the netatalk server needs the following:

- **Kernel 2.2 or later.** Earlier versions of the kernel will not work with the netatalk+asun package.
- **AppleTalk DDP support.** Most Linux distributions enable DDP by default. Still, you should make sure that this support is enabled in the kernel configuration you are using. To do this, open a terminal window, switch to /usr/src/linux, type make xmenuconfig, and press Enter; you will see the Linux Kernel Configuration dialog box. Click Networking Options, and make sure AppleTalk DDP is enabled as a module (M). If this option is not enabled, check M, and follow the on-screen instructions to recompile the modules on your system.
- **User directories.** Create user names and home directories for each of the Macintosh users who will be given access to file storage space on the server. To create a shared storage space, create a group named mac, and give this group ownership of a directory named /home/public.

Obtaining Netatalk+asun

You will find the latest versions of netatalk+asun at the following locations:

- **Source code (tarballs).** ftp.cobaltnet.com/pub/users /asun/release
- **Red Hat packages.** ftp://contrib.redhat.com/pub/ contrib/libc6/SRPMS/
- **Debian packages.** http://cgi.debian.org/www.master/ debian.org/Packages/stable/net/netatalk.html

---

TIP If you have an RPM-compatible system, you should install netatalk+asun from the RPM packages, if possible. Source code installation is complex and requires quite a bit of configuration; for more information, see the Netatalk HOW-TO (http://thehamptons. com/anders/netatalk).

Configuring Netatalk

Once you have installed netatalk, you probably do not need to do any configuration to get your AppleTalk server running. By default, the server enables Macintosh users to access their home directories on the server's filesystem.

The following provides an overview of the netatalk configuration files. If you have installed netatalk+asun from the RPM version, you will find them in /etc/atalk. If you installed netatalk+asun from source, you will find them in /usr/local/atalk.

- **config.** Available only in the RPM version of netatalk+asun, this file specifies basic netatalk settings, including the maximum number of clients (5 by default), the name of the AppleTalk server (by default, the server's hostname), the daemons that are run by default (papd and afpd), and the execution mode (background execution is enabled by default). You do not need to make any changes to this file. The settings in this file are read by the atalk script, which is installed in /etc/rc.d/init.d.

- **atalkd.conf.** This file defines the AppleTalk interface for the Linux system that is functioning as a Linux server. With most systems, you can simply leave this file blank, as netatalk will automatically detect the network interface and configure itself accordingly.

- **afpd.conf.** This file configures the AppleTalk Filing Protocol daemon. Again, you can leave this file blank. It is needed only if you would like to define more than one server on your system.

- **papd.conf.** This file enables you to make local and network printers available to Macintosh users.

- **AppleVolumes.default.** This file specifies the directories that are mounted when a user logs in. By default, the file contains only one non-commented-out character, a tilde (~), which displays the user's home directory. To make other directories available, type the pathname on a line by itself and save the file.

- **AppleVolumes.system.** This file contains a database that maps file types to their Macintosh equivalents. You do not need to make changes to this file.

Launching the Server

To start netatalk+asun as it is installed from the RPM version, switch to superuser if necessary, type the following, and press Enter:

```
/etc/rc.d/init.d/atalk start
```

You should see the message "Starting AppleTalk services" (backgrounded). It is as simple as that! If you see an error message, make sure that AppleTalk DDP support is enabled by means of the Appletalk module; type

/sbin/modprobe appletalk to load the module if necessary. Try starting netatalk again.

Connecting to the Server with the Chooser

In this section, you will connect a Macintosh to your network. You will need to repeat these actions for each of the Macintoshes you are connecting.

1. Click the Apple menu icon, and click Chooser. You will see the Chooser dialog box.

2. Click AppleShare. You should see the hostname of the Linux system on which you installed netatalk; however, you will want to connect via TCP/IP, which gives superior performance.

3. Click Server IP Address, type the server's IP address in the dialog box, and click OK.

4. Type the user's name and password (these must duplicate the user name and password that you set up on the Linux server), and click OK.

5. Check off the startup options you want, and click OK.

Once the connection is established, you will see a network icon on the Mac desktop. If you double-click this icon, the Mac will open a standard Finder window, showing the files in the user's Linux directory. This directory can be used as if it were an ordinary directory on the Mac's own hard disk.

References and Further Reading

Linux Netatalk HOW-TO. Available online at http://the-hamptons.com /anders/netatalk.

Neon Software. Understanding AppleTalk Routing. Available online at http://www.neon.com/atalk_routing.html.

Netatalk Administrators Mailing List. Available online at http://www.umich .edu/~rsug/netatalk/archive/admins.

Research Systems Unix Group, Univ. of Michigan. Netatalk: The Apple Protocol Suite for Unix. Available online at http://www.umich.edu/~rsug/netatalk. Note: The version of netatalk available from this site will not compile or run on Linux kernel versions 2.2 and later.

Research Systems Unix Group, Univ. of Michigan. Netatalk FAQ. Available online at http://www.umich.edu/ ~rsug/netatalk /faq.html.

Part Three

Connecting Your LAN to the Internet

10

Sharing an Internet Connection

At this point, you have successfully configured your local area network, and you have learned how to share resources, such as directories and printers, so that they are accessible to network users. In this chapter, you will take a step that is vital to completing your network: connecting your network to the Internet so that the connection is shared among all the connected workstations.

If you have already configured one of your Linux systems to access the Internet by means of a modem, you may be wondering why the procedures in this chapter are necessary. The reason is that this connection is not shared—at least, not yet. This chapter details the methods you can use to make this connection accessible to other network users.

Although it is possible to connect LANs to the Internet in a variety of ways, this chapter focuses on the most common one: connecting your network to the Internet via a modem. To do so, you will configure one of the machines on your network—the one with the modem—to function as the modem server. The technique described in this section will work for PPP connections with a modem. It will also work for ISDN connections with an ISDN adapter that masquerades as an analog modem for installation purposes.

NOTE If you have not already done so, install your modem and configure your system so that you can connect to your Internet service provider's system and access the Internet. For information and instructions, see Chapter 1. This chapter assumes that your modem is installed and working.

Obtaining and Installing the Software You Need

You need several utilities on your Linux modem computer to test and set up modem sharing on your network. Check to see whether these utilities are already installed; if not, install them from your Linux distribution's CD-ROM or from your Linux distribution's FTP site.

- **diald.** The diald16 utility initiates dialing automatically whenever any of the computers on your network initiates an Internet connection.
- **dctrl.** Once you set up diald on your Server, this GUI utility allows you to monitor and control activity on your modem. It is installed as part of the diald pack-

age. For more information and downloads of diald and dctrl, see the utility's home page at http://diald.sourceforge.net.

- **diald-config.** The diald16-config utility provides a user interface to the configuration file.

NOTE The diald and diald-config packages are designed for use with Red Hat Linux, which is included in the CD that comes with this book. If you are using another distribution, you will probably need the diald16 and diald16-config packages. Go to your Linux distribution's CD-ROM or their Web site for download information on the appropriate packages.

First, you will install and configure these packages on the Linux computer with your modem. This computer is your modem server. You will set up the diald configuration files on your modem server to dial and logon to your ISP. Then you can set up your modem server with the IP addresses for your ISP's DNS server and gateway. Your ISP's gateway is your modem server's route to the Internet.

Then you will set up the other computers on your network to look to your modem server for Internet access. You will configure each of these computers with the IP address of your ISP's DNS Server. As your modem server is the gateway for your other computers to your ISP, you will make your modem server's internal IP address the gateway address for these computers.

Configuring Dialup-on-Demand (diald)

The following section assumes that your PPP connection and modem are installed and working correctly; if not, please turn to Chapter 1. In this section, you will learn how to configure diald, which initiates dialing automatically whenever an Internet connection is needed by any of the computers on your network.

To set up diald, you need to modify two configuration files: connect and diald.conf. When you install the diald rpm packages, these files are located in the /etc/diald/ directory. The diald.conf file sets up how your modem server communicates with your ISP. It then calls up the connect file to initialize your modem, dial your ISP, and login.

Once you are finished editing, you will move these files to the directories where they will be read by Linux as needed.

Diald Connect Configuration

Before you start editing, back up the /etc/diald/connect configuration file. For example, the following command backs up the connect file in the current directory:

```
cp -i connect connect.bak
```

Open up /etc/diald/connect in a text editor such as emacs, vi, or any text editor in your Start menu. If you installed the diald16 rpm packages, you will see 10 different variables that you can modify. These variables are detailed in the following steps:

1. Look for the MODEM_INIT variable. The default should work for most modems. If you have a problem connecting and do not hear the "beeps" associated with a dialing telephone, check this parameter against your modem's documentation.

2. Review the PHONE_NUMBER variable. Set this to the phone number of your ISP. If you need to dial a number such as "9" to access an outside line, there is a short delay before you get a dial tone for an outside line. In this case you should add a comma, for example, if your ISP's number is 555-4321, set the PHONE_NUMBER variable to: 9,555-4321. This makes your modem wait 2 s between dialing 9 and dialing your ISP.

3. Look for the USER_CHAT_SEQ variable. Most ISPs send "ogin:—ogin—:ogin" to indicate that it is looking for your user name. Talk to your ISP to make sure that is appropriate for you. When you talk to your ISP, also review steps 4, 5, 7 and 8. Modify this variable if directed to do so by your ISP.

4. What follows should be the USER_NAME variable. Enter your username for your ISP here.

5. Review the PASSWORD_CHAT_SEQ option. Once your ISP receives your username, it will send a request for your password. In most cases, this will look like "ssword:". Check with your ISP to make sure this is the case for you.

6. Look for the PASSWORD variable. Enter the password that you use to logon to your ISP here.

7. Go to the PROMPT variable. Talk to your ISP. If your ISP sends a message to your computer after accepting your password, enter it here. In most cases, there will be no message.

8. Move on to the PROTOCOL_START variable. In most cases this will be PPP.

These settings assume that your ISP wants you to send your username and password in "clear text," that is, without encryption.

If you are not using encryption, you will only enter data for PHONE_NUMBER, USER_NAME, and PASS-WORD. If necessary, you can refer to KPPP for this information using the commands you learned in Chapter 1.

Once you have modified this file to your satisfaction, copy it to your /etc/ppp directory. The PPP dameon reads this configuration file here.

In the next section, you will look at the settings that you need to change if you are using the two most common methods for username and password encryption.

Encryption

There are two major methods for encryption when you are logging on to the Internet. They are known as the Password Authentication Protocol (PAP) and the Challenge Handshake Authentication Protocol (CHAP).

Although PAP usernames and passwords are encrypted at your ISP, they are sent through your connection without encryption; CHAP usernames and passwords are encrypted when sent, using a encryption key sent by your ISP.

If your ISP uses either PAP or CHAP for logins, add the following line to your connect script:

```
pppd-options name username@isp.net
```

where isp.net represents the domain of your Internet service provider. This part is not always required. Consult your ISP for the username message that they expect.

If you're setting up your connect file for PAP or CHAP, you can now "comment out" other variables related to logon, USER_CHAT_SEQ, USER_NAME, PASSWORD_CHAT_SEQ, and PASSWORD. In other words, when you add a "#" in front of the lines with these variables, diald won't read them when it connects to the Internet.

Diald Configuration

Now you will edit the diald configuration file to tell diald how to communicate with your modem. Once again, before you start editing back up your /etc/diald/diald.conf file.

Now open up the diald.conf file in a text editor such as emacs, vi, or any text editor in your Start menu. If you installed the diald16 rpm packages, most of these variables are already set up for you. If you are not sure what to do with some of these variables, check the KPPP configuration that you set up in Chapter 1.

The following steps detail only those variables that you may need to change. There are several dozen other variables that may be part of the default diald.conf file for your distribution:

1. Look for the device variable. This is the device assigned to your modem, usually /dev/modem. If

you are not sure, check the Device Tab of the KPPP Configuration dialog box from Chapter 1.

2. Next, check the speed variable. This is the communication speed between your computer and the modem. Speed is typically about twice the rated speed of your modem. Normal options for a 56 and 33.6 kbps modem are 115,200 and 57,600 bps. If you are having trouble staying connected, you might try a slower speed.

3. Move on to the dynamic variable. It's required if your ISP dynamically assigns you an IP address when you connect. If your ISP has assigned you a static IP address, add a "#" at the beginning of this line. (This "comments out" the line, which keeps diald from reading it.)

4. Continue to the local variable. If your ISP assigned you a static IP address, enter it here. For example, if your IP address is 191.12.132.1, enter:

```
local 191.12.132.1
```

Otherwise, enter one of the special use IP addresses listed in Chapter 5. If your IP address is dynamically assigned, it does not matter what address you use, as long as it is not a real IP address on the Internet.

5. Move on to the remote variable. Set this to the static IP address for the ISP side of the connection. If you do not have this IP address, enter one of the special use IP addresses listed in Chapter 5.

6. Next, review the up-delay variable. By default, this is set to 5 (seconds). If you are having trouble connecting to your ISP, you might increase this number.

7. Check the crtscts variable. This is the default for a modem with hardware control. If your modem does not use hardware control, and you know it works with Linux, review your modem documentation for the flow control variable to use here.

8. Move on to the connect variable. Set this to the location of the diald configuration file that you just edited:

```
connect /etc/ppp/connect
```

For more information, refer to the diald manual page. You can find this online at http://www.loonie.net/~eschenk/diald.html.

Once you have finished editing this diald.conf file, copy it to the /etc/ directory.

```
/etc/rc.d/init.d/diald start
```

You need to be in root or superuser mode to make this work. You can also substitute other commands for "start" such as "restart" and "status."

Testing the Connection

Now you can see if everything works. Check your physical connections from your computer to your telephone line. Make sure that your telephone line has a dial tone.

A useful graphical tool for testing your connection is Diald Control. Open up a command line interface and enter the /usr/bin/dctrl command. You will see the Diald Control Tool on-screen.

There are five sections shown in the Diald Control Tool:

- **Detailed Status.** The current status for your modem.
- **Numeric Load Monitor.** TX and RX loads are based on data that is Transmitted and Received through your modem.
- **Graphical Load Monitor.** TX and RX loads are mapped graphically over time.
- **Packet Queue.** Data to be sent through your modem.
- **Dialing Log.** When diald sets up your modem to dial, the progress is shown in this window.

Now you can test how diald works with your connection. Click Control on the Diald Control toolbar, then click Up request. If your configuration works and everything is properly connected, you will now see something resembling the following messages:

```
Initializing Modem

Dialing 5555555
```

Diald will dial the number of your ISP as you entered it into the /etc/ppp/connect configuration file. Your modem should now establish a connection with your ISP. If there is a problem, you will see a message such as "no dialtone" or "no answer." If you have a problem, there are a number of steps you can take to troubleshoot your system.

Troubleshooting Your Connection

When you troubleshoot a connection, always first check physical connections. Then use special tools such as dctrl to help you diagnose a problem. Only then does it make sense to check your software, such as your diald configuration files, because this is the least likely source of a problem.

Most connection problems are physical; in other words, something is not connected between your computer and the telephone line.

If your modem has a speaker, you may hear a dial tone and dialing pulses when it dials your ISP. If this is your situation, there is probably no physical problem with your connection.

The message that you get from Diald Control can help you diagnose most problems. Review the following messages for what you can do.

- **Failed to Initialize Modem.** Your modem may be disconnected from your computer. Check your connections. If you are using an internal modem, you will have to shut down your computer first. Once your computer is off, take the precautions to avoid static electricity as discussed in Chapter 1. Try removing and reinstalling your modem.
- **No Dial Tone.** There is a good connection between your computer and modem. However, there is something wrong with the connection between your modem and the telephone line.

NOTE If you have no dial tone, check your telephone wires. Many modems have two different sockets. One modem socket is used for the wire that runs to the telephone jack, usually in your wall. The other socket is used to connect to your telephone. Make sure you are connected to the right socket. If there is no label on your modem, you may simply have to try the other socket.

- **No Answer.** Check your telephone number. If the number is correct, there may be a problem with your ISP.
- **Busy.** The line is busy. Try again later.
- **Chat Timeout.** Check the telephone number shown in Diald Control. Make sure it corresponds to the number of your ISP. You get this message if the telephone on the other end of the line is suddenly disconnected, or is a fax machine. If the number is correct, there may be a problem with your ISP.
- **Failed to log in.** Your modem reached a good number, but could not connect to your ISP. Recheck your number; it might be someone's home telephone number. If it is a good number for your ISP, they may be having problems. Look for an alternate number and try again.
- **Other Problems.** If you can not even start one of the Diald Control drop-down menus, that means diald is not working in some way. The next step is to recheck the diald configuration files.

Once you have diagnosed your problem, try setting up Diald Control again. Restart diald whenever you change your configuration files. Repeat what you did in the last section. If you still have a problem, the next step is to check your software. There are a number of steps you can take:

- **Check your adapters with the ifconfig command.** The results should show a loopback (lo), ethernet (eth0), and serial connection (sl0). The serial connection communicates with your modem. If one of these adapters is missing, your modem server can't communicate through that adapter.
- **Check to see if kppp is still working.** Despite the files that you set up for diald and the modem server, kppp should still work. Refer to Chapter 1 if required, and use KPPP to try to connect to your ISP. If kppp works and diald does not, review the previous sections and recheck your configuration files.
- **Check your diald configuration files.** The key files are /etc/diald.conf and /etc/ppp/connect. Check these files against the settings that you used for KPPP in Chapter 1. Even if you did not set up KPPP, Chapter 1 explains the information that you need from your ISP.

Once you have addressed any open issues, you know that diald works. You are now ready to move on to the next step, that is, testing the modem server on the local computer. Open up a command line in root or superuser mode. Start the Diald Control screen with the dctrl command. In the Diald Control toolbar, click Options, then activate Dialing Log.

Now open up another command line interface. Enter the following command: ping www.mkp.com. You can substitute the Web site of your choice. If everything is working as it should, your modem server should now get diald to dial your ISP. If it does not connect, it will retry the number you added to your /etc/ppp/connect configuration file.

Setting Up the Rest of Your Network

The last step is to set up the right gateway and DNS server(s) for each of your other computers.

To set up your modem server as the gateway for the other computers on your network, review your /etc/hosts file. Write down the IP address of your modem server computer. You will also need to set up your ISP's DNS server(s) in each of your other computers.

Go to the other computers on your network. Set up your gateway. The steps you take depend on whether you are setting up a Linux, Windows, or Macintosh computer.

- If you are setting up a Linux computer, you can set up your gateway and DNS servers with the tool appropriate for your distribution, for example: Red Hat's LinuxConf, Corel's Control Center, Caldera's COAS, or S.u.S.E.'s YaST. You will need to be in superuser mode or have the root password available for these tools. In some of these tools, DNS servers are also known as nameservers. Once you activate the changes, each computer should be ready to connect to the Internet through your modem server.
- If you are setting up a Windows computer, click on the Start button, point to Settings, then click Control Panel. In your Control Panel, double click the Network icon. In the Network dialog box, scroll down to and then double-click TCP/IP. In the TCP/IP Properties dialog box, click the Gateway tab. Enter the IP address of your modem server in the New gateway text box and click Add. Click the DNS Configuration tab. Enter your ISP's domain name, such as isp.net, in the Domain text box. Enter your ISP's DNS server IP

address in the DNS Server Search order text box. Click Add. Repeat if your ISP has more than one DNS server. Click OK and OK again. Restart your computer when prompted.

- If you are setting up a Macintosh computer, go to the Apple menu bar, click Control Panels, then click MacTCP. Highlight PPP and then click More. In the Obtain Address section, highlight Server. In the Gateway Address section, enter the IP address of your modem server. In the Domain Name Server Information section, enter your ISP's domain name, such as isp.net, and its DNS server's IP address. Click OK, close MacTCP, and restart your computer.

However, this is not enough. After the next section, you will set up IP Address Masquerading. This will keep others from using your Internal IP Network addresses to access your modem (and other data).

Automatic Configuration

Now that you have set up diald on your modem server, you can choose to have it dial your ISP whenever you start your Linux computer.

When you start your Linux computer, it runs through a number of scripts located in the rc.d directory. A script is a file with a series of commands. The scripts that are run depend on your Linux distribution and are documented in the /etc/inittab file. You will find a group of "rc" files listed here. Look through these files. You will find an appropriate script such as rc.local or rc.sysvinit to add the diald command.

Open up the appropriate "rc" file in a text editor such as vi, emacs, or a GUI editor that you access through the

Main Menu button. Add the diald command, making sure to include the full directory path to that command. For example, if diald is located in the /etc/rc.d/init.d directory, enter /etc/rc.d/init.d/diald start command in the file.

Setting Up IP Masquerading

As there are over 1000 channels of data in TCP/IP, masquerading is a complex topic. With the right masquerading commands, you can defend your internal network against attack from the Internet. In this section, you will learn some simple commands to protect your network and allow access to the World Wide Web. In Chapter 15, you will learn to modify these commands to allow access to more Internet services such as FTP, ICQ, and Secure Servers.

There are three possible commands that you can use depending on your Linux distribution:

- **ipfwadm.** Linux distributions such as Red Hat version 5.x are based on the Linux 2.0 kernel, which uses the IP FireWall ADMinistration tool.
- **ipchains.** Linux distributions such as Red Hat version 6.x are based on the Linux 2.2 kernel, which uses the IP Chains management tool.
- **ipnatctl.** Linux distributions to be released in the second half of the year 2000 will be based on the Linux 2.4 kernel, which uses the IP Network Address Translation ConTroL tool. As new security problems are found, developers update the packages for each of these commands. If you want to defend your network against attack, you will want to keep the package that you use up to date. The Web Find option in

GnoRPM can help you find the latest version of each package. You will learn more about keeping your security packages up to date in Chapter 15.

IP Forwarding

Before the other computers on your network can use your modem to communicate with the Internet, you need to set up forwarding.

In Red Hat or Caldera Linux, open up the /etc/sysconfig/network file in a text editor such as vi, emacs, or a GUI editor through the Main Menu button. Check this file to make sure "FORWARD_IPV4" is set to "yes."

In other distributions, you will probably need to run the following command to activate IP forwarding:

```
echo 1 > /proc/sys/net/ipv4/ip_forward
```

Then reboot Linux to activate forwarding on your computer.

Setting Up Your Firewall

Anyone with a private network connected to the Internet needs a firewall. A properly configured firewall prevents unauthorized users from getting to your system. All data that passes through your firewall has to meet specific criteria, which you will start to learn about here.

You may already have a firewall. On Red Hat Linux, your firewall commands are located in the /etc/rc.d/rc.firewall file. On Caldera systems, they are located in the /etc/rc.d/rc.firewallup file. Go to your modem server computer. If you are not using Red Hat or Caldera, you can find this file from a command line interface using the

/etc/isp/rc.firewall

locate **rc. firewall** command. Review this file in a text editor such as vi, emacs, or a GUI editor that you can access through the Main Menu button.

NOTE As of this writing, the default Red Hat Version of this file includes basic ipfwadm commands that clear any previously set firewall rules. If you use this file, your modem server will not block any data. In other words, the default Red Hat commands do not protect your network.

Firewalls will be covered in more detail in Chapter 15. These will include commands to allow access to other Internet services such as FTP and IRC. The following are some basic rules that you should set up to allow you to browse the World Wide Web from your Linux computer.

Review the following commands. They are the first entries that you will need in the /etc/rc.d/rc.firewall file.

```
if [ -f /etc/dhcpc/pump.info ]; then
    . /etc/dhcpc/pump.info
elif [ -f /etc/dhcpc/hostinfo-ppp0 ]; then
    . /etc/dhcpc/hostinfo-ppp0
elif [ -f /etc/dhcpc/dhcpc-ppp0.info ];
then
    . /etc/dhcpc/dhcpc-ppp0.info
else
    echo "rc.firewall: dhcp is not config
    ured."
```

Use these lines if your ISP assigns your IP address dynamically through a DHCP Server. The three listed files are where Linux might store the IP address assigned by your ISP.

If your ISP assigns you an IP address dynamically only when you connect, make sure these lines are part of your rc.firewall file. Use a text editor such as vi, emacs, or a GUI text editor that you can start through the Main Menu button.

Now look at the first ipchains commands in a typical rc.firewall file. These seven commands, in this order, block all traffic. Once you understand these commands, check them against your rc.firewall file.

- **ipchains –F.** Eliminate ("flush") any previous ip chains commands.
- **ipchains –P input DENY.** Stops all data from coming to your modem server.
- **ipchains –P output REJECT.** Stops all data from your local computer.
- **ipchains –P forward DENY.** Stops all data coming from the other computers on your network intended for the Internet.
- **ipchains –A input –i lo –j ACCEPT.** Allows input to your loopback interface.
- **ipchains –A output –i lo –j ACCEPT.** Allows output from your loopback interface back to your computer.
- **ipchains –A input –i eth0 –j ACCEPT.** Accepts input from your local network, assuming it is set up on the eth0 device. Substitute accordingly if you are using another device to connect to your local network.
- **ipchains –A output –i eth0 –j ACCEPT.** Allows output from your modem server to your local network, assuming it is set up on the eth0 device.

TIP If you prefer to use the ipfwadm commands, you will actually find information in the IP Chains-HOWTO and the Firewall and Proxy Server-HOWTO, available online at http://www.linuxdoc.org.

To summarize, the first four commands stop all access to your modem server computer. Then the last three commands modify these rules by allowing access through your loopback and local network interfaces.

Now you can add the command that allows you to send and receive basic information to the Internet:

```
ipchains -A forward -i ppp0 -s
192.168.0.0/24 -j MASQ
```

This is an important command. Review how it works, from the standpoint of your modem server, in the following steps.

1. **ipchains.** Tells Linux to execute this command, with any modifications that follow.

2. **-A.** Adds the following (IP Chains) rule to any that you have set up so far.

3. **forward.** Linux applies this rule to any data forwarded through your modem server.

4. **-i.** Linux applies this rule to the following network interface.

5. **ppp0.** The network interface. This is the most common device name for a modem. If you are using a different device, substitute accordingly.

6. **-s.** Short for source. Linux applies this rule for any data that comes from the following IP addresses.

7. **192.168.0.0/24.** The source addresses. This specifies a source network address of 192.168.0.0. The /24 corresponds to a subnet mask of

255.255.255.0. In other words, this rule applies to all computers on your internal network with IP addresses between 192.168.0.0 and 192.168.0.255. If you are using a different internal network address, substitute accordingly.

8. **–j.** If the data comes from your internal netwokr (as defined in step 7), act on the next command.

9. **MASQ.** Enable masquerading.

In other words, this command sets up masquerading for all of the computers on your internal network. Any data from computers inside your network are sent out through your modem (ppp0). From the outside, it appears that the data are coming from your modem server. Because others on the Internet can not identify the computers behind your modem server, they cannot attack them as easily.

This command also works for the reverse process, that is, for information coming to your internal computers from the Internet.

Once you have saved these changes to your rc.firewall file, restart diald to activate these changes.

To make sure your firewall rules are read when you reboot Linux, you'll need to add the following command to the same file where you added the diald command in the Automatic Configuration section of this chapter.

```
echo "Loading the re.firewall ruleset.."
/etc/rc.d/rc.firewall
```

If your firewall script has a different name or location, substitute accordingly. Remember to make and save your changes with a text editor.

TIP A great source of information for setting up a firewall is located at the Linux LAN & Internet Firewall Security FAQ, located online at http://www.linux-firewall-tools.com. You will set up more of these tools in Chapter 15.

NetFilter (Linux 2.4)

Linux distributions released starting about the middle of the year 2000 will be based on Linux Kernel 2.4. With this Kernel comes a new Firewall and Masquerading tool known as ipnatctl, short for IP Network Address Translation ConTroL. This is part of a package tenatively known as NetFilter.

If you have already set up IP Chains on your Linux computer, you will not need to make major changes. If and when you load NetFilter on your Linux computer, you can keep most of the IP Chains rules that you have already set up. You will only need to load a special IP Chains module. The command is similar to what you used to load your modem through ppp:

```
/sbin/insmod ipchains
```

The only thing that you will have to change is your masquerading command. The NetFilter command that corresponds to the IP Chains command from the last section is:

```
ipnatctl -I -0 ppp0 -b 192.168.0.0/24 -m
masquerade
```

Sharing Windows and Macintosh Modems

If your modem is connected to a Microsoft Windows computer, you can share modems from Windows NT 4.0, Windows 2000, or Windows 98 Second Edition. A good guide to sharing modems on Windows NT is located at http://www.ezine.com/EZNTRouter.html. Windows 98 Second Edition and 2000 include a service known as Internet Connection Sharing, which can be activated through the Add/Remove Programs program in the Windows Control Panel.

NOTE Microsoft does not provide any modem sharing software with the first release of Windows 98, Windows 95, or earlier operating systems.

Alternately, there are third-party modem-sharing solutions for Windows, including Sygate (http:// www. sygate.com), WinGate (http://wingate. deerfield.com) and WinProxy at (http://www. winproxy.com). These options are easier to set up than Internet Connection Sharing; they also work with more kinds of modems.

NOTE As of this writing, Windows Internet Connection Sharing does not work with all the latest network interfaces, especially in the USB area.

Apple does not provide any modem-sharing software. However, there are two third-party options for sharing a modem connected to a Macintosh computer. Vicomsoft (http://www.vicomsoft.com) has two products: SurfDoubler for a very small (2-3 computer) network, and SurfRouter Plus for larger networks. These products use the 192.168.1.0 network by default. Alternately, Sustainable Softworks offers an IPNetRouter software.

References and Further Reading

Baitinger, Friedemann. (1999). *Linux Modem Sharing mini-HOWTO*. Linux Documentation Project. Available online at http://www.linuxdoc.org.

Ranch, D., and Ambrose, A. (2000). *Linux IP Masquerade HOWTO*. Linux Documentation Project. Available online at http://www.linuxdoc.org.

Schenk, E., and G. Soukoreff. (1997). *The Linux Diald FAQ*. Available onilne at http://www.loonie.net/~eschenk/diald/diald-faq.html.

Wright, C. (1999). *The Masqdialer Server*. Documentation available online at http://www.cpwright.com/mserver. A different developer may take over stewardship of Masqdialer. If you can not find Masqdialer information here, look for a link or through the search engine of your choice.

Ziegler, R. L. (1999).Configuring an Internet Firewall and Home LAN with Linux. *Linux LAN & Firewall FAQ* (September 28, 1999). Available online at http://www.linux-firewall-tools.com.

11

Sharing High-Speed Connections

In Chapter 10, you set up your network to share a telephone modem connection to the Internet. In this chapter, you will explore the many options for faster connections.

The good news is that setting up a shared high-speed connection on your network is often easier than setting up a modem connection. The bad news is that high-speed connections are usually more expensive, not only in monthly fees, but also in installation costs.

This chapter first helps you measure what you need from a high-speed connection. Next, it examines the wide variety of affordable high-speed technologies so that you can determine what is best for you.

Your choice determines the hardware you need, which leads to the software that you must have to set up on your Linux system. Only then can you connect your computer and then your network to the Internet through a high-speed connection.

Finding the Speed You Need

There are a number of different technologies that you can use for high-speed Internet access. The differences can seem intimidating. Even after you choose a technology, you may have to choose between a number of different companies competing for your business. What they offer usually depends on the speed that you need.

Before you make a choice, you need to determine your needs in the following areas:

1. **Download Speed.** How much data do you and the other users on your network take from the Internet? How much delay can you tolerate?

2. **Upload Speed.** How much data do you and your users send to the Internet?

3. **Budget.** What are you willing to spend for equipment, special installation services, and monthly fees?

4. **Type of connection.** Do you and your users need instant and reliable access to the Internet?

5. **Address.** Do you have a use for a permanent Internet (IP) address?

6. **Protection.** Can you dedicate a computer to protect your network from attack through the Internet?

7. **Number of Users.** Did you take into account that the number of users you have also drives the speed you need?

In the following sections you can find the information that you need to address each of these issues.

Download Speed

Any data that you receive on your network is a "download." The speed you need depends on the amount of data that you take and the time that you are willing to wait. While requirements change constantly, review Table 11.1 for guidance on the speed you need.

Table 11.1 **Internet Speed Requirements**

Service	Speed
Internet Surfing	28-128 kbps, mostly download
CD Quality Sound	40-80 kbps, Mostly download unless two-way sound (e.g., an Internet telephone call) is desired.
Video Conferencing	384 kbps, upload and download
Uploads / Downloads	Size of file / Time to wait

For example, if you and your users simply "surf" the Internet, according to Table 11.1, each user needs an average download speed of between 28 kbps and 128 kbps. If you are looking for high sound quality for Internet telephone calls, you want 40 to 80 kbps per user in each direction. The speed that you need for video conferencing increases rapidly if you want larger pictures (i.e., greater than 4 inches square).

When you are calculating the time to download a file, you need to know that data transfer speeds, such as for your modem, are measured in *bits*, while files are sized in *bytes*. There are 8 bits in a byte. In other words, if you are downloading a 1 Mega*byte* file over a 56-kilo*bits*-per-second modem, you're actually downloading 8-Mega*bits* of data. Also, networks usually work at half their rated speed (or less). While a 1-Megabyte file download *theoretically* takes only 2.5 min, in practice, this download can take 5 min (or more). If anyone else is using your network, your wait will increase.

Upload Speed

If you are simply "browsing" the World Wide Web, your users are only sending text information to your ISP, text that contains the Web addresses (also known as URLs or Uniform Resource Locators) of the sites you want to visit. Even a telephone modem connection is good enough for this purpose. However, if you are sending a lot of data, such as through a video camera, you will need more upload speed than many "high-speed" services can provide.

Budget

High-speed equipment can be expensive. When you start considering routers and satellite dishes, equipment costs can run into the thousands of (US) dollars before costs for installation.

Where there is heavy competition for high-speed customers, a number of companies waive the costs of equipment and or installation, usually in exchange for an agreement to use their services for a certain period of time.

Type of Connection

Some high-speed ISPs require that you use a modem to connect before you can upload and download data. Others offer an "always on" connection, which can save you that hassle. However, this convenience may come with a higher price tag.

Type of Address

Some high-speed ISPs give you one IP address that you use as long as you subscribe to their service. This is also known as a Static IP address.

Static IP addresses are easier to configure because they do not require you to install the DHCP client daemon (dhcpcd). Static IP addresses make two-way communication such as video conferencing, more convenient because others can use it as your telephone number to call you.

If you have a Dynamic IP address, you can set up a static host name on the Internet by joining a currently free service at http://www.dyndns.org. This sevice keeps track of your IP address when it changes; the static host name allows others to contact you.

Protection

High-speed connections are tempting targets for crackers. If they can break into your computer or network, they can use your connection to attack other users and Web sites. A firewall protects your network against attack from outside your network. However, it may not completely protect the computer where you set up the firewall. A dedicated firewall is a device where you store no critical information. There are two kinds of dedicated firewalls:

- **A Dedicated Computer.** You can set up an older computer as a firewall. Set up Linux on that computer, use the commands you learned in Chapter 10 (and what you will learn in Chapter 14), and connect it as the gateway between the Internet and your network. If you set up your firewall correctly, the worst that can happen is that others find that you have not stored anything important on your firewall.
- **Router as a Firewall.** Alternately, you can use a specialized network device known as a router. Routers are designed as junctions between networks, usually with firewalls. Some high-speed Internet services may even supply a router as a firewall for your network. One advantage of a router is that you can connect all of your computers directly to it.

Once you have addressed these issues, you are ready to consider the available options for high-speed Internet service.

Number of Users

In figuring the requirements for your own system you need to consider the following current and future needs of your users:

- **Number of Simultaneous Users.** If you have a network, you may have more than one user surfing the

Internet at the same time. However, they may not be downloading large files simultaneously. In other words, you do not need to multiply the maximum needs of each user by the maximum number of users.

- **Patience of Your Users.** This is subjective. Some users are willing to wait a little longer to get their Internet information.
- **Growth.** Other users may discover the advantages of videoconferencing after you upgrade your Internet connection. You may need to adjust the service that you use depending on the changing needs of your users.

As for growth, in the next few years, there will be a "convergence" of information technologies, all delivered through the Internet. In other words, you will be able to get telephone, television, and Internet service through one connection. The speeds that you will need will go up as well; for example, you may need as much as 6 Megabytes (48 Megabits) per second of information for a full-size High-Definition Television (HDTV) signal.

Examining High-Speed Connection Options

Now that you have some idea about the Internet connection speed you need, the next step is to examine the variety of services available. Each service makes different demands on your facilities, your wallet, and finally your Linux system and network.

Most high-speed connection options are set up to connect to your computer through Ethernet (10 Mbps), and Fast Ethernet (100 Mbps) Network cards as well as regular telephone modems. You have learned to install each of these components in previous chapters.

While there are many different types of high-speed service, three parameters determine what you need to install:

- **One-Way or Two-Way.** If you have "two-way" service, you get high-speed access for uploads as well as for downloads. Ethernet network cards are designed to work with two-way connections. If you have "one-way" service, your have high-speed access only for downloads. You would need a regular telephone modem for uploads.
- **Static or Dynamic IP Address.** Some services come with a Static IP address, which means that you do not need to install the DHCP service.
- **Maximum or Minimum Speed.** Some ISPs who provide high-speed service offer a guarantee that you can always transmit and receive at some minimum speed.

The following table can help you compare the speeds available. There is serious competition between these services in many markets, so it is important to check with your local providers.

You already learned to set up a telephone modem to connect your network in Chapter 10. You will learn about most of these options in the following sections. The exceptions are wireless modems because of their relatively slow speed and ISDN because of their comparatively higher cost.

See Table 11.2 for high-speed service possibilities.

Table 11.2 High-Speed Services

Option	Speed
Wireless Modems	28.8 and 128 kbps. Wireless modems are not limited to 53 kbps as are telephone modems. However, their speeds pale in comparison to high-speed wireless service.
ISDN	128 kbps. As of this writing, ISDN lines are much more expensive than DSL or Cable. Because of DSL, telephone companies no longer appear interested in promoting this service.
Cable (One-Way)	Up to 5 Mbps download. May be much slower depending on local demand. Uploads limited by the speed of telephone modems.
Cable (Two-Way)	Up to 5 Mbps download. Can be much slower depending on local demand. Upload speeds usually limited to 128 kbps. With a "splitter," you can receive Cable TV signals over the same wires.
High-speed Wireless	Up to 6 Mbps. Two-way wireless systems are currently set up at upload speeds up to 1 Mbps. One-way wireless systems use telephone modems for uploads.
Satellite	400 kbps download maximum. As only one-way service is available, satellite Internet requires a telephone modem for uploads.
DSL	128 kbps and up as a guaranteed minimum speed. Higher speeds are available. Upload speeds are commonly slower. With a "splitter," you can connect a regular telephone to the same line.
Tx Lines	ISPs connect to the Internet with T1 (1.5 Mbps), T3 (44 Mbps) and faster lines. You can too, but this option currently

	requires expensive equipment. You can divide a Tx line into data and several regular telephone lines.
Fiber	Faster. If you are willing to pay the price, fiberoptic data speeds are available in gigabits per second, but are currently not practical for home or small business use. However, this could change.

In each of the following sections, you will review the basics of each service. Then you will review what you need in four categories: Computer hardware; wire installation; software; and any special issues unique to Linux.

As you visualize your Local Area Network connection, there are two basic options. You can set up one computer as an Internet server, similar to how you set up one computer as a modem server in Chapter 10. If available, you can alternately use a router as your Internet server as well as a hub that connects directly to all of the computers on your network.

Two-Way Cable Internet

When you have a two-way cable modem, your gateway computer or router sends uploads and downloads through this modem.

Some of you may know that the wires for cable television service are virtually identical to the wires used for an older version of Ethernet. Unfortunately, older cable television service is set up only for one-way transmission of data. A number of cable companies are building new two-way networks for television signals and Internet data.

To determine if two-way cable modem service is available for your location, contact your local cable company.

If you choose two-way cable modem service, you will need to consider the following factors. Consult your cable company about how they handle each issue.

1. **Equipment.** You will need a cable modem and Ethernet card to connect a single computer on your network. Cable ISPs often provide this equipment as part of the service. Alternately, some cable ISPs have a dedicated router, which provides firewall services as well as a connection for multiple computers on your network.

2. **Wiring.** The cable company provides cable line up to your cable modem. From there you may need to provide the Ethernet cable to connect to your card and your other computers.

3. **Software.** The following Linux packages: gated, ipchains to set up your computer as a gateway and a firewall. If you have to use a Dynamic IP address, use dhcpcd.

Before you choose a cable modem, check the experience of other Linux users. Most are documented in the Cable Modem Providers HOWTO. Specific experiences for a number of different cable modem providers (including many outside the US) are listed here. Unlike most HOWTO, the latest version of this document can be found on the Open Source Writers Group Web page at http://www.oswg.org.

NOTE As of this writing, some governments are trying to open the cable Internet network to some or all Internet service providers.

One-Way Cable Internet

Some cable TV companies provide cable modem service for downloads only. In other words, you need a telephone modem for everything that you send to the Internet, from requests for specific Web pages to e-mail that you send. Because uploads through telephone modems are normally limited to 33 kbps, you cannot take advantage of two-way high-speed services such as videoconferencing.

NOTE The 33 kbps upload speed limit is standard even if you are using a 56-kbps telephone modem.

With a one-way cable conneciton, uploads proceed at a maximum of 33 kbps, and downloads occur at a maximum of 5 Mbps. You can also see that the computer requires three cards for networking: two Ethernet cards (eth0, eth1), and one telephone modem (ppp0). You need to know if your computer has room for all three cards.

To determine if one-way cable Internet service is available for your location, contact your local cable company.

If you choose one-way cable Internet service, you will need to consider the following factors. Consult your cable company about how they handle each issue.

1. **Equipment.** You will need a cable modem, a telephone modem, and Ethernet card to connect a single computer on your network. Cable ISPs often provide this equipment as part of the service.

Alternately, some cable ISPs have a dedicated router, which provides firewall services as well as a connection for multiple computers on your network. Otherwise the connection to your other computers is left up to you.

2. **Wiring.** The cable company provides a cable line up to your cable modem. From there you may need to provide the Ethernet cable to connect to your card and your other computers. You will also need to provide the wiring from your telephone modem.

3. **Software.** You will need the following Linux packages: gated, ipchains to set up your computer as a gateway and a firewall. If you have to use a Dynamic IP address, dhcpcd.

4. **Open Channels.** ISA cards are easier to install in Linux; as most newer computers are limited to one or two slots, you may need to use some PCI cards and slots as well. Each card also requires IRQ, DMA and I/O resources that you might have already dedicated to other purposes such as printers and drives.

Before you choose one-way cable Internet service, check the experience of other Linux users. Most are documented in the Cable Modem Providers HOWTO. Specific experiences for a number of different cable Internet providers (including many outside the US) are listed here. Unlike most HOWTOs, the latest version of this document can be found on the Open Source Writers Group Web page at http://www.oswg.org.

Wireless Cable

Wireless cable Internet service is also available in some areas. Depending on the provider, the setup is similar to one-way or two-way cable Internet service. The difference is that wireless service uses broadcast frequencies in the same way as regular broadcast television service.

The general hardware requirements are similar to that for cable Internet service. Some wireless cable operators in fact use the same cable modems. However, you will need a receiver that looks like an antenna or satellite dish. You will also need a transmitter or telephone modem for your uploads.

Digital Subscriber Line (xDSL)

A Digital Subscriber Line (DSL) uses your telephone line to transmit digital data. It can work on the same wires as a telephone because it transmits data on different frequencies. All telephone lines are connected to central offices of the telephone company. As you can tune into different stations on a radio, the right equipment in a telephone company central office can route your telephone call or DSL data.

As implied by the "x" in the title of this section, there are different types of DSL service available:

- **Asymmetric.** ADSL service means that the speed of your uploads is slower than the speed of your downloads.
- **Symmetric.** SDSL service means that the minimum speed of uploads is the same as the minimum speed of downloads. This is suitable for users who need two-way services such as video conferencing.

- **Very High Speed.** VDSL service is sometimes available if you have less than one mile of wire between your telephone and your local telephone central office; VDSL service offers speeds from 13 to 55 Mbps. As of this writing, VDSL is available in very few areas. It is currently intended as a way to deliver enough data for HDTV. Nevertheless, it certainly could be used as an Internet connection for a larger office.

To determine if DSL service is available for your location, contact the DSL provider of your choice or your local telephone company.

It is certainly possible to set up one telephone line for your DSL and your regular telephone. A typical configuration when you use DSL service involves the use of a "splitter," which allows you to connect a telephone to the same line.

Where available, there is often heavy competition to provide DSL service. A number of different DSL providers provide service over the same local telephone lines to many of the same metropolitian areas.

The DSL speed that you get is deceiving. Unlike other high-speed services, the DSL speed that you get is a *minimum* speed. In other words, a 144 kbps DSL line can sometimes be faster than a 5 Mbps cable modem connection depending on the traffic on the local cable network.

- **Distance.** Generally, DSL adapters are not designed to work if they are more than 17,500 feet (5300 m) from a telephone company central office.

- **Equipment.** Your telephone company needs special equipment to filter DSL signals from regular telephone calls.
- **Access.** The DSL provider of your choice must have some connection to your telephone company's central office.
- **Quality of Line.** Even if you meet the distance requirement, some telephone lines are too old or poor to transmit the quantity of data required for DSL.

If you choose DSL service, you will need to consider the following factors. Consult your DSL provider to learn how they handle each issue.

1. **Equipment.** You will need a DSL adapter and an Ethernet card. If you want a telephone that uses the same line, you will also need a splitter. Sometimes a DSL provider will provide a network card that functions as both a DSL adapter and an Ethernet card.

2. **Wiring.** The telephone company provides wiring to your telephone jack. Your DSL provider wires your connection to your DSL adapter. From there you may need to provide the Ethernet cable from the DSL adapter to your Ethernet card(s).

3. **Software.** You will need the following Linux packages: gated, ipchains to set up your computer as a gateway and a firewall. If you have to use a Dynamic IP address, dhcpcd.

4. **Hardware.** Some DSL providers supply a network card that does not work with Linux. Ask for an ISA Ethernet card or a PCI card with a Linux

driver. If such is not available, that DSL provider might not be for you.

With the large number of DSL providers, there are variations in the service that you will get. Sometimes you may need a separate telephone lines for your DSL and telephone service. If you need to set up any wiring yourself, refer to the ADSL mini-HOWTO, available online at http://www.linuxdoc.org.

Satellite

Yes, you can receive your Internet data via satellite. The data moves through one of three satellites in geosynchronous orbit, 22,500 miles (36,000 km) above the earth. Unfortunately, these satellites are set up only for one-way transmission of Internet data. You will need a telephone modem for uploads.

If you want satellite Internet service, you will need a satellite dish. Different dishes are available for Internet service only, or for both Internet and television service. Separate subscription charges are required for Internet and television; if you want your own ISP, you will have to pay a charge for that as well.

Currently, Hughes Network Systems (now a part of the Boeing Company) is the main satellite Internet provider. While their documentation states that satellite Internet connection software is only available for Windows, there is a router designed to connect the Hughes satellite dish with your Linux system.

More information on this router is available online at http://www.helius.com.

To determine if satellite Internet service is available for you, navigate to http://www.direcpc.com. As of this writing, service is available in most of North America, Europe, and Japan.

If you choose satellite Internet service, you will need to consider the following issues. Contact Hughes to learn how they handle each issue.

1. **Equipment.** You need a satellite dish, mounting hardware, and a Helius router. You also need a satellite modem (similar to a cable modem), as well as an Ethernet card. You also need an unobstucted line of sight towards the equator from where you mount the dish.

2. **Wiring.** Connections to your satellite dish and router.

3. **Software.** The Helius router is currently designed to work only with Red Hat and Caldera Linux. If you have to use a Dynamic IP address, dhcpcd.

4. **Hardware.** Linux connections to DirecPC are available at this time only through a Helius router.

One problem with current satellite Internet technolgy is distance. Because geosynchronous satellites are so far away, data takes an extra one-third of a second to get to your computer. The delay makes two-way videoconferencing difficult, even if two-way satellite Internet service were available.

Future Options

The only sure thing is that faster connections are on the way. Within the next five to ten years, high-speed Internet connections will become the standard. With one connection, you will be able to use your telephone, watch the television program of your choice when you want, work from home effectively with the help of videoconferencing, and get all of the conveniences of the Internet.

There are a number of companies working on Internet "appliances" to make this happen all over the home. Many current efforts involve setting up Linux with a Web browser or customized menu. Little or no customer configuration will be required.

Future high-speed Internet access may be based on one or more of the following technologies:

- **Fiber.** Currently, fiberoptic cables transmit the largest amount of data over a practical physical medium.
- **Cellular.** As we currently communicate digitally over "cell phones," we may soon get our HDTV signals and Internet information digitally using the same basic technology.
- **Two-Way Satellites.** Satellites are being deployed in "low" orbit, hundreds of miles above the earth's surface. They are currently being used for satellite telephones; the same technology can be adapted for any two-way data transmission.

In previous chapters, you learned to set up everything you need for a higher-speed connection: Network (Ethernet) cards; IP addresses on a private network; forwarding across a Linux computer set up as a modem server.

In the next section, you will review the tools that you need to set up the hardware and software you need. While many providers of higher-speed Internet access do not "officially" support Linux, many can still help. A number of different ISPs use Linux to run their own systems. Some higher-speed ISPs even have their own "HOWTO" designed for the Linux user.

Configuring High-Speed Connections

There are two basic ways to connect your network to the Internet. You can take one of the computers on your network and turn it into an "Internet server" by connecting it to the Internet. Other computers access the Internet through this Internet server.

NOTE The term "Internet server" is used to describe one computer on a network that you use to get access to the Internet. Do not confuse this with a "Web server," which is a computer where you can create and store Web pages for use by others.

Alternately, you can get a router. The router includes the direct connection to the Internet. Each of your computers is directly connected to the router.

In the following sections, you will examine each option in more detail. Whether you are configuring a computer or a router as an "Internet server," you need to configure many of the same things such as IP addresses and gateways.

Create Your Own Internet Server

You can take one of your computers and turn it into an "Internet Server." Similar to the modem server that you set up in Chapter 10, it has both a connection to your network and a connection to your ISP. The difference is that you have a high-speed connection instead of a regular modem to get your data from the Internet.

Depending on the high-speed service that you choose, you need a card to connect to your network and one or two cards to connect to your high-speed service. The predominant network card in use by high-speed providers is the same Ethernet card that you learned about in Chapter 4 and set up in Chapter 5.

Then you need to configure the software on your Internet server. It gets two IP addresses, one for the connection to the Internet, and one for the connection to your internal network. You then set up IP forwarding in the same way that you did for your modem server in Chapter 10. You need to set up the IP gateway address as assigned by your ISP. Finally, you need Firewall and Masquerading software based on the same commands as you see in Chapter 10 and 15.

You will also need to configure the other computers on your network to look to your Internet server as a gateway. When it can not find what it wants on your local network (e.g., the www.linux.com Web site), it looks to the gateway, which then transmits your request on to the Internet.

You can also use a router as an Internet server. The router gets the direct connection to the Internet. It also gets connected to each of the computers on your network.

If you have more computers than connections or ports on a router, you can connect one of the router ports to the uplink port on a hub. Consult the documentation for your hub if you need help identifying your uplink port.

As with an Internet server, you need to configure IP addresses, forwarding, gateway, masquerading, and fire-walling on a router. Many routers include special software for this purpose that you need to install on one of the Linux or Windows computers on your network.

You then configure the computers on your network to look to your router as the gateway computer. The router then transmits requests for information not on your local network on to the Internet.

Configuring Your IP Address

One key issue with high-speed Internet service is how you get your IP address. Generally, with a telephone modem connection, you do not have a choice; an IP address is dynamically assigned to you when you connect to your ISP. However, many high-speed Internet providers give you at least the option of using a Static IP address. There are several advantages:

- **No DHCP.** You do not have to set up a DHCP client to find your IP address.
- **Easier Network Setup.** You can assign your static IP address to the network card connected to the Internet.
- **Simpler Firewalls.** You do not have to include the search for DHCP addresses as discussed in Chapter 10.

This option drives the way you configure the gateway computer on your network. You will explore this issue in more detail in the next section.

Configuring the Gateway Device

When you set up a network connection to the Internet, the key is the Gateway from your network. Dedicated routers make this job easier; you do not need to "sacrifice" a computer for this purpose. On the other hand, routers can be expensive and are usually unnecessary based on what you can do to configure Linux on older systems.

As you did in Chapter 5, you need your Linux distribution's network configuration utility to assign a hostname, domain, gateway and IP addresses to the Ethernet card that is connected to your high-speed service. If you can not get a static IP address, you will also need to include the IP address of your ISPs DHCP server.

You will also use your network configuration utility to set up IP forwarding. Finally, use the techniques from Chapters 10 and 15 to set up a firewall and masquerading on your network.

Configuring the Other Computers

Now it is time to configure the other computers on your network. If the computer is set up for Linux, use your distribution's network configuration utility to assign a gateway IP address. The address you use should be your Internet server's IP address on your local network.

Remember, your Internet server has two IP addresses— one assigned by your ISP for the high-speed connection, the other assigned by you for its connection to your local network.

Now you are ready to start enjoying high-speed Internet access from every computer on your network.

Using a Dedicated Computer as a Firewall

It is possible to set up a "Firewall" computer for regular use. However, computers have limited resources. If you cannot sacrifice a computer for use as a firewall, there are a number of things to consider about your firewall computer.

- **Limited Slots.** Setting up hardware for Linux is easier when you have ISA cards. However, if you want to use a service such as one-way cable modem, you may need two Ethernet cards and a telephone modem. Many newer computers have only one or two ISA slots available. For more information about ISA and PCI cards, refer to Chapter 1.
- **Limited Channels.** If you connect a large number of components to your firewall computer, such as printers, CD-ROMs, DVD players, etc., you may not have enough IRQ channels for the Ethernet cards and modems that you need to install. One way to review the channels you have available is through the KDE Control Center. Click on the Main Menu button, then click KDE Control Center. Click on the plus sign next to Information, then click Interrupts. The currently used IRQs will be listed here.
- **Security.** Any firewall you set up can protect the computers on your internal network very well. However, the computer that you use as a firewall can sometimes be at risk.

If you cannot dedicate a computer as a firewall, you will probably have to move your peripherals. Because you can share access on your network, you do not absolutely have to have the following equipment on your firewall computer: floppy drives; printers; CD-ROMs; second hard drives, etc. Move these devices to other computers on your network and share them through Samba or NFS as appropriate.

Improving Your Network's Performance

Once you have set up your network, there are a couple of things that you can do with Netscape Navigator to optimize your Internet experience. You can cache commonly used Web pages on your local computer. You can also use the proxy servers common to many high-speed Internet service providers.

Adjusting Netscape's Cache Settings

By default, Web browsers such as Netscape Communicator use their own cache of Web pages. You can set them up to store the most recently used Web pages in your Random Access Memory (RAM) or on your local hard drive. For example, when I review the various HOWTOs related to Firewalls, Netscape first looks for the applicable pages on my local hard drive before going out to the Internet.

Using cache can reduce the load on a busy network. However, it requires considerable free memory. Unfortunately, the settings you use for Netscape cache work only for the local computer. However, you can set up similar caches for each computer on your network.

To set up Netscape caching, open up Netscape on your computer. Depending on your distribution and Graphical User Interface, click on the Netscape button on your desktop menu bar or navigate to Netscape through your Main Menu button. In the Netscape toolbar, click Edit, then click Preferences. This opens up the Netscape: Preferences dialog box. In the Category column, click on the arrow next to Advanced. You will see two options under Advanced: Cache and Proxies.

Click on Cache. There are four decisions that you need to make for your cache, as described in the following sections.

Memory Caching

Your memory cache is the amount of RAM that you can dedicate to storing the most recently accessed Web pages. Generally, you need a *lot* of free RAM on your computer to use a Memory Cache. One way to check for free RAM is to open up a command line interface and run the **top** command. Then check the amount of memory listed as free in the "Mem" line.

TIP One problem with too much Netscape memory cache is that Web pages stay in your computer memory even *after* you close Netscape. This deprives other applications of the RAM that might be needed to run properly.

Disk Caching

Your Disk Cache is the amount of hard drive space that you want to dedicate to storing the most recently accessed Web pages. If you have a lot of extra hard disk space available and use certain Web pages frequently, you can store them in your hard drive for easy retrieval.

Cache Folder

You can set up your disk cache in the folder of your choice. You can even set up a dedicated partition for this purpose.

Cache Refreshing

The "Document in cache is compared..." setting specifies when you use your cache.

If you choose "Every time," Netscape gets your Web page from the network every time there has been a change. You can then set your cache sizes to zero. If you work with time-sensitive information, you do not want a cache in any case.

If you choose "Once per session," your browser compares your cache with the Web page on the network only once after you start Netscape. If you return to that Web page, the page comes from your cache, unless you then click on Refresh in the Netscape toolbar.

Setting Up Netscape Proxies

This section applies if your ISP uses a Proxy Server. Many high-speed ISPs use Proxy Servers to increase their effective speed.

You can set up how you interact with Proxy Servers in Netscape preferences. If you are still in the Netscape preferences window from the last section, click on Proxies.

In the setup dialog box for proxy servers, there are four decisions that you need to make regarding how you relate to your Proxy Server, as discussed in the following sections.

Bypass Your Proxy Server

If you want to bypass your Proxy Server, select Direct Connection to the Internet. This option bypasses your ISP Proxy Server for all information that you get from the Internet. While this may be slower, the information that you get will be more up to date.

NOTE This option may violate the policy of some high-speed ISPs. Ask your ISP for more information.

Automatic Proxy Configuration

The setup for some ISPs proxy servers can be complex. If you choose the Automatic Proxy Configuration option, Netscape looks to your ISPs Proxy Server setup file for all Web pages. You will also need to include your ISP proxy server address in the text box, which typically appears something like, http://proxy:8080. Consult your ISP to see if it has a proxy server and the address you need here. Some proxy servers may have trouble with sites such as Web-based e-mail. Some ISPs have custom proxy files available at a specific Web address to manage this issue.

Manual Proxy Configuration

If you are ready to do a bit of work, the middle option— manual proxy configuration—is for you.

A manual proxy setup is essential if you access many Web-based mail servers. Select the manual proxy configuration option and click View. This brings you to the Netscape: View Manual Proxy Configuraton dialog box. The entries that you see here apply to the @Home cable modem service.

Consult your ISP for the name to enter for each of the noted Internet Protocols. You will also want their IP addresses for reference. Because Gopher and WAIS are rarely used today, you should be able to leave these blank.

TIP If Netscape does not recognize your ISP Proxy Server, add the IP address of that server to your /etc/hosts file.

TIP Based on the firewall that you set up in Chapter 10, you should be able to only read regular Web pages. You will not be able to connect to secure Web sites or FTP sites until you allow access through the appropriate *ipchains* commands. You will learn to do this in Chapter 15.

Caching Web Documents Locally

If your high-speed Internet setup is not good enough for you, you can set up your own proxy server on your local area network. A proxy server stores Internet data on a computer closer to those who need the information, in this case, on your local area network.

With your own proxy server, you do not have to worry about your ISP proxy server configuration. You can save your high-speed Internet access for such uses as video conferencing, and you do not need a Netscape cache on any of the computers on your network.

When the first person on your network looks for a Web page for the first time, such as http://www.yahoo.com, your proxy server cannot find it in its cache. It looks to the Internet for a copy of the Yahoo Web page, serves it to the requesting computer, and stores a copy in its cache.

When the second person on your network looks for the Yahoo Web page, your proxy server finds it on its network and serves it directly to the requesting computer without accessing the Internet.

The proxy server for Linux is known as Squid. After several years of development, it was finally released in September of 1998.

You can set up Squid behind a firewall to manage all kinds of Internet information, including Web pages, secure Web pages, FTP servers, mail and newsgroups, and more. You can also set up Squid to filter out what you do not want, including Web banners and the sites that you do not want your users to see on your local network.

You can get more information about Squid, including its users' guide and latest downloads from the Squid Web Proxy Cache home page at http://www.squid-cache.org.

Alternately, you can download rpms or compressed files suitable for Squid installation from your Linux distribution's Web site.

References and Further Reading

Fannin, D. (1999). ADSL HOWTO For Linux Systems. Available online at http://www.linuxdoc.org.

Hughes Network Systems. (2000). *DirecPC Help*. Available online at http://www2.direcpc.com/helpfiles /index.html.

Kiracofe, D. (2000). Transparent Proxy with Squid mini-HOWTO. Available online at http://www.linuxdoc.org.

Tourrilhes, J. (1999). *Linux Wireless LAN HOWTO*. Available online at http://www.hpl.hp.com/personal /Jean_Tourrilhes/Linux/Wireless.html.

Vuskan, V. (2000). *Cable Modem Providers HOWTO*. Available online at http://www.oswg.org.

Part Four

Creating an Intranet

12

Running an Intranet Web Server

Now that you have set up your network connection to the Internet, everyone on your network is happily surfing. It is time to bring advatages of the Internet to your own network. It is also time to set up an internal internet, or *intranet*, with Web pages only for your users.

One way in which intranets have changed the corporate world is in how people communicate within their organizations. An internal Web page is a way to send a joint message, to ensure that everyone is working towards the same goal.

An intranet is a network inside a company or other organization. In contrast, an internet is any group of networks that are connected together. The Internet is the worldwide group of interconnected public networks.

The key to communication on any of these networks is a Web server, which is any computer setup with software to "serve" Web pages to other computers. The Web server used for Linux computers is known as Apache.

You will get enough information from this chapter to create your own intranet. In addition, you will set up a Linux package known as Apache as Web server. Although Apache is currently the most popular Web server on the Internet, what you set up is limited to your internal network, or intranet.

If you want to set up your own Web site on the Internet, there are many good ISPs who can help. Whether they use Linux, Unix, or some variant of Windows, you can also learn enough from this chapter to be an intelligent customer for their services.

Introducing Apache

The first Apache server was developed in 1995 at the National Center for Supercomputing Applications (NCSA). The name Apache is loosely derived from the large number of software "patches" or fixes that was made to the original NCSA Web server ("A PatCHy sErver").

Similar to most other Linux applications, Apache is an open source, which means that you can copy and use it for free. Although it comes with no warranty, there is a substantial community of users ready and willing to help.

Although Apache is complex, starting Apache is fairly simple. In this chapter, you learn to get Apache up and running. Later, you will learn some of the features that come with this application.

Resources

The work on the Apache Web server is rich and extensive. You can find a host of resources, including documentation, the latest downloads, and several different kinds of help on the Apache Web site at http://www.apache.org/httpd.

Apache is included with most major Linux distributions. Alternately, you can download the latest version of Apache in rpm or tar.gz formats from your distribution's Web site or from major Linux download sites such as www.rpmfind.net and www.linuxberg.org.

The pattern of the following sections should now be familiar. First, you will check for and then install Apache if required. Then you will choose what directories to share for your Web service, and finally decide how to share with different computers on (or outside) your network.

Installation

You may already have Apache installed on your computer. If it is running, you will see it from the following command:

```
ps -ax | grep http
```

If Apache is running, you will see a number of lines with "httpd" at the end. That means the http daemon, which is the program that runs Apache, is operational. The number of "httpd" is related to the number of users who can connect simultaneously.

Another way to check is to open up your Web browser, then type localhost in the Location text box. If you are connected to the Internet, and Apache is not working, you will be sent to www.localhost.com.

It is possible that Apache is not even installed. Open up a command line interface. Go into root or superuser mode. In Red Hat Linux, look for httpd in the *etc/rc.d/init.d/* directory. If you are using another distribution, use its package manager to see if Apache or "httpd" is installed.

The most reliable way to install Apache is based on the instructions that come with your Linux distribution. As different distributions expect key Apache files in different directories, consult your documentation for instructions on how to install Apache from the source files on your CD-ROM or downloaded from your distribution's Web site.

If you are installing a slightly older version of Apache, you will find a long list of packages. Do not be intimidated by this list. You will not need most of these packages, which are commands written in a computer language called perl. You will only need the rpm or tar.gz files for the commands that you use. The packages that you absolutely need to run Apache are:

- **Apache.** If you need the latest version, download it from http://www.apache.org.
- **Perl.** You need the basic perl package if you want to use any of the perl commands. Perl is currently installed by default on most Linux distributions.
- **Mod-Perl.** Allows your Apache server to read Perl commands from your Apache configuration file. This package is automatically installed with newer versions of Apache.
- **Perl-Apache-xxx.** You only need to load the packages associated with the commands that you use. You probably already have the Perl modules that you need. However, if you run into an error when you try to start Apache, review the error message and your Apache configuration file. In Red Hat Linux, this text file is located at /etc/httpd/conf/httpd.conf. This should give you a clue as to what additional module(s) you need to install. Most Perl-Apache modules are automatically installed with newer versions of Apache.

Because newer versions of Apache include Perl modules, they are easier to download and install. Once installed, you can start Apache by starting the http daemon, also known as httpd. In Red Hat Linux, for example, it is located in the /etc/rc.d/init.d/ directory. Start Apache by running the *etc/rc.d/init.d/httpd start* command. Consult your distribution's documentation for the appropriate start command if you have another type of Linux.

TIP If you are using Caldera Linux 2.4 or above, use the graphical Webmin tool to manage Apache.

Configuring Apache for Basic Web Services

When you download and install Apache, it is set up in such a way that it should work. If you do not get an error when you start the http daemon (httpd), you should be able to open Netscape on your computer, type in http://localhost in the Location text box, and you should get the default Web page, which confirms that Apache is working.

When you install Apache, it may not be quite ready to serve Web pages on your internal network. What you need to do is similar to turning on the switches on your computer.

The switches are located in three different configuration files:

- **access.conf.** Determines the computers that can access your Apache Web server, as well as directories they are allowed to use. You will place your Web pages, pictures, etc. in these directories, as defined in srm.conf.
- **httpd.conf.** The main Apache configuration file, which configures usable Perl commands. You can also use this file to set the number of simultaneous users on your Web server.
- **srm.conf.** Defines where your Web page files, pictures, etc. are located.

These files are located in their own directory, which vary by Linux distribution. If you cannot find these files, use the file-finding utility associated with your graphical user interface.

In most Linux distributions, the content of all three files is consolidated in the httpd.conf file. If you do not see any content in your access.conf or srm.conf files, look in your httpd.conf file.

Preconfigured versions of Apache do not always work. If you see an error message when you try to launch Apache, you will need to make changes to the Apache configuration file.

Before opening this file, back it up. In Red Hat Linux, the Apache configuration file httpd.conf is located in the /etc/httpd/conf directory. In Caldera Linux, this file is located in the /etc/httpd/apache/conf directory. Open up httpd.conf in a text editor such as vi, emacs, or one of the editors available through the main menu button. Note the problem cited when you tried to start httpd.

If you have installed a newer version of Apache, that means you should reload the whole package. Save any work that you have done so far in a different directory before reloading Apache.

The next step is to save the httpd.conf file, and then restart httpd. If you are using Red Hat Linux, restart httpd with the **/etc/rc.d/init.d/httpd restart** command. In S.U.S.E. Linux, use the **/usr/sbin/apachectl restart** command.

Because of the large number of Perl modules, a full explanation on how to address this particular issue issue is beyond the scope of this book.

TIP You do not need everything in the Apache configuration file to make Apache work. If you encounter problems in the httpd.conf file and there is no obvious solution, try commenting out the offending lines.

Security

Whether or not Apache is working, the next step is to look at security. If Apache is working, you want to keep unauthorized users out. If Apache is not working, your configuration file may also be keeping authorized users out. Open up your Web browser. Navigate to http://localhost. If you managed to start Apache, you should not see the localhost.com Web site. If you see an error page, then you probably need to change either user permissions on your Web directories or your Apache configuration file to let in authorized users.

By default, Apache Web directories are located in your /home/httpd directory. Open up a command line interface and navigate to this directory. Check the permissions with the ls –la command. You should see lines such as:

```
drwxr-xr-x3     root   root   4096   Jan  3  15.03
cgi-bin

drwxr-xr-x3     root   root   4096   Jan  3  15.03
html

drwxr-xr-x3     root   root   4096   Jan  3  15.03
icons
```

These lines show that everyone has at least read (r) and execute (x) access to your Apache directories. You can change permissions on any directory with the *chmod* command using the techniques that you learned in

Chapter 6. For example, if you need to change the permissions on the icons directory, go into root or superuser mode and run the following command:

```
chmod 755 /home/html/icons
```

When everyone has at least read and execute access, they still may not be able to get in; Open the httpd.conf file in your text editor.

Look for the line associated with "DocumentRoot." In Red Hat Linux, it is the /home/httpd/html director, which is the root directory as far as Apache is concerned. Now look for the <Directory "/home/httpd/html"> line. Below it, you can find another line that appears as "order deny, allow."

The following lines limit access to your Apache Web pages to computers inside your network. Edit the lines in your httpd.conf file under the <Directory "/home/httpd/html"> heading to match.

- **order deny, allow.** Apache applies the rule from the line that starts with deny. Then it modifies the rule from the line that starts with allow.
- **deny from all.** This line denies access to your Web server from all computers. If your network is connected to the Internet, you do not want unauthorized outsiders to connect to your Intranet.
- **allow from 127. localhost 192.168.0.0/ 255.255.255.0.** This line allows access from the 127.0.0.0 subnet and localhost. It also allows access from the 192.168.0.0 network. If your subnet is on a different IP address, substitute accordingly to give access to all computers on your Local Area Network (LAN).

Make the changes that you need to conform to these guidelines, and then save this file.

Testing Your Work

Open up a command line interface. Go into root or superuser mode. Restart Apache with the */etc/rc.d/init.d/httpd restart* command, or the command appropriate to your distribution. Return to your Web browser, type **http://localhost** in the Address or Location box, and press Enter. You should see a Web page proclaiming that Apache is working.

Look up the IP address for your Apache server in your /etc/hosts file. Record it and then go to any other computer on your network. It does not matter if it is a Linux, Windows or Macintosh computer. Open up the browser of your choice. In the location text box, type in the IP address for your Apache server. When you press enter, you should be able to see the same Apache test Web page.

Setting Up Web Pages

Now that you have Apache running, you can start planning your Web pages. The page that you see when you have started Apache successfully is the *index.html* file in the directory specified as the DocumentRoot; for Red Hat Linux, that is the /home/httpd/html directory. Other pages are located in the /home/httpd/cgi-bin and the /home/httpd/icons directories. These particular Red Hat directories are designed to contain html files, CGI scripts for data interfaces, and pictures, respectively. Other distributions include these and more categories in different directories.

When you create your Web page, you can use this directory structure, or create your own based on the modifications that you make to the Apache configuration files.

There are a number of tools available to create Web pages, including Netscape Composer and Microsoft Front Page. Now that you know how to transfer files through Samba and Netatalk, you are not limited to Linux-based tools.

Because Web pages are based on text files, you can even use a text editor to create your Web page. Some Web page creation tools have Web page templates. Whatever tool you use, save your desired home page to the index.html file in your DocumentRoot directory.

Examining Apache Options

Now you will examine some of the other options associated with Apache. This list is far from extensive; some books on Apache alone are twice the size of this book.

To help guide your review, reopen your Apache configuration file(s). The following sections divide some of the parameters in your configuration file(s) into the following categories:

- **Basic Setup.** Important parameters for every Apache Web site.
- **Tuning.** Performance related parameters.
- **Features.** Parameters that you can add for more sophisticated Web sites.
- **Advanced.** Other parameters.

You can review some of the parameters in each category in the following sections.

Basic Apache Setup Options

The Apache configuration file includes a long list of settings. You probably will not need to make any changes simply for serving Web pages on your local network. If you want to set up a Web site, you will generally want to work through your ISP. If you understand these settings, you can ensure that your ISP is meeting your needs.

The following is based on the Red Hat 6.2 Apache httpd.conf configuration file. If you are working from a different Linux distribution, you may find a slightly different set of parameters.

Each of these parameters are variables; for example, once you set ServerAdmin to an email address, any reference to ServerAdmin in any other part of Apache returns that email address.

- **ServerAdmin.** Set this to the email address of the Web site administrator. This address appears in a number of error messages such as when a specific Web page cannot be found. Your users can use it to contact you when they see a problem.
- **ServerName.** Set this to the hostname of your computer. If you have a working /etc/hosts file or DNS, leave this blank. If your ISP runs your Web site, they set the ServerName.
- **DocumentRoot.** The root directory for your Web server; other directories with Web pages are subdirectories of the Document Root.
- **CustomLog.** There are four basic custom log files: access, referer, agent, and error. The access log lists

each time someone goes to your Web site. The referer log lists each time someone goes to your Web site from a link. The agent log notes the browser that access your Web page. The error log notes every time an error message such as "file not found" is sent to a user.

- **ScriptAlias.** Set this variable to the location of your Common Gateway Interface (CGI) Scripts. These are small programs that primarily help your Web sites process user requests, such as search information from a database.
- **User, Group.** People who access your Web site get some level of user privileges on your Linux computer. By default, this should be set to no one. If you limit your Web site to an intranet, you can set these variables to a specific user and group.

Apache Tuning Options

There are three features you can modify to help "tune" Apache for better performance.

- **Port.** TCP/IP has 1023 different channels, which are technically known as ports. By default, Web sites use channel 80. For greater security, you could use a different channel, as long as it is above 1024. As long as your users did not share this information with others, you would then have a private channel for your Intranet Web site.
- **Timeout.** When you're connected to a Web site, there is almost always data going back and forth between your computer and the Web site. If Apache does not see data for the Timeout period, in seconds, it disconnects the user. If you run a Web site with many

lost connections, you may want to reduce this number to allow others to connect more quickly.

- **HostnameLookups.** By default, Apache reads the IP addresses of computers that browse your Web pages. If you activate host name lookups, it will also check your databases (/etc/hosts and DNS) for the associated computer host names. This can help you identify from where the users of your Web site are coming. However, this option can slow the responsiveness of your Web server.

Additional Apache Features

There are a number of features that you can set up for specific files and directories on your Apache Web Server. If you want these features, set the Options variable under the applicable directory to each feature:

- **May Execute CGI.** You only need to activate this in any directory with CGI files.
- **Includes.** Refers to Server Side Includes (SSIs), which insert files or programs into your Web pages. If you have a ".shtml" web page, you need this option because your Web page has Server Side Includes.
- **Includes NOEXEC.** Another way to use SSI commands, except "#exec" and "#include."
- **Multi views.** Allows Apache to serve different types of programs (e.g., CGI or SSIs) depending on the preferences set on the user's Web browser.
- **Indexes.** You can use this option to turn Apache into a file server. By default, Apache gives users the "index.htm" page from the applicable directory on your Server. If there is no index.htm page in that directory, and this is active, Apache sends out a current list of files in that directory.

- **May follow symlinks.** If you activate the Indexes option to share files, this allows your users to follow any symbolic links that you have set up between your Linux files.
- **Follow symlink if owner matches.** Modifies the previous option, based on the owner of each linked file.

Advanced Apache Options

The following is simply a brief overview of the other modules that you can set up on your Apache server.

- **Virtual Domains.** If you have more than one Web site on your Apache server, you need to set up a different Virtual Domain for each server. While the options for each Virtual Domain are similar to those shown in the last section, you should set up each Virtual Domain(s) in its own directory.
- **Modules.** You can review a list of modules that Apache loads. If you know how to use Apache modules, review this list against what you see in the Apache configuration file.
- **Secure Modules.** With Secure Modules, you can configure Apache for secure Web pages, also known as the Secure Sockets Layer, or https.

For more information on these and other modules that you can use with Apache, refer to the Apache Web page. You can also review the references listed in the next section for more information.

References and Further Reading

The Apache Group. (1999). Apache 1.3 User's Guide. Available online at http://www.apache.org/docs.

The Apache-SSL Team. (2000). Apache-SSL. Available online at http://www.apache-ssl.org.

Covalent Technologies. (2000). The Apache Module Registry. Available online at http://modules.apache.org.

Faure, M. (1998). Linux Apache SSL PHP/FI frontpage mini-HOWTO. Available online at http://www.faure.de.

The Java Apache Project. (2000). Apache JServ. Available online at http://java.apache.org.

Stein, L., and MacEachern, D. (1999). Apache Modules. Petaluma, CA: O'Reilly. Several chapters available online at http://www.modperl.com.

13

Creating an Intranet FTP Server

Now that you have learned different ways to share files between Linux, Windows, and Macintosh computers, it is time to discover an easier way to share files on your local network: the File Transfer Protocol, also known as FTP.

Unlike NFS, samba, or netatalk, you cannot share printers or Internet connections with FTP. However, you can set up reasonably secure file transfers with FTP software.

If file sharing is all you need on your network, FTP is the simplest choice. You do not need to share or mount directories and folders with FTP. You can simply log on, and then download and upload the files you need. As FTP is dedicated to file transfer, it is faster and more reliable than the alternatives.

There are two main components to ftp: a server and a client. The main server used on the Internet is known as wu-ftpd, short for the Washington University (in St. Louis, Missouri) FTP daemon.

Introducing Wu-ftpd

To use FTP on your network, you need a server and a client. All Linux distributions include one or more FTP clients. By default, several distributions install the Washington University FTP Daemon (wu-ftpd) as an FTP server.

Washington University released wu-ftpd version 2.4 in 1994. It was so successful that version 2.5 was not released until 1999. By that time, the WU-FTPD Development Group took over stewardship of this open source tool.

The wu-ftpd package, along with a FAQ, is available online from the WU-FTPD Development Group at http://www.wu-ftpd.org. Additional documentation is available on Kurt Lanfield's site at http://www. lanfield.com/wu-ftpd.

Even if wu-ftp is installed as part of your Linux distribution, you can not check if it is already running. It does not run as a separate process the way Apache, NFS, or samba does.

The only way to check if wu-ftpd is installed is with the package manager for your distribution. For example, you can use GnoRPM on Red Hat Linux, COAS on Caldera,

YaST on S.u.S.E., or Corel's Package Manager. You should also ensure that you have FTP or another FTP client installed.

Running an FTP server can create a security hazard. When wrongly configured, an FTP server may allow users from other computers to browse through and download files from anywhere on your computer. Be aware that the wu-ftpd server is a popular target for crackers. To ensure security on your network, check the wu-ftpd Web sites frequently for security updates and patches.

You can also set up wu-ftpd for anonymous users. When you set up an anonymous FTP server, users do not need a user name or password on your computer. This is useful if you want to distribute larger files to the general public.

Anonymous FTP can be a special security hazard. If you need to give anonymous users access to your FTP Server, it is best to set it up through your ISP.

Configuring Wu-ftpd

Once you have installed wu-ftpd and ftp, the next step is to configure the TCP/IP superserver. In the next section, you will change the superserver configuration file /etc/inetd.conf so that your computer can listen for messages from FTP clients.

In the following section, you set up wu-ftpd configuration files for access permissions, file compression, password encryption, and default users.

The Superserver Configuration File

When you set up your Linux computer as a server, it listens for messages from clients. Linux servers listen as defined in the superserver configuration file.

To modify the superserver file:

1. Get your distribution's documentation for the wu-ftpd server. The change that you make to the superserver configuration file varies with your distribution.

2. Before modifying any configuration file, you should back it up. Copy your superserver configuration file, /etc/inetd.conf, in your home directory.

3. If you did not log in as the root user, go into the superuser mode.

4. Open the /etc/inetd.conf file in a text editor such as vi, emacs, or any text editor accessible through the Main Menu button.

5. Search for a line that starts with ftp. It should appear somewhat as follows:

```
ftp stream tcp nowait root
/usr/sbin/tcpd    in.ftpd
```

6. Cross-check the line against your distribution's instructions for starting the wu-ftpd server. The variation is in the final part of the command; you may need to substitute in.ftpd -a, in.ftpd –l –a, or wu.ftpd –a.

7. Save the /etc/inetd.conf file.

8. Make Linux reread this file. Open a command line interface. Go into root or superuser mode and enter the killall –HUP inetd command.

9. If Linux returns a message such as "inetd is stopped," start the superserver. In Red Hat Linux, use the /etc/rc.d/init.d/inetd start command. If you are not using Red Hat, consult your distribution's documentation for the command to start your internet superserver.

TIP In Red Hat Linux 6.2 and above, you may see only a few (if any) lines in your /etc/inetd.conf file. If this is your situation, install inted networking. Then you can set up the FTP server. Use a package manager such as GnoRPM to download and install this package.

Now that you have set up the superserver, it searches for FTP clients. In the next section, you set up wu-ftpd as the FTP server.

Wu-ftpd Configuration Files

Depending on your distribution, you may have as many as five wu-ftpd configuration files in the /etc directory.

- **ftpaccess.** Sets up what different users can do through your server.
- **ftpconversions.** Default FTP settings for compressed or archived files.
- **ftpgroups.** Sets up encryption for your user's passwords.
- **ftphosts.** Lists users that are allowed or denied access to your FTP server. In Caldera Linux, the

/etc/hosts.allow and /etc/hosts.deny files serve this purpose.

- **ftpusers.** Sets up default users, in addition to the standard users already set up on your Linux computer.

Typically, you will only need to revise the /etc/ftphosts file to govern access to your FTP server. If you are using Caldera Linux, access to wu-ftpd is governed by the /etc/hosts.allow and /etc/hosts.deny files.

To confirm this, check the other configuration files against the samples from the WU-FTPD Resource Center. As of this writing, it is located at http://www. lanfield.com/wu-ftpd. Change your configuration files to match these sample files as required.

You also need the correct user names on your FTP server. When others try to connect to your FTP server, they will need a username and password on your FTP server computer.

In the ftphosts file, use the allow and deny commands to set up the computers allowed to access your FTP Server. Unlike the configuration files for Samba, NFS, and Apache, the allow list does not supersede what you put in the deny list.

For your small network, it is simplest to add to this file a line similar to the following:

```
allow    localhost   127.
192.168.0.0/255.255.255.0
```

This particular line allows you to access the FTP server from the local computer (localhost), through the loopback address (127.0.0.1), and all computers on the

192.168.0.0 subnet. If you use a different subnet for your local network, substitute accordingly.

Once you have modified the /etc/ftphosts file, restart the Internet superserver. Run the *kill –HUP inetd* command.

Now you can start your FTP server with the */usr/sbin/ ftprestart* command. In the next section, you can test your new FTP server.

Using FTP Clients

Now that you have set up the FTP server, you need an FTP client. Once both are set up, you can transfer files between server and client. In this section, you learn about one of the major Linux graphical FTP clients known as gFTP.

The gFTP tool was developed by the Simple End User Linux project as part of the GNOME graphical user interface. You can download the latest version of this tool from the gFTP homepage at http://www.gftp.seul.org.

If gFTP is already installed, you can find it through your Main Menu button or by navigating to your /usr/bin directory. If necessary, you can install it using the instructions on the gFTP homepage or by using the package manager for your distribution.

You started the wu-ftpd FTP server in the last section. Go to a different Linux computer on your network and start gFTP.

To connect to your FTP server, fill in the following text boxes in the gFTP window:

1. **Host.** The hostname of your FTP server.

2. **Port.** The FTP port number, usually 21.

3. **User.** Your username on the FTP server.

4. **Pass.** Your password on the FTP server.

Once you input the proper information in each text box, press Enter. The gFTP client attempts to connect to your FTP server. When successful, gFTP takes you to the home directory of the User on the FTP server.

To transfer a file from client to server, highlight a file in the Local (client) list. Click Transfers on the toolbar, then click Put Files.

To transfer a file from server to client, highlight a file in the server list. Click Transfers on the toolbar, then click Retrieve Files.

Looking Under the Hood

You can use a command-line interface utility called ftp to connect with an FTP site. Once you launch this utility, it becomes interactive and displays a special prompt. Try the following commands:

1. **ftp *server*.** This command starts the FTP client. It also attempts to connect to the computer named by *server*.

2. ***username*.** Type your username for gaining access to the FTP server. You will see a request for the password.

3. *password.* When prompted to do so, type your password. The server checks the username and password against its /etc/passwd database. When successful, you see the line "User *username* logged in."

4. **put** *filename.* As you saw in the last section, the put command sends files from the FTP client to the FTP server. For *filename,* use a file in the working directory. This command opens a connection between client and server. The data is sent in ASCII mode. When the file transfer is complete, ftp tells you the number of bytes that were sent. If you want to send (or receive) a binary file, type **binary** and press Enter. Type **ascii** to change the default file transfer mode back to plain text.

5. **get** *filename.* This command retrieves the specified *filename* from the FTP server.

6. **quit**. This command logs off from the FTP server named linux-desktop.

Common errors when connecting to an FTP server include "Connection Refused" and "Service not available." If you're unable to connect to your FTP server, review the last section and recheck your work on the /etc/inetd.conf and /etc/ftphosts files.

Table 13.1 summarizes the commands you can use with the ftp utility.

Table 13.1 Typical FTP Commands

Command	Function
ascii	Sets file transfers to ASCII (text) mode.
binary	Sets file transfers to binary mode.
cd	The Linux change directory command works normally.
delete	Deletes a file on the FTP server. This is a good reason to make users log into FTP.
get	Copies a file from the FTP server.
ls	Lists the files in the current directory.
pwd	The Linux present working directory command identifies the current directory on the FTP server.
put	Copies a file from the client computer to the FTP server.
quit	Logs off from the FTP Server.

References and Further Reading

Borowski, M. (2000). FTP mini-HOWTO. Linux Documentation Project. Available online at http://www.linuxdoc.org.

Landfield, K. (2000). WU-FTPD Resource Center. Available online at http:///www.landfield.com/wu-ftpd.

Lundberg, G. A. (1999). "upload.configuration .HOWTO." Available online at ftp://ftp.wu-ftpd.org/pub/wu-ftpd/upload.configuration.HOWTO.

Part Five

Managing Your Network

14

Archiving Your Data Automatically

Now that you have learned how to share directories over your network, you can make use of this capability by backing up your users' data. To do so, you will create a *backup server*, a computer that has been set aside for backup purposes. You will then configure each users' computer with the tar and cron utilities, which will automatically create backups of each user's data at times you specify each evening.

Creating Your Backup Server

You can use a workstation as a backup server, but it is best to use a dedicated system. Here is a great use for an older, slower system, such as a 486 or a Pentium 90. Equip the computer with a slow but capacious drive—you can get 26 GB hard drives at present for as little as $150—and set the machine aside as a backup device. Install Linux on this machine, create user accounts for all the users on your network, and export the users' home directories with NFS or Samba. Once you have set up the machine this way, you can configure tar and cron, as explained in the next section, to back up users' data automatically.

Backing Up with Tar and Cron: An Overview

Here is an overview of the backup solution described in this chapter. As you will see, it is simple, and very easy to implement.

- **Tar.** You will use the tar (tape archiver) utility to back up your users' home directories to the backup system. As you will see, the backup approach involves making an initial full backup of the user's home directory, followed by daily incremental backups of any new or altered files. Full backups are repeated each week, beginning a new backup cycle.
- **Cron.** The cron daemon performs the task of launching the needed backups, both the weekly full backups and the daily incremental ones. You can use the backup schedule suggested in this book, or substitute your own, if you wish, at more or less frequent intervals.

Archiving Data with Tar

The Linux version of the venerable Unix tape archive program tar can write to directories as well as tape devices. Once you have set up your network, you can use tar to create backup archives of your data.

Understanding Fundamental Tar Concepts

If you are used to using Windows archiving programs such as WinZip, you need to understand that tar does not include file compression capabilities; it is strictly an archiving program, which means that it collects one or more files and stores them as a unit. Once you have created the archive, you can compress it using gzip, the GNU compression utility discussed in the next section.

Creating an Archive

To create an archive with tar, you will make use of three basic command options: —create, —verbose, and —file.

- **Create (—create or –c).** The –c option tells tar to make a new archive file.
- **Verbose (—verbose or –v).** The –v option tells tar to give you information about what it's doing.
- **File (—file or –f).** The –f option enables you to specify the name of the file to be created.
- **Extract (—extract or –x).** The –x option enables you to take the files from an archive and restore them to their original, separate condition.

In addition, you must also list the files to be archived. You can do so by listing them individually, separated by a space. As an alternative, you can use wildcards. For example, the following command creates an archive containing all the GIF graphics in the current directory:

```
tar -cvf  gif-collection.tar *.gif
```

Note that you can use the short form of the option names (-cvf) instead of typing the lengthier versions (—create —verbose —file). When you use the short version, type only one hyphen, not two.

Additional Options for Backup Actions

Once you have specified one of the required options (-c or -v), you will need to add one or more of the options shown in Table 14.1.

Table 14.1 Additional Backup Options (tar)

Option	Description
–f *filename*	Use the specified archive file or device name. You can specify an external location using the form hostname:filename.
–h	Do not archive symbolic links; instead, archive the files to which they point.
–W	Verify the archive after creating it.
-p	Keep the permissions found on the source files.
-P	Keep the full path information for each file.

Listing and Extracting Archives

Over time, you may have created a considerable archive. If you need to check the contents of a specific archive, you can examine the files in an archive such as art.tar with the following command:

```
tar -lt art.tar
```

If a disaster strikes, you can restore files from an archive with the following command (note that this example also uses the --verbose and --file options):

```
tar -xvf art.tar
```

By default, this command extracts the entire archive and places the files in the current directory.

CAUTION Be careful when you are extracting archives. If any file in the current directory has the same name as a file in the tar archive, tar will overwrite the existing file, even if it is more recent than the archived version. Unless you are restoring all of the files in a tar backup, play it safe. Create a new subdirectory, move the tar archive to that subdirectory, and extract the archive there.

Alternately, you can extract individual files from an archive. For example, if you wanted to extract great-art.gif from a tar of your entire home directory, use the following command:

```
tar -xvf home.tar great-art.gif
```

Only the file(s) named at the end of the command will be extracted from the archive.

Creating a Backup Routine

To safeguard the work you create on your Linux system, you should perform regular backups. You can use your network to back up your more important files on different computers.

Full and Incremental Backups

A good backup begins with a *full backup*, which makes a copy of all of your valuable files. If you have a backup tape drive or CD-R drive, you can back up your entire hard disk—and that is not a bad idea unless you are comfortable starting almost from scratch (and reinstalling everything) in the event of a hard disk failure.

At minimum, you should make a full backup of your home directory. This directory should contain the work and configuration files of each of your users.

TIP It is not a bad idea to perform a full backup on your /etc directory as well. This directory contains system-wide configuration files, including settings for the X Window system, your network, and connections to the Internet. These files can be difficult to configure, so it is wise to back them up once you have them working.

You do not need to perform a full backup every time. With an *incremental backup*, you can back up only the files that have been altered or created since your last backup.

Performing the Full Backup

To perform a full backup, use a command such as the following:

```
tar -cWPpf lothlorien:suzanne.tar
/home/suzanne
```

This command backs up all the files in /home/suzanne; if you specify a directory name as this command does, tar operates in recursive mode by default. In other words, the utility backs up all the files in /home/suzanne, as well as all associated directories. The utility writes these (via NFS) to this user's directory on the server named lothlorien. The options tell tar to preserve the user's permissions (-p) and to store the full path information for each file (-P); this information will be needed to restore the filesystem should the user's disk fail. Once the backup archive has been written, it is verified against the original files. Note that this command will not work unless both of the following are true: lothlorien must be running, and Suzanne must have permission to write to her directory on lothlorien.

Performing an Incremental Backup

Once you have performed a full backup, you can now perform incremental backups for new or revised files. These backups make copies of only those files that have changed since the last full backup was made.

To perform an incremental backup, use the —newer (-N) option. The following example backs up all the files in the /home/mj directory created after March 12, 2000, the date of the last full backup:

```
tar -cvNWf'12 Mar 2000'
/home/mj/shares/home1.tar
```

When you have successfully completed the incremental backup, record the date and file location, followed by the date of the associated full backup.

How often should you perform an incremental backup? If you were running a multiuser Linux system, you would perform incremental backups daily. With a network, this process should be relatively painless, especially as you could perform this process automatically (see "Automating Backups with Cron," later in this chapter).

Repeating the Full Backup

Periodically, you will want to repeat the full backup in such a way that tar erases the last incremental backup. Here is why. When you perform incremental backups with tar, tar adds new or altered files to the archive—but it does not remove any of the files that have been deleted since the last update occurred. As a result, tar archives tend to grow in ways that make invasive vines and grasses appear as amateurs. Moreover, the archive may contain copies of sensitive or confidential files that the user thought had been deleted. Thus this unfortunate feature of tar can pose confidentiality risks that may matter a great deal to some users. When you perform a full backup on top of an incremental backup, and you use the same archive name for the repeated full backup, tar erases the previous copy of the archive and writes a new one. The new archive will not contain any of the files that the user deleted since the time of the last backup.

Scheduling Backups with Cron

The cron daemon, installed by default on most Linux distributions, polls the system once per minute to determine whether any jobs have been scheduled to run at that time. The utility checks for jobs at two levels, that of the system administrator and that of the user. Leaving aside the use of cron for system administration purposes, let us examine the procedure users can apply to set up a cron schedule. If you are setting up a user's system for backup purposes, switch to the user's account before running crontab, the utility that is used to create the cron configuration file.

Learning the Essentials of Cron Syntax

To use crontab, you will need to learn the syntax required to specify job schedules and commands with cron. In brief, each job is specified in a one-line statement, which consists of six fields. From left to right, they are the following:

- **Minute.** Possible values are 0 to 59.
- **Hour.** Possible values are 0 to 23.
- **Day of the month.** Possible values are 0 to 31.
- **Month.** Possible values are 0 to 12. You can also type the first three letters of the name of the month.
- **Day of week.** Possible values are 0 to 7. You can also type the first three letters of the day name of the day.
- **Command.** This is the same command you would type at the bash prompt.

To leave a field blank, type an asterisk (*) instead of one of the possible values.

The following is an example of a cron statement:

```
0 23 * * fri tar -xPpf /tmp/net/lothlorien
/home/suzanne
```

This command performs a full backup of the user's home directory and writes the archive file (home.tar) to the remote directory currently mounted on /tmp/net/lothlorien. Furthermore, it does so at precisely 11:00 PM every Friday.

The following specifies a complete backup regimen, beginning with a full backup that occurs every Friday, and continues with incremental backups on Monday through Thursday:

```
0 23 * *fri tar -xWPpf /tmp/net/home.tar
/home/suzanne
    0   23   *  *   mon tar -uWPpf
/tmp/net/home.tar /home/suzanne
    0   23   *  *   tue tar -uWPpf
/tmp/net/home.tar /home/suzanne
    0   23   *  *   wed tar -uWPpf
/tmp/net/home.tar /home/suzanne
    0   23   *  *   thu tar -uWPpf
/tmp/net/home.tar /home/suzanne
```

Note that this command assumes that the remote system (lothlorien) is indeed online and that this user (Suzanne) has write permissions to the mounted directory.

Using Crontab

To use crontab to create the backup schedule, do the following:

1. Log in as the user whose files you want to back up.

2. In a terminal window (or at the console), type crontab -e and press Enter. You will see the crontab editor, which makes use of your system's default text editor (such as vi). If you are using vi, type i to begin inserting text.

3. Type the cron commands, one to each line; be sure to press Enter at the end of each line.

4. Exit the editor. With vi, press Esc to exit the insert mode, and type :x (and press Enter) to save the file and exit the editor. When you have exited the editor, cron automatically writes the necessary files and adjusts the system configuration accordingly.

References and Further Reading

Scotney, P. (1999). Linux Backup HOYWTO. Available online at http://foo.medstu.unimelb.edu.au/~pierre/backup/BackupHOWTO.html.

15

Troubleshooting Your Network

When you experience some sort of difficulty with your network, you find yourself face-to-face with a good deal of complexity. The problem could be caused by a myriad of factors, including hardware glitches, poor connections, a configuration error, a disk that is filled to capacity so that temporary files cannot be written, and many more. Network problems can prove very difficult to solve, especially if you are not used to problem-solving in a networking environment.

This chapter introduces a problem-solving methodology based on real-world networking experience. You will start learning the basic principles of this method. Subsequently, you will learn to use the same problem-solving tools used by professional network administrators.

Configuration vs. Troubleshooting

Before you get started, be aware that this chapter is about *troubleshooting*, not *configuration*.

Configuration involves all the steps that lead to successful network functionality in the first instance. If you have had trouble getting something to work, you need to go back over the configuration steps, and make sure you have done everything correctly.

In contrast, troubleshooting involves problem-solving when a successfully functioning network stops working. For example, suppose you've set up an NFS server to export directories to a client. Due to a power outage, the server and the client lose power and, when power is restored, they reboot. After the user logs in to the client and attempts to access the remote directory formerly made available by NFS, the user discovers that this directory is no longer available.

This problem illustrates the type of problem tackled by a problem-solving procedure. There is nothing wrong with the configuration; formerly, the connection worked fine.

Observe, Theorize, Test

If you are not experienced with diagnosing network problems with Linux, the best place to start is the basic scientific method for problem-solving outlined here.

Identifying the Problem Through Observation

In this step, you identify the problem—specifically, the what and the where. Does the problem occur in other applications on the user's machine? Does it occur with only one of the computers on the network, or are all of them affected? Does the problem occur only when Internet connections are involved? You can observe some problems directly, such as physical connections; others will require the use of network analysis tools, which you will learn about in this chapter.

Returning to the example just mentioned, suppose you discover that other workstations cannot access remote NFS directories, either. This strongly suggests that the server for some reason was not available when the clients tried to log on.

Why start with observation? Identifying the problem correctly is not as easy as you might think. For example, if one of your users cannot get a network printer to work, there are a number of possible causes:

- **Bad connection.** Check your cables and plugs.
- **Problem with hardware.** Check the lights on your network card, hub, modem, and/or high-speed adapter.
- **Network card setup.** Several Linux commands can help you check how your network card is setup.
- **Network setup.** Make sure your computers know each other's addresses, etc. on your network.
- **Network software setup.** Make sure Samba, NFS, or other software is working.

- **Application setup.** Make sure your print command is set up to print to your printer. And make sure you are printing to the right printer.

Developing a Theory About the Underlying Cause

Make an educated guess on the cause. In particular, ask this question: "What has just happened that may have caused this problem?" Here, logical reasoning comes in very handy. For example, suppose you are using an older, slower Pentium as a file server on your network. This machine boots much more slowly than your top-of-the-line client workstations. Perhaps this is why your workstations are not able to access remote NFS directories. The workstations booted before the server became available. In consequence, they were not able to mount the remote directories.

Testing a Potential Solution

Once you have made a guess as to the cause, you can test a solution. To test your theory concerning why clients can not access NFS-exported directories, go to one of the clients, open a terminal window, type **dmesg | less**, and press Enter. If the NFS mount failed because the server was not available, you will see an error message. Now try mounting the remote filesystems (on Red Hat and Red Hat-derived systems, type **/etc/rc.d/init.d/netfs restart** and press Enter). If the mount is successful, you will have additional evidence that you have identified the problem. To verify your theory, shut down all the systems, including the NFS server. Restart the NFS server first. *Then* restart the clients. If all the clients can access remotes directories, you have successfully identified the cause of the problem.

Start with the Physical

When you troubleshoot a problem, the right way to proceed is in this general order. In other words, start with the physical, then check your basic network software, and then check your applications.

There are two advantages to this process. First, most network problems are physical. Second, if you have a physical or a network software/setup problem, any change that you make to your application, *at best*, will not help you. In the sections to come, you will learn how this works in more detail.

Checking Physical Connections

Most problems that pop up in a previously functioning network are physical in nature. To isolate such problems, determine whether your network cables are transmitted data—and if they are not, check to see whether they are properly connected.

To determine whether your network is transferring data, check the lights on network interface cards. A green light on your Ethernet card usually means that it is properly connected both to your computer and to the rest of your network. If it flashes when you send or receive data on your network, that is another good sign. Make the same checks on your hub, cable modem, and/or DSL adapter.

TIP A number of network components, including hubs, switches, routers, cable modems, and DSL adapters have separate power lines that also should be checked.

Next, examine the cables. Make sure that the connections between your Ethernet (or other network) cards and cables are secure. Even if all lights seem to be working, do not be afraid to disconnect and reconnect each cable.

NOTE If the lights are active on your network cards and hubs, that does not mean that data can flow over your cables. There are eight wires in a standard Ethernet cable; only one needs to be active to turn on the light.

If you suspect a problem with your connection to the Internet, check your modem or adapter and all its connections. Most high-speed connections (cable modems, DSL adapters, etc.) can be reset. If this is not covered in your documentation, ask your service provider for instructions.

Be aware that cables sometimes deteriorate to the point that they interfere with the flow of data, or stop carrying data altogether. If you have determined that just one of the workstations is not working properly, try swapping the workstation's Ethernet cable for a fresh, new one.

NOTE If you suspect a problem with your cable, special cable testers are available. Alternately, you can use a standard electrical continuity tester (available in most hardware stores) to check the wires in your cable. Remember, the lessons from Chapter 4. Do not bend your cables too sharply. And keep your cables away from rotating machinery.

Checking Network Activity

Once you are certain that all the physical connections are intact, check for network activity. You can do so by means of a network activity monitor. If you are using the GNOME desktop, for example, you can use the NetLoad applet to monitor network activity; if the network is functioning, you will see spikes that indicate that packet transfers are indeed occurring. Another useful utility is wmnet, a network activity monitor available with Window Manager (one of several alternative window managers you can use with X).

Checking the Interface Configuration

Once you are sure your network is functioning, go to the workstation that is experiencing the problem, open a terminal window, type **/sbin/ifconfig,** and press Enter. You will see a screenful of information.

You will find a guide to the ifconfig's output later in this section, but for now, this is what to look for:

- **IP address.** Is the workstation's IP address correct? Does it correspond exactly to the IP address entered in the /etc/hosts files of every workstation on the network?
- **Subnet address.** Is the subnet address correct? For a class C network, this should be 255.255.255.0.
- **Is the interface UP and RUNNING?** Look for these uppercase messages; if you do not see them, the interface is not functioning.

Here is more information on what you are seeing when you run ifconfig. The output from the ifconfig command falls in the following categories:

- **Link encap.** The type of network, usually Ethernet.
- **Hwaddr.** The hardware address of your network card. You can cross check this with next section's arp

command as well as the diagnostic program for your network card.

- **inet addr.** Your IP address. This should correspond to the IP address in your /etc/hosts file, unless your IP address is assigned by a DHCP server.
- **Bcast.** The broadcast address for your local network.
- **Mask.** The subnet mask for your local network. If you have followed the guidelines for network addresses in this book, this should be 255.255.255.0.
- **UP.** If it is DOWN, your Ethernet card is not operational.
- **BROADCAST.** If you are using Ethernet, this should be active, by definition.
- **RUNNING.** If you do not see this flag, try using the techniques from Chapter 5 again to get Linux to recognize your card.
- **MULTICAST.** If this is on, you can use this card for multicasts. In other words, you can connect to special IP addresses for data transfer to a group of computers. A common use for multicasting is videoconferences. If MULTICAST is off, your network can still work.
- **MTU.** If you have an Ethernet network, the Maximum Transmission Unit of data should be 1500 bytes. This is sometimes known as a packet.
- **RX, TX.** Lists the number of data packets received and transmitted through your network card. The number of errors, etc. in each category should be small relative to the total number of packets.
- **collisions.** If two different computers on an Ethernet network send messages at the same time, the data from each message will collide on your network. If the collisions exceed approximately 5% of your total

traffic (RX, TX), you may need to consider subdividing your network.

If there is a problem with your network card or modem, it may not show up in the output to an *ifconfig* command. However, Linux may still recognize your card; the next section can help.

Restarting Network Interfaces

One of the strengths of Linux is that reboots are rarely required. If a network card does not appear in the output from the *ifconfig* command, you can try restarting the network interface. On Red Hat and Red Hat-derived systems, you can do so by opening a terminal window, switching to superuser, typing **/etc/rc.d/init.d/inet restart**, and pressing Enter. Check your distribution's documentation to determine how to restart network services on your system.

Once you have restarted the network interfaces, check to see whether the problem has been solved. If not, you have successfully determined that the network is functioning, and that this workstation's network interface card is working correctly; the next section examines the next level at which problems can occur.

Checking Network Address Translation

If a workstation is experiencing difficulty accessing resources on another workstation on the network, there may be a problem with *address resolution*. In brief, address resolution maps numerical Ethernet card identification numbers (MAP numbers) to IP addresses. Such problems are almost always caused by two workstations configured to use the same IP address. If you inadvertently assigned the same IP address to two computers, your network will still work, but you may experience a variety of problems.

To determine whether address resolution is working correctly on your network, go to the workstation that is experiencing connection problems, open a terminal window, log in as superuser, type **arp -a,** and press Enter. If address resolution is working, you will see which IP addresses are currently mapped to functioning Ethernet interfaces.

To check for address resolution problems, use ifconfig to determine the hardware addresses of each machine on the network, and make a list of these addresses. With the output from arp, check to make sure that the assigned IP address is the correct one. If you discover that two machines are using the same IP address, configure one of them to use an address that is not already taken.

Using Ping

Now you can check whether the computers on your network can hear each other. The key command is known as *ping*, which sends a message to a specific IP address, requesting a reply. If your ping is successful, you will see responses that indicate the server is returning packets successfully. You will need to use the Ctrl + C command to stop the responses. Open up a command line interface. When using *ping,* you should use the following commands in order:

- **ping 127.0.0.1.** The 127.0.0.1 address is known as the loopback address. If you can ping your loopback address, TCP/IP is installed (but not necessarily configured) correctly on your computer.

- **ping** *your_ip_address*. Substitute the IP address for your computer. If you do not know your IP address, use the *ifconfig* command. If this "ping" is successful, your IP address is properly connected to your network card. If the computer you are using has two network cards (e.g., your gateway computer), ping each IP address in separate commands.

- **ping** *your_computer_name*. Substitute the host name of your computer. If you do not know your computer host name, check your /etc/hosts or /etc/HOSTNAME file. If this does not work, you may have a problem with these files on your local computer.

- **ping** *other_ip_address*. Substitute another IP address on your local network. Refer to your /etc/hosts file if required. If there is a problem here, check the connections and cables between your computer and the computer with this address. If your network is not too large, repeat this command for the other computers on your network.

- **ping** *other_computer_name*. Substitute the host name of another computer on your network. Refer to your /etc/hosts file as required. If there is a problem here, make sure your /etc/hosts file matches the hostname of your other computers.

- **ping** *dns_server_ip_address*. Use the IP address of your ISP's DNS server. You should have recorded this in your /etc/resolv.conf file. (Another name for a DNS server is a "nameserver.") If you have a problem here, report it to your ISP. If a DNS server is down, the ISP's other customers will also have problems navigating to Web sites on the Internet.

- **ping** *internet_website*. Substitute the name of some popular Internet site such as http://www.momma-bears.com. Since you have already "pinged" the IP address and host name of your default gateway, this message should travel to your ISP's DNS server and finally to the "pinged" internet Web site. Any problem here is a job for the next command.

TIP When you stop the ping response with a <Ctrl-C>, you will stop the response to one packet. Therefore, it is normal to have one fewer packet received than transmitted. Also, note the time for each ping. That is the time, in milliseconds, for the Web site in question to respond to your ping. If this time goes up in the future, you may have trouble connecting to that particular Web site.

To summarize, if you can ping successfully, your network can communicate with the destination computer. However, you should look out for the following messages:

- **Unknown Host.** If this is from a ping to a computer on your local network, check your /etc/hosts and /etc/HOSTNAME files on each computer. If this is from a ping to a computer outside your network, check the IP address for your DNS server in your /etc/resolv.conf. These addresses should match those given by your ISP. If you still have a problem, you are trying to ping a bad hostname, or at least a computer that has not been working for several days.

- **100% Packet Loss.** The host is known, but your ping could not reach the destination computer. If the destination is on your local network, check your physical connections. If the destination is on the Internet, the Web site you are looking for may be down.

- **Network Unreachable.** Your ISP's DNS server works, but your ping cannot reach your desired computer or Web site. Review the next section for more information.

Tracing Internet Connections

You have pinged everything in sight. You can share on your network just fine, but cannot reach anyone on the Internet. You can think of the *traceroute* command as an advanced version of ping. In essence, it asks for a response from every computer in its path. If *traceroute* finds a problem, you will see something like the following message:

```
unknown host www.unknown.com
```

There are two issues that a traceroute can address. If the traceroute cannot get past your ISP, go to your gateway computer. Check the gateway IP address. If you are using Red Hat Linux, it is listed in your /etc/sysconfig/network file. If you are using another distribution, check your documentation for the configuration tool or file to check. This address should match the gateway given by your ISP.

If the traceroute stops somewhere else, there may be a traffic problem on the Internet. Either the ISP for the Web site you want to reach is down, or there is a lot of traffic between your ISP and that Web site. Both problems are usually beyond your control.

Testing Your DNS Server

Typically, you will be relying on your ISP's DNS server. Even if you can "ping" or "traceroute" to that server, it may not be working. The direct way to check your DNS Server is with the nslookup command. This command uses one of the DNS servers listed in your /etc/resolv.conf file (see next section). When you start nslookup from the command line interface, you will see your DNS Server name and IP address followed by a different prompt:

>

Type **help** and press Enter to see the available commands. Once you've set the type of test to be an ns (short for name server), you can enter the Web site of your choice. If your DNS is working, it should return the "authoritative" DNS for that Web site. Otherwise, contact your ISP. They may be having problems with their DNS servers.

NOTE The Internet is divided up into Zones of Authority such as .com, .gov, .org, and .jp. There are several DNSs that are "authoritative" for all ".com" addresses. Each Web site is governed by the ISP that hosts that site. That ISP's DNS server is "authoritative" for that Web site.

Checking Your Network Setup: Configuration Files

You have set up a number of different files to get your network going. If you have a problem, and have run through the previous physical and command checks on your network, now is the time to recheck your configuration files. The following are your key network configuration files and their respective functions. Remember, if you are not using Red Hat Linux, you will probably find these files in different directories.

- **/etc/HOSTNAME.** Lists the hostname of your local computer.
- **/etc/hosts.** Lists the hostnames and IP addresses of at least the computers on your local network.

- **/etc/host.conf.** Lists the order of files where Linux checks for computer hostnames. The first line in this file should normally be *order hosts, bind,* which means that Linux checks your /etc/hosts file first before looking at the DNS servers shown in your /etc/resolv.conf file.
- **/etc/resolv.conf.** Lists the IP addresses of your DNS Servers. If your network is properly connected to your ISP, these *nameservers* should correspond to the IP addresses of your ISP's DNS servers.
- **/etc/hosts.allow.** The list of computers allowed to connect to your TCP/IP network. Remember, this should include **127.** to allow your local computer to access your network. Works with the /etc/hosts.deny file.
- **/etc/sysconfig/network.** In this file, you need Networking and IP forwarding set to yes. Unless this computer has a telephone modem connection to the Internet, the Gateway should specify the IP address and Network card that is your path to the World Wide Web.

This is strictly review, as you have already learned to set up these files in previous chapters.

Checking Network Services: Restarting Network Software

Just as you restarted your network cards earlier in this chapter, you can also try to restart the software that allows communication on your network. Sometimes, you may have a temporary problem that can be addressed by restarting Samba or NFS.

Most Red Hat network services are located in the /etc/rc.d/init.d/ directory. For example, if you are having a problem between a Linux and a Windows computer, you may want to restart Samba with the following command:

```
/etc/rc.d/init.d/samba restart
```

Other services that you might restart (and their commands) include the following. Remember, each of these commands is located in the /etc/rc.d/init.d directory in Red Hat Linux.

- **Samba.** (Linux-Windows networking) smb restart
- **Network File System(Linux networks).** *nfs restart*
- **Modem Dial-Up.** diald restart
- **Apache (The Linux Web Server).** httpd restart
- **Basic Networking.** inet restart

Checking Applications: Browser Setup

You pinged and traced every route. You know that your network card works well. But you still cannot get through to your Web site. Common problems include:

- **Blocking.** It is common to use a proxy server such as Squid to block access to "undesirable" Web sites such as sexually explicit ones. In this section, you will see how you can set up blocking through Netscape Communicator.
- **Proxies.** Some Web sites do not work with proxy servers, whether they be on your local network or at your ISP. You will set up Netscape to bypass proxy servers for specific Web sites in Chapter 16.

NOTE This can also be a problem if you have a firewall such as IP chains from Chapter 16. By default, the IP chains setup in Chapter 10 blocks all channels except for addresses that start with "http:". In

Chapter 14, you will learn to use IP chains to let in the other channels of data that you want, such as FTP, Internet Chat, and Real Audio.

You can also set up Netscape to block "undesirable" Web sites. Open up Netscape on your computer. Click on the Main Menu button, point to Red Hat, point to Internet, and then click Netscape Communicator.

In the Netscape menu bar, click Help (in the upper right corner) and then click NetWatch. If you are connected to the Internet, this brings you to a series of menus on Netscape's Web site that help you set up blocking of different kinds of Web sites. Follow the instructions given in the following Web pages.

As of this writing, Netscape uses two different rating systems:

- **RSAC.** Short for the Recreational Software Advisory Council, this group rates Web sites in four different areas: Language, Violence, Nudity, and Sex. You can find more information on their ratings at http://www.rsac.org.
- **SafeSurf.** This group has a more extensive set of filters in 11 different areas. For more information on their rating system, navigate to their site at http://www.safesurf.com.

Both systems depend on Web masters to set up ratings for their sites. While RSAC depends on a Web master filling out a questionnaire, SafeSurf depends on Web masters adding certain numbers to "Meta Tags" in the code for their Web sites.

While it is possible to abuse these systems, it is generally believed that Web masters of adult-oriented sites are motivated to help. First, it is believed that users of adult sites use these tags to help them find the content they desire. Second, helping others filter out their Web sites reduces the risk of governmental regulation.

NOTE This section just covers setting up Netscape to block Web sites on your local computer. Many other applications also can be used to block Web sites. For more information, consult the documentation for your application.

Network Slowdowns and Stoppages

You cannot control traffic on the Internet. So when you have a problem reaching a Web site, the problem may be unrelated to the conditions on your network. One way to check this is through the "Internet Weather Report," which you can review at http://www.mids.org/weather.

Internet traffic varies by location and by domain. If the Internet Weather Report shows that a particular area is experiencing problems, you may not be able to connect to a Web site in that area.

You can also use the Internet Weather Report to check traffic in a number of more specific geographical areas, such as the United Kingdom or the Silicon Valley of California.

Deeper Analysis

The IP traffic utility allows you to observe the start and end points of each message, as well as the format of each message.

Open up a command line interface. Go into root or super-user mode if required. Start the IP traffic utility with the **/usr/sbin/iptraf** command. If you see the following message, your command line window is not large enough. Resize or maximize the command line interface window and try the **/usr/sbin/iptraf** command again.

```
This program requires a screen size of at
least 80 columns by 24 lines. Please resize
your window.
```

If you have set up IP masquerading on this computer, you will see a message suggesting that you start iptraf on a different computer. Iptraf will still work on an IP masquerading computer, but it will list this computer as the source for all messages from the Internet.

When you get to the first menu screen, use your arrow keys to highlight "IP traffic monitor," and then press Enter. You will see information about each of the connections that are currently in progress

Look at the number after each IP address. The addresses from the Internet are all associated with port 80. This happens to be the standard Internet channel for transmitting Web sites. If you are using an ISP's proxy server, that means these Web sites are bypassing that proxy server. The ISPs often use proxy servers to help protect their users from attack.

In other words, the data that you get from these Web sites may be putting your network at risk.

Detailed Analysis

The next tool to check your traffic is Ethereal, a network protocol analyzer—also known as a *packet sniffer*. This application allows you to read the data traveling over your network in more detail. If Ethereal is not installed on your system, you can obtain a copy from the program's home page at http://ethereal.zing.org/download.html.

To start Ethereal, open a terminal window, type **ethereal,** and press Enter.

When Ethereal opens, click Capture in the toolbar, then click Start. When the Ethereal: Capture preferences window opens, check your Interface. Change it to the network interface that you want to check, then click OK.

Transmit some data over your network. You will see a small window with a number of different letters. When you have finished your data transmission, click Stop in this window. You will see a series of lines that represent the data going to and from your network.

If you see something suspicious, highlight the IP address and look at the data in more detail. Note the source of the data; if you suspect that someone is trying to break into your network, the IP address that your attacker is using is shown here.

NOTE People who break into networks can hide their actual IP address. In fact, if someone breaks into your network, they may use your IP address to initiate other attacks. Therefore, if you have a static

IP address, the IP chains commands that you will learn about in Chapter 16 are especially important.

The middle window shows a lot of strange looking information related to this particular data packet. The "Source port" and "Destination port" show that the IP masquerading set up in Chapter 16 is working.

On the Internet, there are 1024 standard (and 65,536 total) "ports." You can think of a port as like a channel on a television. Source port 80 is the standard for data from Internet Web sites. The IP masquerading sets the Destination port to a random "channel" above 1024, which helps hide your information from intruders.

The bottom window helps you analyze your data. The "destination" is highlighted in the middle window. As you can see, the destination IP address is 192.168.0.1. The highlighted numbers in the bottom window give the destination IP address, in hexadecimal (base 16) notation.

There are many tools available to troubleshoot networking in Linux. In this chapter, you have learned about a few of these tools. You have also learned to use the scientific method to determine what to check, and in the best possible order.

Some of these tools also help you determine if you have a security problem with your network connection to the Internet. Many of these problems can be addressed through the IP chains commands that you will learn about in the next chapter.

References and Further Reading

Kirch, Olaf. (1996). *Linux Network Administrator's Guide.* Linux Documentation Project. Available online at http://www.linuxdoc.org.

Mourani, Gerhard. (2000). *Securing and Optimizing Red Hat Linux.* Linux Documentation Project. Available online at http://www.linuxdoc.org.

16

Securing Your Network

There is a frontier element when you connect to the Internet. The opportunities are fabulous. However, the security risks are fabulous as well. There is no one tool that can address all security issues. In this chapter, you will learn to take a layered approach to security.

First, you will review the ways in which you are vulnerable to attack. Not all security issues destroy files on your computer; you will learn to monitor the activity on your network for problems.

If you are connecting to the Internet through an ISP, you are not working alone. The ISPs will help you by filtering some of the content from the Internet. But they cannot help you if you bypass their security gates.

Later, you will look at the things that you can do to protect your network. First, you will learn to keep your network as simple as possible. Fewer active network programs mean fewer ways to break into your network.

Finally, you will also learn about setting up a firewall with various *ipchains* commands.

Understanding the Risk

Perhaps you are thinking that your network is safe from attack because it contains little or nothing of value, at least to outsiders. If so, it is time for a wake-up call. *Any* network that is connected to the Internet is vulnerable to attacks from the following unsavory individuals:

- **Computer virus authors.** A computer virus is a rogue program that attaches to executable programs in such a way that the virus "infects" other executable programs on the victim's computer. Many viruses are designed to destroy data as well as embarrass the affected user (for example, by posting the user's documents to the Internet with subject headings such as "Child pornography—click here"). When infected, executable files are transferred via the Internet, and the chaos spreads.
- **Script kiddies.** Thanks to the proliferation of the necessary scripts by means of the Internet, youthful computer enthusiasts—even those lacking in technical knowledge—can scan the Internet automatically, looking for poorly protected systems. If they find one and are able to gain entry to it, they can use the com-

promised system as a launching pad for attacks on other systems—and those affected will believe that the attack is coming from your network! To do so, the intruder will plant *trojan horses* on your system. A trojan horse is a program that is named after, and functions like, a useful utility. However, it contains code that performs malicious functions, such as gathering all the passwords in use on your network and sending them to the intruder.

- **Crackers.** More knowledgeable intruders, called crackers, may specifically target your system; for crackers, it is something of a challenge to try to gain entry to a system, especially one that is reasonably well-protected. (Note that the popular press uses the term hacker to refer to people who break into other computer systems. However, the term *hacker* properly refers only to a computer enthusiast who enjoys "tweaking" a program or network to extract the maximum performance.) Should you become the target of a knowledgeable cracker, it is bad news indeed; you would need to be a security mastermind to defend a network against the better crackers. Fortunately, there is little chance that a cracker would target a low-profile home or small business network; in general, they are after bigger fish. From the foregoing, it should be clear that every computer network is at risk. You must clearly understand that the world contains rather large numbers of people who are not nice; they take satisfaction in causing harm to others.

Has Your Network Been Compromised?

You cannot stop all attacks, but at least you can learn about some of the symptoms of an attack. In the following sections, you will look at three basic diagnostic tools. While these tools may not seem "high-tech," they can help you diagnose problems more quickly.

- **Behavior.** Know your network. Be suspicious when you see something unusual happening, such as an unusually slow "high-speed" connection. A cracker may have planted a trojan horse on your system that allows him/her to launch an attack against someone else.
- **Logs.** Linux provides log files for everything from how your system loads network cards to the amount of time your users are on your system. The log files may contain evidence of intrusion attempts.
- **Files.** If intruders have managed to place trojan horses on your system, there are ways to find out.

The following sections detail the procedures you can use to determine whether your network has been compromised.

Examining Network Behavior

While the following signs do not necessarily mean that you have a problem, they could be an indicator of suspicious activity:

- **Constant Hard Disk Activity.** This means either that you are running too many programs relative to your available memory, or someone is trying to read the data on your hard drive.
- **Constant Network Activity.** On smaller networks, there will be times when no one is accessing the Internet. If the lights on your telephone or cable modem or DSL adapter still flash during these periods of inactivity, someone may be using your network as a base to attack someone else.

Not all strange network activity is a sign of a security problem. There are a number of possible causes for slower network connections. Just a few legitimate explanations are included here.

- **Cable modems.** If you have a cable modem, others in your neighborhood may have just acquired cable modem service and are sharing the capacity (a.k.a. bandwidth) of your neighborhood connection to the Internet. Suddenly, your Internet access is slower—but it is not because an intruder has gained access to your system.

- **E-mail clients.** Some e-mail clients are automatically configured to check for new mail as often as once every minute. Even if your users are not working on their computers, their computers keep accessing the Internet for mail. You should reconfigure the clients so that they check for mail once every half hour or once an hour.

- **TCP/IP configuration errors.** If one of your computers is set up with an IP address that is not part of your subnetwork, it will load up your Ethernet network looking for other computers. In this case, you would check the IP address assigned to each computer. Make sure that all of them are part of the same subnetwork and that they all match what you see in the /etc/hosts files.

- **Problems with exported directories.** If you are using NFS or Samba to share directories, you may have a problem when the NFS or Samba server is down. Other computers set up to connect to an NFS or Samba shared directory may keep trying to connect. Your network will be busy as a result. All you can do in this case is reboot the server or deactivate Samba or NFS.

Configuring Log Files

Many network services and applications maintain *log files,* which contain confirmation and error messages. You will find the various log files in the /var/log directory.

As with everything else in Linux, log files are controlled by a configuration file. In Red Hat Linux, they are configured in the */etc/syslog.conf* file. By default, the configuration file sends network messages to the /var/log/messages file. Go into root or superuser mode and review your log messages by typing the following and pressing Enter:

```
_cat /var/log/messages | less
```

Chances are good that this is a very long file that scrolls through your screen for some time. Now open up your /etc/syslog.conf file in your favorite text editor. Make sure the following commands are included in this file:

```
_auth.*    /var/log/secure

authpriv* /var/log/secure.a
```

These commands capture any attempt to log on as any user, including the root user. When you review these log files, you can see if someone is trying to log on when no one should be on your network, such as during the middle of the night.

On Red Hat systems, the file called /etc/syslog.conf determines the type of information the kernel records in system logs. This particular log file records key events on your system in the following categories.

- **Kernel.** As Linux loads on your system, the kernel loads various modules, such as for Ethernet adapters (eth0) and modems (ppp0). As you boot Linux, you can see when this process is and is not successful. Alternately, you can observe what happened when you started Linux on your computer with the dmesg command.

- **Info.** Information level messages tell you when Linux daemons such as Samba start, stop, or change settings. Review this on your own computer through the /var/log/messages file.

- **Mail.** Unless you have set up a mail server on your network, you should not see any messages in your mail log file. Check the file set up to receive mail log messages. Unless this file is empty, a mail server such as sendmail is running on your Linux computer. Unless you want to run your own mail server, you should shut it down. You can use the tksysv utility given later in this chapter to deactivate servers such as sendmail.

The default syslog.conf file is very basic. You can divide up each log into different categories. For example, if you want all warnings about users who log on with a bad password in one file, insert the following command in the syslog.conf file:

```
_authpriv, auth.=warning
/var/log/auth/auth.warning
```

This saves all problem logon attempts to the /var/log/auth/auth.warning file. When you edit the /etc/syslog.conf file, you can activate your changes in root or super user mode with the killall –HUP syslogd command. For more information on editing the syslog.conf file, review the syslog.conf manual. Go into a command line interface, and enter the man syslog.conf command.

> **TIP** Unmaintained log files often fill up hard drives. By default, Red Hat Linux uses the *logrotate* utility to keep log files rotated on a weekly basis. If your logs still get too big, you can change how logs are recorded in your */etc/logrotate.conf* file.

Finding Suspicious Activity In Your Logs

Generally, a user needs to log in to do any damage to your system. To log in, users need a password. Any attempt to login with a good or a bad password is recorded in log files. Based on the default /etc/syslog.conf file, logins are recored in /var/log/secure.

To check for login attempts with a bad password, log in as the root user, type the following, and press Enter:

```
_grep refused /var/log/secure*
```

This command tells the grep text-searching utility to examine all the files with names beginning with "secure" in the /var/log directory. These files contain records concerning login attempts.

> **TIP** If /etc/syslog.conf calls for the creation of /var/log/secure, but no such file exists, this is not good news. An intruder may have erased this file—or set its byte count to 0—to cover up the intrusion.

If grep does not find anything, check the /var/log directory to make sure that the secure files exist (you should see secure, secure.1, secure.2, secure.3, and so on). Also, make sure that they contain something; type ls -l and press Enter, and check the file sizes. If all of the files contain zero bytes, and you have been logging in and out fairly regularly, it could spell trouble; intruders cover their tracks by erasing the information in these files.

Another file to check is the */var/log/wtmp* file. Since it is in binary format, you need to convert it with the *utmp-dump* command. Here is an example:

```
_utmpdump /var/log/wtmp > /home/me/logindump
```

Now review the logindump file in a text editor such as vi, emacs, or any text editor accessible through the Main Menu button. Correlate what you see in this file with any suspicious activity from the /var/log/secure file. For example, if you see a problem login at 3 AM on September 26, 2000, check this against the logindump file entry listed for this time.

It is possible for crackers to hide problems deep in your system. Review your log files as far back as possible. Older logfiles, when available, have a name similar to the current logfile, for example: */var/log/secure.1*.

Review the different logfiles available in the /var/log directory. As you review these files on a periodic basis, you will learn to spot anything out of the ordinary.

Examining Executable Files for Suspicious Activity

When intruders gain unauthorized access to poorly secured systems, they may replace certain utilities (including ps, netstat, and top) with doctored versions that hide their activities. If you installed these utilities with RPM, you can quickly and easily find out whether they have been altered since you installed them. To find out, log in as the root user, type the following, and press Enter:

```
_rpm -V procps
```

The procps package contains ps and top, two of the files an intruder is likely to modify. If the files have not been modified since you installed them, you will see the Linux prompt again. If you see output from this command, then the file has indeed been altered since you installed it with RPM. This evidence does not necessarily mean that an intruder has altered these files—perhaps you installed them from a tarball (any file with a tar.gz extension) instead of running RPM—but it is disturbing news. Be sure to check netstat as well by typing the following and pressing Enter:

```
rpm -V net-tools
```

The foregoing package names (procps and net-tools) are those used on Red Hat systems; to find out the name of the corresponding packages on different Linux distributions that use RPM, type **rpm -qf** followed by the path-name and name of the command (as in /rpm -qf /usr/bin/top).

Checking for SUID Executables

An executable file can be given an attribute called set user ID (SUID), which means that any user executing the file receives the privileges of the file's owner. If the file's owner is the root user, that means that anyone executing the file gets the root user's privileges, at least as far as the executable's behavior is concerned.

Some executables need to be SUID. An example is /bin/passwd, the password-changing utility; if this utility was not configured with SUID, users would not be able to change their passwords. Still, SUID executables present a security hazard. Intruders know that if they play around with these executables, they may create an error condition that sets up a shell with root user privileges—which means that they will have unrestricted access to your entire system. Additionally, an intruder may leave behind SUID versions of executables, including a SUID version of the shell, that enable them to gain root user access to your system.

What should you do about SUID executables? Watch them—carefully. Here is how. On a system that is running a clean version of Linux, switch to superuser, type **find / - perm -4000 | lpr**, and press Enter. You will get a printed list of all the executables on your system that have been set to run SUID. Periodically, you should repeat this command. If you notice any new SUID executables—particularly a SUID executable that's located in a directory you rarely inspect—your system may have been compromised. If you are sure that the executables were not altered for a legitimate reason, you would be wise to back up your data and reinstall Linux from your distribution disks.

Asking For Help

If you suspect that your network has been compromised, help is readily available. Search for help in the following order:

1. Search the Web for information about an error message that concerns you. One good search engine for Linux problems is Google, located at http://www.google.com.

2. Search for messages in various Linux-related newsgroups. One way to search many newsgroups

simultaneously is through the Deja Web site at http://www.deja.com.

3. Search through the manual pages and HOWTOs related to the subject in question. If necessary, you can find current versions of manual pages and HOWTOs on the Linux Documentation Web site at http://www.linuxdoc.org.

4. Look for free help. One good source is the articles and discussion groups available on the LinuxNewbie Web site at http://www.linuxnewbie.org. Whether you use LinuxNewbie or another newsgroup, make sure to include your applicable configuration (.conf) files, key log entries, and the steps you have taken so far to try to solve your problem.

5. Consider getting professional help. If you purchased any full distribution of Linux, chances are good that it comes with some sort of technical support. Alternately, LinuxCare offers technical support plans, at a price. You can find out more about LinuxCare support options on their Web site located at http://www.linuxcare.com.

What Should You Do if You Find Evidence of an Intrusion?

If you are convinced that you have found evidence of an unauthorized intrusion into your network, you must do the following:

1. Back up all of your users' data.

2. Reinstall clean versions of Linux from the original distribution CD-ROM.

3. Reinstall clean versions of user applications from freshly downloaded packages or tarballs.

Obviously, this is a lot of work. It could be *days* of work in a network consisting of a dozen or more workstations. But it is necessary. The intruder may have hidden packet sniffers, monitoring programs, trojan horses, and who-knows-what virtually anywhere on your network—and the presence of just one of these compromised files is sufficient to let the intruder back in.

To avoid reinstalling all the software on your network, be proactive. Learn how to secure your network now. In the following sections, you will examine ways your ISP can protect you, and ways you can protect yourself.

Understanding Your ISP's Security Role

Many crackers are smart enough to try to disguise their messages. When they send a virus, trojan horse, or some other malicious program, they often start by cracking someone else's account at another Internet service provider (ISP). When the authorities start their investigation, they will track the message back to that ISP.

Even if the ISP is not at fault, the publicity of an investigation is not good for their business. The publicity could be even worse if the provider is a company, university, or governmental agency. They want to protect their users from crackers as much as possible.

In the following sections, you will look at what ISPs do to help protect their users.

Proxy Servers

One way ISPs help protect their users is through proxy servers. You learned to set up Netscape to work with ISP proxy servers in Chapter 11. Proxy servers have a number of advantages for ISPs. As long as you do not specifically bypass a proxy server, this tool allows an ISP to help protect you in the following ways:

- **Blocking Undesirable Sites.** As you can protect yourself from sites with various levels of sexuality and violence, ISPs and other organizations can do the same through their proxy servers.
- **Blocking Specific IP Addresses.** When an ISP investigates a problem message, they can find the originating IP address for that message. While the problem is being investigated, the ISP can block all messages from that specific IP address.
- **Limiting Access to Specific Sites.** The other way to approach security is to limit Internet access to approved sites. This approach is best for ISPs and organizations that want their Internet access to be suitable for children.

If you do not want this kind of protection, you can bypass a proxy server for specific Web sites using the tools that you learned about in Chapter 11.

Dynamic Addresses

Many ISPs and other organizations make their users share a limited number of IP addresses. After any user disconnects, the IP address that he/she used can be reassigned to a different user, dynamically.

Dynamic IP addresses provide some measure of security against unauthorized intrusions because your network gets a different IP address—at least in theory—every time you log on. Crackers will have difficulty finding their way back to your network. It is as if your telephone had a different number every day; people would find it very hard to reach you!

The protection afforded by dynamic IP addresses is far from complete, however, and that is especially true when you are using high-speed connections such as cable modems and DSL. These services may keep you connected more or less indefinitely, so that your exposure is magnified. There have been many reported instances of break-ins to networks connected via dynamic IP addresses, and the number of such reports is steadily rising.

Securing Your System

Unless you are confident that your ISP defends your network perfectly, you need to work at defending your network. In the following sections, you will look at several different techniques for keeping your computers and data as secure as you can handle.

TIP One option is to ask your ISP to set up security on your network. While this can be expensive, it is often cost effective for larger networks.

Running the Latest and Greatest

Always make sure you are running the latest versions of all the software and utilities provided with your Linux distribution. Often, security flaws are found that lay your system wide open to unauthorized intruders. Word gets around on the 'Net pretty fast, and you can be sure that would-be intruders will get the news very quickly. If you are still running an older version of software that is known to have a vulnerability, you're sending a message that says, in effect, "Here I am! Have fun!" Check your distribution's home page frequently for software updates, and make a habit of visiting sites such as Security Focus (http://www.securityfocus.com), RootShell (http://www .rootshell.com), and CERT (http://www.cert.org).

Fingerprinting Your Files

When intruders break into systems, they leave behind a slew of utilities that have been altered to hide their tracks. It is very difficult to tell that these files have been altered—unless, that is, you create a "fingerprint" of these files in their pristine, unaltered state. You can do this with the md5sum utility, which creates a checksum that uniquely describes the file; if it has been altered, even slightly, the checksum will differ. When you install a clean version of Linux, use the following command to create checksums for all the utilities in /bin, /sbin, /usr/bin, and /usr/sbin:

```
_md5sum /bin/* /sbin/* /usr/bin/* /usr/sbin/*
> /root/clean-check.md5
```

Periodically, perform this check again, but save the output to a different filename:

```
_md5sum /bin/* /sbin/* /usr/bin/* /usr/sbin/*
> /root/new-check.md5
```

To see whether any of the executables have changed, use the following command:

```
_diff clean-check.md5 new-check.md5
```

If the diff utility displays lines that differ, do not panic; you may have installed updated versions of the utilities in question. If not, it is possible that the files have been compromised. You should back up your data and install a fresh version of Linux from your distribution disks.

Backing Up Your Data

The last line of defense in any system is a good backup. In other words, do not haphazardly restore your backup from yesterday, as that might restore whatever viruses or trojan horses might have penetrated your system.

When your system has been cracked, you need a *pristine* backup. This means that you want a backup where the key settings for Linux, as well as any critical data files are unaffected by any known problems.

In general, you can determine if you have a pristine backup by checking your log files. Once you determine the first time a cracker has tried to attack your system (e.g., by logging in at a strange time of day), all you need is a backup before that date.

Using Good Passwords

Although no password is fail-safe, you should encourage your users to set up longer passwords with a mix of letters and numbers. Never use passwords based on dictionary words or a word followed by a number. While a cracker can decipher a password based on a dictionary word in hours, it can take weeks to decipher an alphanumeric password.

One good way to set up an alphanumeric password is based on a favorite sentence. For example, you could use "I shot 2 under par on March 8" to set up the following password: Is2upoM8. Note that each letter (or number) in this password is the first letter in the sentence. And remember, Linux passwords are case sensitive. In other words, *Is2upoM8* is different from *is2upom8*.

Configure /etc/hosts.allow and /etc/hosts.deny

You may have already undertaken this step in previous chapters. Switch to root user or superuser, open a terminal window, and launch a text editor. Open /etc/hosts.deny, and make sure this file contains the following line:

```
ALL:ALL
```

This line effectively denies access to *all* services for *all* outside systems save those that are specifically given access in /etc/hosts.allow.

Open /etc/hosts.allow with a text editor such as vi or emacs, and type your network address and localhost address, as follows:

```
ALL: 192.168.1. 127.
```

If your network address is not 192.168.1.0, substitute accordingly. This line provides access to all TCP/IP services for any of the computers with IP addresses beginning with 192.168.1 or 127 (note the period following these addresses as given in the command; the period functions as a wild card).

Save the files and restart your Internet services. To do so with Red Hat Linux and derived systems, switch to superuser, open a terminal window, type **/etc/rc.d/init.d/inetd restart**, and press Enter.

Safeguard Your Partitions

You may want to limit access to key directories on your Linux computer. This can help protect your system if a cracker somehow finds one of the user names and passwords on your system. The key is through your *letc/fstab* file.

WARNING You cannot create new partitions by adding them to your /etc/fstab file. Revising and adding partitions is a painstaking process most easily done with third-party programs such as Partition Magic or System Commander. Alternately, you can reinstall Linux on your system, but that can be difficult too.

As long as you have the partitions that you want, as shown in your *letc/fstab* file, you can modify the column that starts with "defaults." The settings correspond to the following:

- **defaults.** The default settings for a partition allow read/write access, SUID setup (to allow you to execute programs like KPPP), and dev installation (so Linux can communicate with your hardware). This also limits the mounting of partitions to when you reboot Linux or through a mount command by the root user.
- **noexec.** Prohibits programs from running in this partition. If you have created a partition for /home, it is a good idea to enable this option for all this partition. If a cracker obtains one of your user's passwords,

he/she will not be able to run a malicious program from the intruder's home directory.

- **nodev.** Prohibits setting up a device such as a peripheral on this partition. Keeps crackers from running your hardware.
- **nosuid.** SUID can be dangerous as it can allow any user root equivalent access to critical files.
- **ro.** Read-only. No one, not even the root user, is allowed to write to a read-only partition.
- **noauto.** Does not automatically mount when you boot Linux. This usually is used for the CD-ROM partition, as you do not always have to have a CD in this drive.
- **user.** Anyone is allowed to mount this partition. Useful for CD-ROM drives.

Disabling Unused TCP/IP Services

By default, most Linux versions install a full suite of TCP/IP services, including FTP, HTTP (Web), finger, and so on. It is cool to have all these services available, but it is not so cool to run them if you are not using them. Intruders may be able to gain access to your system through a recently discovered exploit that is only available when a user is thoughtlessly running an unused service.

To disable unneeded TCP/IP services, switch to superuser, launch a text editor, and open /etc/services*all* of the services you are not using. You need to run only those services for which you are running server daemons.

When you have finished disabling services, save the file, and restart the inet daemon (in Red Hat and Red Hat-derived systems, type **/etc/rc.d/init.d/inetd restart** and press Enter).

Disabling Unused Server Daemons

Make sure you are not running any server daemons, such as httpd or wu-ftp, that you do not need. To do so, you can use the SYSV Runlevel Manager, a standard package that is installed by default in most Linux distributions. To start the Runlevel Manager, open a terminal window, switch to superuser, type **tksysv,** and press Enter. (If you are running the K Desktop, use the ksysv command.) As long as this application is installed on your system, you will see the main Runlevel Manager window.

The Runlevel Manager enables you to specify which services are started—and which are stopped—for each of the runlevels defined in your system. Note that Linux distributions vary in the way they define runlevels. The runlevels defined by Red Hat Linux are shown in Table 16.1. When you enter a runlevel, the Runlevel Manager's configuration specifies which daemons are to be started, and which are to be stopped.

Table 16.1 Default Runlevels (Red Hat Linux)

Runlevel	Description
0	Halt
1	Single user
2	Multiuser without NFS or X
3	Full multiuser mode without X
4	Not used
5	Full multiuser with X
6	Reboot

For Red Hat Linux systems, the two runlevels of interest are 3 (Full multiuser without X), and 5 (Full multiuser with X). Make sure these runlevels start only those daemons that you really need. For example, if you are not running Samba, delete smb from the Start list for runlevels 3 and 5.

Do not delete services haphazardly; if you are not careful, you may delete something essential to running your system. If you are not sure what a service does, read its main page.

Securing Your System with IP Chains

The Linux kernel can be set up to serve as a comprehensive and highly effective *firewall,* a barrier between your network and the Internet. You can configure this barrier to make sure that outsiders cannot easily gain entry into your network.

The ideal configuration for a firewall involves the use of a gateway system with two Ethernet cards, each of which has its own, unique IP address. Because all incoming traffic must pass through the gateway machine to reach your network, you can intercept and thwart unwanted accesses. To do so you will need to configure the ipchains utility. The following sections show you how to configure your system using ipchains to act as a highly effective firewall for your network.

Using ipchains can be difficult for novice users. Fortunately, there are tools available that make the process of creating an ipchains-based firewall relatively easy. One such tool is available online at http://www.linux-firewall-tools.com.

You still need a clear understanding of what the ipchains command can do. With it, you can analyze any firewall script for problems.

Preparing Your Kernel

Make sure that your Linux Kernel has the tools that it needs to support ipchains. To find out, log in as root user, type **ls -l /proc/net/ip_fwchains,** and press Enter. If the file exists, then your kernel already has the needed support. If not, you will need to enable the following:

- IP Firewalling
- IP Masquerading
- IP Always Defragment
- Network Firewalls
- IP Masquerading
- IP TCP Syncookie Support

To check whether these kernel parameters are enabled, log in as superuser, switch to /usr/src/linux, type **make xconfig,** and press Enter. You will see the Linux Kernel Configuration window. Enable the need options as modules, and click Save and Exit. Consult your Linux system documentation to learn how to reconfigure your kernel modules so that your choices are in effect when you reboot your system.

If you are using Red Hat Linux, the make xconfig command does not work. To upgrade your kernel, consult the Red Hat Kernel Upgrade HOWTO, available online at http://www.redhat.com/support/docs/howto/kernel-upgrade/kernel-upgrade.html.

Introducing Ipchains

The following commands should be familiar from Chapter 10. You will learn to understand what these mean in more detail in the following sections.

```
_ipchains -F
ipchains -P input DENY
ipchains -P output REJECT
ipchains -P forward REJECT
```

To summarize these commands, Linux first flushes (-F) any IP chains rules stored in memory. Then it stops (DENY, REJECT) any data coming into (input) or out (output) of your system, including anything your gateway computer may *forward* from your other computers. In other words, these rules create a wall between your network and the Internet. Nothing can get out or in unless you explicitly allow it.

As you can see, there are three different kinds of IP chains commands—for data that comes into your network, data coming out of your network, and data that is forwarded through your gateway computer.

Creating the Input Firewall

You want to block messages from several sources, especially private IP addresses as identified in Chapter 5.

You have already used some private IP addresses for your own local network. Although these addresses are not supposed to be used on the Internet, crackers use them to try to break into other networks.

One example command that blocks a series of private IP addresses is shown here:

```
_ipchains -A input -i $EXTERNAL_INTERFACE -s
$CLASS_A -j DENY -l
```

This command adds (-A) a rule and applies it to data coming in (input) through the following interface (-i). You set the $EXTERNAL_INTERFACE to eth0, eth1 or ppp0, whichever interface is directly connected to the Internet. You are looking for data with a source address (-s) as defined by the variable $CLASS_A. You can set the $CLASS_A variable to the Class A private IP addresses as defined in Chapter 5.

If Linux finds data coming from one of these addresses, it jumps (-j) to DENY access. Finally, such attempts are logged (-l) for later analysis.

Output Firewall

As strange as it may sound, you also want to prevent certain kinds of data from leaving your network. For example, you should block the export of shared directories. This applies to the Network File System, Xwindows (the Linux Graphical User Interface), and SOCKS, which is how most traffic travels through a proxy server. An example of the IP Chains command that stops exports is:

```
_ipchains -A input -i $EXTERNAL_INTERFACE -p
tcp -y \

    —destination-port $NFS_PORT -j DENY -l
```

This command adds (-A) the following rule to data coming in (input) through the network interface (-i) connected to the Internet ($EXTERNAL_INTERFACE). IP chains then checks your data for the TCP protocol (-p). If it sees a TCP packet, it checks if the data coming in is an attempt to connect to your computer (-y) through the destination port for your NFS Server ($NFS_PORT). If all of these conditions are met, IP chains jumps (-j) to DENY and then logs (-l) the request.

Creating the Forwarding Firewall

You want your gateway computer to forward data from the computers inside your network to the Internet. This allows your users to send requests such as to browse the www.linux.com Web page.

But you do not want your gateway computer to forward the internal IP address of your computer that is sending a request to the Internet. That IP address would help a cracker break into your network.

With the following command, you can set up masquerading; in other words, all requests from inside your network look like they are coming from your gateway computer.

```
ipchains -A forward -i $EXTERNAL_INTERFACE -s
$LOCALNET -j MASQ
```

This command adds (-A) a rule and applies it to data that is forwarded through the following interface (-i). You set the $EXTERNAL_INTERFACE to eth0, eth1 or ppp0, whichever interface is directly connected to the Internet.

Linux applies this rule to all data from (-s, for source) your local network. Masquerading (MASQ) substitutes your $EXTERNAL_INTERFACE's IP address for the source computer on your network.

Once your gateway computer gets an answer from the Internet, it automatically substitutes the source IP address on your local network, before forwarding.

IP Chains Basic Syntax

Now that you have analyzed the three different kinds of ipchains commands, you can understand what happens when you substitute different switches and actions.

The basic switches that you can use with IP chains are listed in Table 16.2. The actions that you can take with IP chains are listed in Table 16.3. More information is available in the IPCHAINS-HOWTO, available online at http://www.linuxdoc.org.

Table 16.2 Ipchains Commands

Switch	Function
-A	Append, or add this rule to the ones created before it
-D	Delete the following rule
-d	Destination. Specifies the destination IP address
-F	Flush all previously set rules. Allows you to start fresh
-i	Specifies the network interface, such as eth0 or ppp0
-j	Jump to an action, if all of the conditions in this rule are met
-L	Lists all current rules. Typically run at the command line
-l	Log every packet that meets the conditions of this rule

-P	Specifies default policies. The final rule in any ipchains set
-p	Look for data that matches the following protocol, such as TCP or UDP
-y	Check if the data is an attempt to connect. If it is "! −y", check if the data is being transferred on an existing connection

Table 16.3 Ipchains Actions

Action	Function
ACCEPT	If the data meets the requirements in this rule, let it through
DENY	If the data meets the requirements in this rule, stop it. No message is sent to the computer sending this data
MASQ	If the data meets the requirements in this rule, substitute the local IP address for the source address
REDIRECT	If the data meets the requirements in this rule, send it to the specified port
REJECT	If the data meets the requirements in this rule, stop it. A message is sent to the originating computer

Managing Your Channels

There are 65,536 channels associated with TCP/IP. If any of these channels are open, a cracker can use them as a way to break into your network.

When you use IP chains on TCP/IP channels, there are three objectives. The first objective is to block the export of shared directories, as discussed in a previous section. The second objective is to open the channels associated with the services that you do use. Important channels (port numbers) are shown in Table 16.4.

Table 16.4 Key Port Numbers for Internet Data

Data Type	Port Number
DNS (To help find Web pages)	53
HTTP (Web page data)	80
HTTPS (Secure Web page data)	443
proxy server Cache	8080
NNTP (To access newsgroups)	119
IMAP (Special Mail Services)	143
SMTP (Sending Mail)	25
SSH (Secure Connections)	22
TELNET	23
FTP (Downloading Files)	21
IRC (Internet Relay Chat)	6667
ICQ (Alternate Chat Software)	4000

You will want to let data in and out for any of these Services that you use on the Internet. For example, to manage secure server data (https), run the following commands:

```
ipchains -A output -i $EXTERNAL_INTERFACE -p
tcp \
-s $IPADDR $UNPRIVPORTS -destination-port 443
-j ACCEPT
  ipchains -A input -i $EXTERNAL_INTERFACE -p
! -y \
-d $IPADDR $UNPRIVPORTS -j ACCEPT
```

Each command adds (-A) a new rule. The first command is for data going out (output); the second command is for data coming in (input). Both rules apply to the network interface (-i) connected to the Internet ($EXTERNAL _INTERFACE). The IP Chains then checks your data for the TCP protocol (-p).

The output command uses your gateway's IP address ($IPADDR) as the source address, using undesignated ports or channels ($UNPRIVPORTS). If the destination port is 443, the standard for secure server (HTTPS) data, IP chains jumps (-j) to ACCEPT the output.

The input command looks for data that matches what left your computer (! −y). The destination address is your IP address ($IPADDR). It comes in through undesignated channels ($UNPRIVPORTS). If all these conditions are met, IP chains jumps (-j) to ACCEPT the input.

The third objective is to manage the data coming and going through the ping and traceroute commands from Chapter 15. The firewall script that you can create at http://www.linux-firewalls.com prevents crackers from identifying IP addresses inside your network. It also prevents "denial of service" attacks, which can keep you from accessing the Internet even with a high-speed connection.

IP Tables

At the time of this writing, work on the *iptables* command for the next major Linux releases such as Red Hat 7.0 is not complete. However, the firewall that you build from this command promises to be quite simple; it is hoped that the following script will protect your network just as well as the *ipchains* script in Appendix A.

These commands assume that connection tracking is already built into the Linux kernel. The first four commands block all connections unless they come from your connection to the Internet:

```
iptables -N block
iptables -A block -m state —state ESTAB-
LISHED,RELATED -j ACCEPT
iptables -A block -m state —state NEW -i !
eth1 -j ACCEPT
iptables -A block -j DROP
```

The last two commands block data input or forwarded to your network:

```
iptables -A INPUT -j block
iptables -A FORWARD -j block
```

When Red Hat 7.x is released, review the Packet Filtering HOWTO for the latest information on how to set up the *iptables* command.

Looking Under the Hood

Table 16.5 lists all the parameters you can define with ipchains. As you analyze firewall rules, these parameters tell you about the traffic that you are managing.

Table 16.5 Firewall Parameters

Parameter	Function
EXTERNAL_INTERFACE	Specifies the network card on your gateway computer that is connected directly to the Internet.
LOOPBACK_INTERFACE	Specifies the loopback network card, normally "lo."
LOCAL_INTERFACE_1	Specifies the network card on your

	gateway computer that is connected to your Local Network.
IP_ADDR	Sets up your IP address on the Internet. This is unrelated to the private internal IP addresses on your network. This address is linked to your EXTERNAL_INTERFACE.
LOCALNET_1	Sets up your local subnetwork. The network shown in Figure 16.6 covers the addresses from 192.168.1.0 through 192.168.1.255.
ANYWHERE	Any IP address. Generally not used, unless you want to restrict access to all locations on the Internet.
NAMESERVER_1	Specifies the IP address for your ISP's DNS server. As this is essential for navigating the Internet, you do no't want to block any information to or from this computer.
NAMESERVER_2	Specifies the IP address for your ISP's backup DNS server.
SMTP_SERVER	Specifies the host name for your ISP's outgoing mail server. See the note after the end of this table.
IMAP_SERVER	Use this parameter only if your e-mail comes in through an Internet Message Access Protocol Server. Most e-mail systems still use POP, or the Post Office Protocol to receive mail.
NEWS_SERVER	Use the host name of your news server. See note after this table.
WEB_PROXY_SERVER	You will need the host name of your ISP's proxy server here.
LOOPBACK	All addresses in the class A network 127.0.0.0 are reserved for loopback functions.

CLASS_A	Standard IP Class A addresses reserved for private networks. CLASS_A through CLASS_E are set up to prevent crackers from using these addresses to attack your network.
CLASS_B	Set to cover the standard Class B private network addresses.
CLASS_C	Set to cover the standard Class C private network addresses.
CLASS_D	Set to cover the standard Class D multicast addresses. These IP addresses are not legal for source computers.
CLASS_E_RESERVED_NET	Set to cover the standard Class E experimental addresses. These IP addresses are not allowed for use anywhere on the Internet.
BROADCAST_SRC	Set to the Broadcast Source Address. While this is the normal way for computers inside your network to identify each other, you do not want people on other networks to identify the IP addresses that you use inside your network.
BROADCAST_DEST	Set to the Broadcast Destination Address. See BROADCAST_SRC.
PRIVPORTS	Set to the reserved channels for TCP/IP.
UNPRIVPORTS	These channels are available for use by any TCP/IP service.
NFS_PORT	Makes sure that when you export NFS directories, the exports stay within your local network.
SOCKS_PORT	This is just another channel that a cracker could use to manipulate your system.

XWINDOW_PORTS	Set to the Linux standard ports for remote users that want to connect to your Graphical User Interface.
SSH_LOCAL_PORTS	SSH, or the Secure SHell, is a way to connect two computers with encrypted logons and commands. This specifies the channels that can be used on the local computer.
SSH_REMOTE_PORTS	Specifies the channels that can be used on a remote end of a SSH connection.
TRACEROUTE_SRC_PORTS	Sets up the channels for the traceroute command, which you used to trace the route of your data on the Internet. You do not want a cracker to trace the data that you send all the way back to your computer.
TRACEROUTE_DEST_PORTS	The other end of the traceroute command.

From Here

This chapter concludes *Linux Networking Clearly Explained*. You have now learned all the concepts and skills you need to set up a network based on Red Hat Linux. With this solid foundation behind you, you will be able to set up reliable small networks, secure from the dangers inherent to the Internet. Congratulations!

References and Further Reading

Mann, S. and Mitchell, E. L. (2000). *Linux System Security,* Upple Saddle River, NJ: Prentice-Hall.

Red Hat Support. (2000). *Upgrading the Linux Kernel on Red Hat Linux systems.* Available online at http://www. redhat.com/support/docs/howto/kernel-upgrade/kernel-upgrade.html.

Russell, P. (1999). *IPCHAINS-HOWTO.* Linux Documentation Project. Available online at http://www.rust-corp.com.

Russell, R. (1999). *Packet Filtering HOWTO.* Linux Documentation Project. Available online at http://netfilter.kernelnotes.org. Once Linux Kernel 2.4 (and probably Red Hat 7.x) is released, this should also be available online at http://www.linuxdoc.org.

Ziegler, R. L. (2000). *Linux LAN & Firewall FAQ.* Available online at http://www.linux-firewall-tools.com/linux/faq/index.html.

Index